Security for Web Developers

John Paul Mueller

Beijing · Boston · Farnham · Sebastopol · Tokyo

Security for Web Developers

by John Paul Mueller

Copyright © 2016 John Mueller. All rights reserved.

Printed in the United States of America.

Published by O'Reilly Media, Inc., 1005 Gravenstein Highway North, Sebastopol, CA 95472.

O'Reilly books may be purchased for educational, business, or sales promotional use. Online editions are also available for most titles (*http://safaribooksonline.com*). For more information, contact our corporate/institutional sales department: 800-998-9938 or *corporate@oreilly.com*.

Editor: Meg Foley
Technical Editors: Russ Mullen, Billy Rios, and Wade Woolwine
Production Editor: Nicole Shelby
Copyeditor: Jasmine Kwityn

Proofreader: Kim Cofer
Indexer: Lucie Haskins
Interior Designer: David Futato
Cover Designer: Randy Comer
Illustrator: Rebecca Demarest

November 2015:   First Edition

Revision History for the First Edition

2015-11-09:   First Release

See *http://oreilly.com/catalog/errata.csp?isbn=9781491928646* for release details.

978-1-491-92864-6

[LSI]

This book is dedicated to the medical professionals who have helped restore my health—who have listened to all my woes and found ways to address them. Yes, I did need to follow the advice, but they were the ones who offered it. Good health is an exceptionally grand gift.

Table of Contents

Part I.   Developing a Security Plan

Part II.   Applying Successful Coding Practices

Part IV.   Implementing a Maintenance Cycle

Part V. Locating Security Resources

Preface

Ransomware, viruses, distributed denial-of-service (DDoS) attacks, man-in-the-middle attacks, security breaches, and the like all bring to mind the one thing that anyone involved in managing applications hates—nightmares. It gets to the point where anyone who does anything to affect the security of an application or its associated data becomes gun shy—conservative to the point of absurdity. You don't actually want the responsibility for securing the application—it just comes with the territory.

Adding to your burden, the disastrous results of any sort of mistake could haunt you for the rest of your life. Unlike most mistakes, you likely won't sweep this one under the carpet either, because it'll appear in the trade press where everyone can see it. Even if your name doesn't become synonymous with security failure, there are always the ramifications of a security issue—legal woes, loss of job, and so on. So, how do you deal with this issue?

Hiding your head in the sand doesn't appear to provide a solution—at least, not for very long. *Security for Web Developers* isn't intended to tell you about every threat out there or resolve every security woe you'll ever encounter. Instead, it provides you with guidelines and tools you need to resolve any security issue on your own—to be able to see a light at the end of the tunnel that doesn't have something to do with a train. What this book is really about is being able to get a good night's sleep knowing that you have what you need to get the job done right.

About This Book

Security for Web Developers provides you with the resources you need to work through web application security problems. Yes, you also see some information about platforms, because browsers run on specific platforms. In addition, you might see some of these security issues when working with desktop applications simply because the security landscape occupies both application domains. However, this book focuses on security for web applications, no matter where those applications run. You can find information on everything from the latest smartphone to an older desktop, and everything in-between. The book breaks the information into the following parts, each of which takes you another step along the path to creating a better security plan for your organization:

Part I

Nothing works well without planning. However, some of the worst disasters in the computer industry occurred due to a bad plan, rather than no planning at all. This part of the book helps you create a good security plan for your organization —one that considers all the latest user devices and user needs as part of the picture. This part of the book also discusses the need for third-party support, because let's face it: the complex security environment really does make it hard to create a secure environment alone. The materials help you locate the right sort of third-party help and ensure you actually get the value you need from it.

Part II

Creating applications today means relying on third-party code found in libraries, APIs, and microservices. This part of the book helps you consider coding issues. You won't find bits and bytes for the most part, but instead find helpful tips for incorporating these elements into your application successfully. This part of the book helps you manage your applications, rather than allowing them to manage you.

Part III

You have a number of ways to test applications and a number of means to do it. For example, you can create your own test suites or you could rely on one produced by someone else. A third party could do the testing for you. Perhaps you want to know how best to combine different strategies to ensure you have your entire application covered. This part of the book answers all your questions about modern testing strategies and details what you can do to make your efforts more efficient.

Part IV

At some point, your application is in production and running smoothly. Some applications continue to run for years this way without getting the proper maintenance. Unfortunately, modern application development means performing updates regularly because the hackers are constantly creating new strategies for accessing your system. Adding to this mess are all the updates to those third-party libraries, APIs, and microservices that you use. This part of the book provides you a map through the update maze and makes it possible to keep everything running smoothly without losing your mind first.

Part V

Security threats constantly evolve, which means that you need some means to keep updated. One method is to track security threats. Of course, if you track every threat, you never get anything done. This part of the book describes techniques you can use to avoid information overflow. The second technique is to obtain additional training. In fact, your entire organization needs training of some sort to keep abreast of current security issues and techniques for dealing with them. This part of the book also discusses training requirements in a way that every organization can use—even if you're a one-person business or a recent startup.

What You Need to Know

The readers of this book could have any of a number of titles, such as web designer, frontend developer, UI designer, UX designer, interaction designer, art director, content strategist, dev ops, product manager, SEO specialist, data scientist, software engineer, or computer scientist. What you all have in common is a need to create web applications of some sort that are safe for users to interact with in a meaningful way. You're all professionals who have created web applications before. What you may really need is to brush up on your security skills given the new climate of major application intrusions through nontraditional means, such as contaminating third-party APIs and libraries.

Security for Web Developers provides you with an end-to-end treatment of security, but it doesn't provide a lot of handholding. This book assumes that you want the latest information on how to thwart security threats at several levels, including a reading of precisely which categories those threats occupy, and how hackers use them to thwart your security measures.

The book does include a few security programming examples. In order to use these examples, you need to have a good knowledge of CSS3, HTML5, and JavaScript programming techniques. However, if you don't possess these skills, you can skip the programming examples and still obtain a considerable amount of information from the book. The programming examples provide details that only programmers will really care about.

Beyond the programming skills, it's more important that you have some level of security training already. For example, if you don't have any idea of what a man-in-the-middle attack is, you really need to read a more basic book first. This book obviously doesn't assume you're an expert who knows everything about man-in-the-middle attacks, but it does assume you've encountered the term before.

Development Environment Considerations

All you need to use the programming examples in this book is a text editor and browser. The text editor must output pure text, without any sort of formatting. It must also allow you to save the files using the correct file extensions for the example file (*.html*, *.css*, and *.js*). The various book editors, beta readers, and I tested the examples using the most popular browsers on the Linux, Mac, and Windows platforms. In fact, the examples were even tested using the Edge browser for Windows 10.

Icons Used in This Book

Icons provide emphasis of various sorts. This book uses a minimum of icons, but you need to know about each of them:

A note provides emphasis for important content that is slightly off-topic or perhaps of a nature where it would disrupt the normal flow of the text in the chapter. You need to read the notes because they usually provide pointers to additional information required to perform security tasks well. Notes also make it easier to find the important content you remember is in a certain location, but would have a hard time finding otherwise.

A warning contains information you must know about or you could suffer some dire fate. As with a note, the warning provides emphasis for special text, but this text tells you about potential issues that could cause you significant problems at some point. If you get nothing else out of a chapter, make sure you commit the meaning behind warnings to memory so that you can avoid costly errors later.

Sidebars

A sidebar contains helpful information that you don't necessarily need to know to work with web applications. You should read all of the sidebars at some point because they really are interesting, but you also don't need to read them immediately. The sidebars contain good information that complements the current topic, but isn't necessarily precisely on topic.

Conventions Used in This Book

The following typographical conventions are used in this book:

Italic
> Indicates new terms, URLs, email addresses, filenames, and file extensions.

Constant width

> Used for program listings, as well as within paragraphs to refer to program elements such as variable or function names, databases, data types, environment variables, statements, and keywords.

Constant width bold

> Shows commands or other text that should be typed literally by the user.

Constant width italic

> Shows text that should be replaced with user-supplied values or by values determined by context.

Some of the text in this book receives special treatment. Here are a few of the conventions you need to know about:

```
Source code appears in special paragraphs in most cases to
make it easier to read and use.
```

Sometimes, you see `source code` in a regular paragraph. The special formatting makes it easier to see.

URLs, such as *http://blog.johnmuellerbooks.com*, appear in a special font to make them easier to find. This book uses many URLs so that you can find a lot of related information without having to search for it yourself.

Where to Get More Information

I want to be sure you have the best reading experience possible. Please be sure to send any book-specific questions you might have to *John@JohnMuellerBooks.com*. You can also check out the blog posts for this book at *http://blog.johnmuellerbooks.com/category/technical/security-for-web-developers/*. The blog posts provide you with additional content and answer questions that readers commonly ask. If there are errata in the book, you can find the fixes on the blog as well.

Using Code Examples

Supplemental material (code examples, exercises, etc.) is available for download at *https://github.com/oreillymedia/Security_for_Web_Developers*.

This book is here to help you get your job done. In general, if example code is offered with this book, you may use it in your programs and documentation. You do not need to contact us for permission unless you're reproducing a significant portion of the code. For example, writing a program that uses several chunks of code from this book does not require permission. Selling or distributing a CD-ROM of examples from O'Reilly books does require permission. Answering a question by citing this book and quoting example code does not require permission. Incorporating a significant amount of example code from this book into your product's documentation does require permission.

We appreciate, but do not require, attribution. An attribution usually includes the title, author, publisher, and ISBN. For example: "*Security for Web Developers* by John Paul Mueller (O'Reilly). Copyright 2016 John Paul Mueller, 978-1-49192-864-6."

If you feel your use of code examples falls outside fair use or the permission given above, feel free to contact us at *permissions@oreilly.com*.

Safari® Books Online

 *Safari Books Online* is an on-demand digital library that delivers expert content in both book and video form from the world's leading authors in technology and business.

Technology professionals, software developers, web designers, and business and creative professionals use Safari Books Online as their primary resource for research, problem solving, learning, and certification training.

Safari Books Online offers a range of plans and pricing for enterprise, government, education, and individuals.

Members have access to thousands of books, training videos, and prepublication manuscripts in one fully searchable database from publishers like O'Reilly Media, Prentice Hall Professional, Addison-Wesley Professional, Microsoft Press, Sams, Que, Peachpit Press, Focal Press, Cisco Press, John Wiley & Sons, Syngress, Morgan Kaufmann, IBM Redbooks, Packt, Adobe Press, FT Press, Apress, Manning, New Riders, McGraw-Hill, Jones & Bartlett, Course Technology, and hundreds more. For more information about Safari Books Online, please visit us online.

How to Contact Us

Please address comments and questions concerning this book to the publisher:

O'Reilly Media, Inc.
1005 Gravenstein Highway North
Sebastopol, CA 95472
800-998-9938 (in the United States or Canada)
707-829-0515 (international or local)
707-829-0104 (fax)

We have a web page for this book, where we list errata, examples, and any additional information. You can access this page at *http://bit.ly/security-web-dev*.

To comment or ask technical questions about this book, send email to *bookquestions@oreilly.com*.

For more information about our books, courses, conferences, and news, see our website at *http://www.oreilly.com*.

Find us on Facebook: *http://facebook.com/oreilly*

Follow us on Twitter: *http://twitter.com/oreillymedia*

Watch us on YouTube: *http://www.youtube.com/oreillymedia*

Acknowledgments

Thanks to my wife, Rebecca. Although she is gone now, her spirit is in every book I write, in every word that appears on the page. She believed in me when no one else would.

Russ Mullen, Billy Rios, and Wade Woolwine deserve thanks for their technical edit of this book. All three technical editors greatly added to the accuracy and depth of the material you see here. In many cases, I was able to bounce ideas off them and ask for their help in researching essential book topics.

Matt Wagner, my agent, deserves credit for helping me get the contract in the first place and taking care of all the details that most authors don't really consider. I always appreciate his assistance. It's good to know that someone wants to help.

A number of people read all or part of this book to help me refine the approach, test scripts, and generally provide input that all readers wish they could have. These unpaid volunteers helped in ways too numerous to mention here. I especially appreciate the efforts of Eva Beattie, Glenn A. Russell, and Luca Massaron, who provided general input, read the entire book, and selflessly devoted themselves to this project.

Finally, I would like to thank Meg Foley, Nicole Shelby, Jasmine Kwityn, and the rest of the editorial and production staff.

PART I

Developing a Security Plan

In this part of the book, you discover how to create a security plan that you can use when writing applications. Having a good security plan ensures that your application actually meets specific goals and that others can discuss how to implement security with the development team. Without a good security plan in place, hackers often find easy access to the application and cause all kinds of problems for your organization. Chapter 1 gets you started by helping you understand the components of a good security plan.

It's important to realize that the security plan doesn't just focus on the application, but also on how users employ the application. Every successful application keeps the user in mind, as described in Chapter 2.

In addition, you need to understand that applications no longer exist in a vacuum—they interact with online data sources and rely on third-party coding. With this in mind, you must also consider how third-party solutions can affect your application, both positively and negatively. Using third-party solutions can also greatly decrease your coding time. Chapter 3 helps you achieve this goal.

CHAPTER 1

Defining the Application Environment

Data is the most important resource that any business owns. It's literally possible to replace any part of a business except the data. When the data is modified, corrupted, stolen, or deleted, a business can suffer serious loss. In fact, a business that has enough go wrong with its data can simply cease to exist. The focus of security, therefore, is not hackers, applications, networks, or anything else someone might have told you—it's data. Therefore, this book is about data security, which encompasses a broad range of other topics, but it's important to get right to the point of what you're really looking to protect when you read about these other topics.

Unfortunately, data isn't much use sitting alone in the dark. No matter how fancy your server is, no matter how capable the database that holds the data, the data isn't worth much until you do something with it. The need to manage data brings applications into the picture and the use of applications to manage data is why this introductory chapter talks about the application environment.

However, before you go any further, it's important to decide precisely how applications and data interact because the rest of the chapter isn't very helpful without this insight. An application performs just four operations on data, no matter how incredibly complex the application might become. You can define these operations by the CRUD acronym:

- Create
- Read
- Update
- Delete

The sections that follow discuss data, applications, and CRUD as they relate to the web environment. You discover how security affects all three aspects of web development, keeping in mind that even though data is the focus, the application performs the required CRUD tasks. Keeping your data safe means understanding the application environment and therefore the threats to the data the application manages.

Specifying Web Application Threats

You can find lists of web application threats all over the Internet. Some of the lists are comprehensive and don't necessarily have a bias, some address what the author feels are the most important threats, some tell you about the most commonly occurring threats, and you can find all sorts of other lists out there. The problem with all these lists is that the author doesn't know your application. A SQL injection attack is only successful when your application uses SQL in some way—perhaps it doesn't.

Obviously you need to get ideas on what to check from somewhere, and these lists do make a good starting place. However, you need to consider the list content in light of your application. In addition, don't rely on just one list—use multiple lists so that you obtain better coverage of the threats that could possibly threaten your application. With this need in mind, here is a list of the most common threats you see with web applications today:

Buffer overflow

> An attacker manages to send enough data in an input buffer to overflow an application or output buffer. As a result, memory outside the buffer becomes corrupted. Some forms of buffer overflow allow the attacker to perform seemingly impossible tasks because the affected memory contains executable code. The best way to overcome this problem is to perform range and size checks on any data, input or output, that your application handles. You can read more about web application buffer overflows at *http://www.upenn.edu/computing/security/swat/ SWAT_Top_Ten_A5.php* and *https://www.owasp.org/index.php/Buffer_Overflows*.

Code injection

> An entity adds code to the data stream flowing between a server and a client (such as a browser) in man-in-the-middle-attack fashion. The target often views the added code as part of the original page, but it could contain anything. Of course, the target may not even see the injected code. It might be lurking in the background ready to cause all sorts of problems for your application. A good way to overcome this attack is to ensure you use encrypted data streams, the HTTPS protocol, and code verification (when possible). Providing a client feedback mechanism is also a good idea.

Code injection occurs more often than you might think. In some cases, the code injection isn't even part of an attack, but it might as well be. A recent article (*http://www.infoworld.com/ article/2925839/net-neutrality/code-injection-new-low- isps.html*) discusses how Internet service providers (ISPs) are injecting JavaScript code into the data stream in order to overlay ads on top of a page. In order to determine what sort of ad to provide, the ISP also monitors the traffic.

Cross-site scripting (XSS)

An attacker injects JavaScript or other executable code into the output stream of your application. The recipient sees your application as the source of the infection, even when it isn't. In most cases, you don't want to allow users to send data directly to one another through your application without strict verification. A moderated format for applications such as blogs is a must to ensure your application doesn't end up serving viruses or worse along with seemingly benign data.

 Few experts remind you to check your output data. However, you don't actually know that your own application is trustworthy. A hacker could modify it to allow tainted output data. Verification checks should include output data as well as input data.

File uploads

Every file upload, even those that might seem otherwise innocuous, is suspect. Hackers sometimes upload backdoors using the file upload capabilities of your server, so the file could contain something nasty. If possible, disallow file uploads to your server. Of course, it isn't always possible to provide this level of security, so you need to allow just certain types of file and then scan the file for problems. Authenticating the file as much as possible is always a good idea. For example, some files contain a signature at the beginning that you can use to ensure the file is legitimate. Don't rely on file extension exclusion alone—hackers often make one file look like another type in order to bypass server security.

Hardcoded authentication

Developers often place authentication information in application initialization files for testing purposes. It's essential to remove these hardcoded authentication entries and rely on a centralized data store for security information instead. Keeping the data store in a secure location, off the server used for web applications, is essential to ensuring that hackers can't simply view the credentials used to access the application in certain ways. If you do need initialization files for the application, make sure these files reside outside the webroot directory to ensure that hackers can't discover them accidentally.

Hidden or restricted file/directory discovery

When your application allows input of special characters such as the forward slash (/) or backslash (\), it's possible for a hacker to discover hidden or restricted files and directories. These locations can contain all sorts of information that a hacker can find useful in attacking your system. Disallowing use of special characters whenever possible is a great idea. In addition, store critical files outside the webroot directory in locations that the operating system can control directly.

Missing or incorrect authentication

It's important to know whom you're dealing with, especially when working with sensitive data. Many web applications rely on common accounts for some tasks, which means it's impossible to know who has accessed the account. Avoid using guest accounts for any purpose and assign each user a specific account to use.

Missing or incorrect authorization

Even if you know the person you're dealing with, it's important to provide only the level of authorization needed to perform a given task. In addition, the authorization should reflect the user's method of access. A desktop system accessing the application from the local network is likely more secure than a smartphone accessing the application from the local coffee shop. Relying on security promotion to assist in sensitive tasks lets you maintain minimal rights the rest of the time. Anything you can do to reduce what the user is authorized to do helps maintain a secure environment.

Missing or incorrect encryption

Use encryption to transmit data of any sort between two endpoints to help keep hackers from listening in on your communication. It's important to keep track of the latest encryption techniques and rely on the best encryption supported by the user's environment. For example, Triple Data Encryption Standard (3DES)isn't secure any longer, yet some organizations continue to use it. The current Advanced Encryption Standard (AES) remains mostly secure, but you want to use the largest key possible to help make it harder to crack.

Operating system command injection

An attacker modifies an operating system command your application uses to perform specific tasks. Your web-based application probably shouldn't use operating system calls in the first place. However, if you absolutely must make operating system calls, make sure the application runs in a sandbox.

Some experts will emphasize validating input data for some uses and leave the requirement off for other uses. Always validate any data you receive from anywhere. You have no way of knowing what vehicle a hacker will use to obtain access to your system or cause damage in other ways. Input data is always suspect, even when the data comes from your own server. Being paranoid is a good thing when you're performing security-related tasks.

Parameter manipulation

Hackers can experiment with parameters passed as part of the request header or URL. For example, when working with Google, you can change the URL and the results of your search. Make sure you encrypt any parameters you pass between the browser and the server. In addition, use secure web page protocols, such as HTTPS, when passing parameters.

Hackers can still manipulate parameters with enough time and effort. It's also important to define parameter value ranges and data types carefully to reduce the potential problems presented by this attack.

Remote code inclusion

Most web applications today rely on included libraries, frameworks, and APIs. In many cases, the include statement contains a relative path or uses a variable containing a hardcoded path to make it easier to change the location of the remote code later. When a hacker is able to gain access to the path information and change it, it's possible to point the remote code inclusion to any code the hacker wants, giving the hacker full access to the application. The best way to avoid this particular problem is to use hardcoded full paths whenever possible, even though this action makes it harder to maintain the code.

Many experts will recommend that you use vetted libraries and frameworks to perform dangerous tasks. However, these add-ons are simply more code. Hackers find methods for corrupting and circumventing library and framework code on a regular basis. You still have a need to ensure your application and any code it relies upon interacts with outside elements safely, which means performing extensive testing. Using libraries and frameworks does reduce your support costs and ensures that you get timely fixes for bugs, but the bugs still exist and you still need to be on guard. There is no security silver bullet. Chapter 6 contains more information about working with libraries and frameworks.

Session hijacking

Every time someone logs in to your web server, the server gives that user a unique session. A session hijacker jumps into the session and intercepts data transferred between the user and the server. The three common places to look for information used to hijack a session are: cookies, URL rewriting, and hidden fields. Hackers look for session information in these places. By keeping the session information encrypted, you can reduce the risk of someone intercepting it. For example, make sure you rely on the HTTPS protocol for logins. You also want to avoid doing things like making your session IDs predictable.

SQL injection

An attacker modifies a query that your application creates as the result of user or other input. In many cases, the application requests query input data, but it receives SQL elements instead. Other forms of SQL injection attack involve the use of escape or other unexpected characters or character sequences. A good way to avoid SQL injection attacks is to avoid dynamically generated queries.

This may look like a lot of different threats, but if you search long enough online, you could easily triple the size of this list and not even begin to scratch the surface of the ways in which a hacker can make your life interesting. As this book progresses, you'll encounter a much larger number of threat types and start to discover ways to overcome them. Don't worry, in most cases the fixes end up being common sense and a single fix can resolve more than one problem. For example, look through the list again and you'll find that simply using HTTPS solves a number of these problems.

Considering the Privacy Aspect of Security

When delving into security, an organization tends to focus first on its own data security. After all, if the organization's data becomes lost, corrupted, modified, or otherwise unusable, the organization could go out of business. The next level of scrutiny usually resides with third parties, such as partners. Often, the security of user data comes last and many organizations don't think too much about customer data security at all. The problem is that many users and customers see the safety of their data as paramount. The whole issue of privacy comes down to the protection of user data such that no one misuses or exposes the information without the user's knowledge and consent. In short, when building an application, you must also consider the privacy of user data as a security issue and an important one at that.

A recent article (*http://www.infoworld.com/article/2925292/internet-privacy/feds-vs-silicon-valley-who-do-you-trust-less.html*) points out that users and customers view the tech industry as poor trustees of their data (). In fact, the tech industry has actually fallen behind the government—people trust the government to safeguard their information more often. Many tech companies publicly support enhanced security policies for other entities (such as the government) and privately build more ways to thwart

---

any notion of privacy that the user or customer might have. This duality makes the situation even worse than it might otherwise be if the tech industry were open about the encroachment on user and customer data.

In order to create a truly secure application, you must be willing to secure every aspect of it, including user and customer data. This act requires that the application only obtain and manage the data necessary to perform its task and that it discard that data when no longer needed. Trust is something that your application can gain only when it adheres to the same set of rules for working with all data, no matter its source.

Understanding Software Security Assurance (SSA)

The purpose of software is to interact with data. However, software itself is a kind of data. In fact, data comes in many forms that you might not otherwise consider, and the effect of data is wider ranging that you might normally think. With the Internet of Things (IoT), it's now possible for data to have both abstract and physical effects in ways that no one could imagine even a few years ago. A hacker gaining access to the right application can do things like damage the electrical grid or poison the water system. On a more personal level, the same hacker could potentially raise the temperature of your home to some terrifying level, turn off all the lights, or spy on you through your webcam, to name just a few examples. The point of SSA is that software needs some type of regulation to ensure it doesn't cause the loss, inaccuracy, alteration, unavailability, or misuse of the data and resources that it uses, controls, and protects. This requirement appears as part of SSA. The following sections discuss SSA in more detail.

SSA isn't an actual standard at this time. It's a concept that many organizations quantify and put into writing based on that organization's needs. The same basic patterns appear in many of these documents and the term SSA refers to the practice of ensuring software remains secure. You can see how SSA affects many organizations, such as Oracle (*http://www.oracle.com/us/support/assurance/over view/index.html*) and Microsoft (*https://msdn.microsoft.com/ library/windows/desktop/ 84aed186-1d75-4366-8e61-8d258746bopq.aspx*), by reviewing their online SSA documentation. In fact, many large organizations now have some form of SSA in place.

Considering the OSSAP

One of the main sites you need to know about in order to make SSA a reality in web applications is the Open Web Application Security Project (OWASP) (*https://*

www.owasp.org/index.php/OWASP_Software_Security_Assurance_Process);   see
Figure 1-1. The site breaks down the process required to make the OWASP Security
Software Assurance Process (OSSAP) part of the Software Development Lifecycle
(SDLC). Yes, that's a whole bunch of alphabet soup, but you need to know about this
group in order to create a process for your application that matches the work done by
other organizations. In addition, the information on this site helps you develop a
security process for your application that actually works, is part of the development
process, and won't cost you a lot of time in creating your own process.

Figure 1-1. The OWASP site tells you about SSA for web applications

Although OSSAP does provide a great framework for ensuring
your application meets SSA requirements, there is no requirement
that you interact with this group in any way. The group does license
its approach to SSA. However, at this time, the group is just getting
underway and you'll find a lot of TBDs on the site which the group
plans to fill in as time passes. Of course, you need a plan for today,
so OWASP and its OSSAP present a place for you to research solutions for now and possibly get additional help later.

The whole reason to apply SSA to your application as part of the SDLC is to ensure that the software is as reliable and error free as you can make it. When talking with some people, the implication is that SSA will fix every potential security problem that you might encounter, but this simply isn't the case. SSA will improve your software, but you can't find any pieces of software anywhere that are error free. Assuming that you did manage to create a piece of error-free software, you still have user, environment, network, and all software of other security issues to consider. Consequently, SSA is simply one piece of a much larger security picture and implementing SSA will only fix so many security issues. The best thing to do is to continue seeing security as an ongoing process.

Defining SSA Requirements

The initial step in implementing SSA as part of your application is to define the SSA requirements. These requirements help you determine the current state of your software, the issues that require resolution, and the severity of those issues. After the issues are defined, you can determine the remediation process and any other requirements needed to ensure that the software remains secure. In fact, you can break SSA down into eight steps:

1. Evaluate the software and develop a plan to remediate it.
2. Define the risks that the security issues represent to the data and categorize these risks to remediate the worst risks first.
3. Perform a complete code review.
4. Implement the required changes.
5. Test the fixes you create and verify that they actually do work on the production system.
6. Define a defense for protecting application access and therefore the data that the application manages.
7. Measure the effectiveness of the changes you have made.
8. Educate management, users, and developers in the proper methods to ensure good application security.

An Alternative SSA Strategy

When it comes to security, you can find any number of ways to deal with a particular issue. Depending on your organization's culture and method of working through security issues, you might find an alternative technique for ensuring SSA works better. Some security experts suggest these steps:

---

1. Define security requirements to overlay the product requirements (you only need to perform this step for new software).

2. Define and communicate secure coding requirements that developers must use when writing code.

3. Perform automated code reviews as developers create new code.

4. Perform a complete code review after completing the application.

5. Perform penetration testing and vulnerability assessment of the complete application.

6. Evaluate the test findings to find a balance between security and business risks. Plan fixes for any vulnerabilities identified as too risky for the business.

7. Implement any required security fixes.

8. Repeat Step 5.

Categorizing Data and Resources

This process involves identifying the various pieces of data that your application touches in some way, including its own code and configuration information. Once you identify every piece of data, you categorize it to identify the level of security required to protect that data. Data can have many levels of categorization and the way in which you categorize the data depends on your organization's needs and the orientation of the data. For example, some data may simply inconvenience the organization, while other data could potentially cause harm to humans. The definition of how data security breaches affects the security environment as a whole is essential.

After the data categorization process is complete, it's possible to begin using the information to perform a variety of tasks. For example, you can consider how to reduce vulnerabilities by:

- Creating coding standards

- Implementing mandatory developer training

- Hiring security leaders within development groups

- Using automated testing procedures that specifically locate security issues

All of these methods point to resources that the organization interacts with and relies upon to ensure the application manages data correctly. Categorizing resources means determining how much emphasis to place on a particular resource. For example, denying developers training will have a bigger impact than denying individual application users training because the developers work with the application as a whole. Of course, training is essential for everyone. In this case, categorizing resources of all sorts helps you determine where and how to spend money in order to obtain the best return on investment (ROI), while still meeting application security goals.

Performing the Required Analysis

As part of SSA, you need to perform an analysis on your application (including threat modeling, user interface flaws, and data presentation flaws). It's important to know precisely what sorts of weaknesses your code could contain. The operative word here is *could*. Until you perform in-depth analysis, you have no way of knowing the actual security problems in your code. Web applications are especially adept at hiding issues because, unlike desktop applications, the code can appear in numerous places and scripts tend to hide problems that compiled applications don't have because the code is interpreted at runtime, rather than compile time.

 It's important to understand that security isn't just about the code— it's also about the tools required to create the code and the skill of the developers employing those tools. When an organization chooses the wrong tools for the job, the risk of a security breach becomes much higher because the tools may not create code that performs precisely as expected. Likewise, when developers using the tool don't have the required skills, it's hardly surprising that the software has security holes that a more skilled developer would avoid.

Some experts claim that there are companies that actually allow substandard work. In most cases, the excuse for allowing such work is that the application development process is behind schedule or that the organization lacks required tools or expertise. The fact that an organization may employ software designed to help address security issues (such as a firewall), doesn't relieve the developer of the responsibility to create secure code. Organizations need to maintain coding standards to ensure a good result.

Logic

Interacting with an application and the data it manages is a process. Although users might perform tasks in a seemingly random fashion, specific tasks follow patterns that occur because the user must follow a procedure in order to obtain a good result. By documenting and understanding these procedures, you can analyze application logic from a practical perspective. Users rely on a particular procedure because of the way in which developers design the application. Changing the design will necessarily change the procedure.

The point of the analysis is to look for security holes in the procedure. For example, the application may allow the user to remain logged in, even if it doesn't detect activity for an extended period. The problem is that the user might not even be present—

someone else could access the application using the user's credentials and no one would be the wiser because everyone would think that the user is logged in using the same system as always.

However, data holes can take other forms. A part number might consist of various quantifiable elements. In order to obtain a good part number, the application could ask for the elements, rather than the part number as a whole, and build the part number from those elements. The idea is to make the procedure cleaner, clearer, and less error prone so that the database doesn't end up containing a lot of bad information.

Data

It may not seem like you can perform much analysis on data from a security perspective, but there really are a lot of issues to consider. In fact, data analysis is one of the areas where organizations fall down most because the emphasis is on how to manage and use the data, rather than on how to secure the data (it's reasonable to assume you need to address all three issues). When analyzing the data, you must consider these issues:

- Who can access the data
- What format is used to store the data
- When the data is accessible
- Where the data is stored
- Why each data item is made available as part of the application
- How the data is broken into components and the result of combining the data for application use

For example, some applications fail to practice data hiding, which is an essential feature of any good application. Data hiding means giving the user only the amount of information actually needed to perform any given task.

Applications also format some data incorrectly. For example, storing passwords as text will almost certainly cause problems if someone manages to break in. A better route is to store the password hash using a secure algorithm (one that hasn't been broken). The hash isn't at all valuable to someone who has broken in because the application needs the password on which the hash is based.

Making all data accessible all the time is also a bad idea. Sensitive data should only appear on screen when someone is available to monitor its use and react immediately should the user do something unexpected.

Storing sensitive data in the cloud is a particularly bad idea. Yes, using cloud storage makes the data more readily available and faster to access as well, but it also makes the data vulnerable. Store sensitive data on local servers when you have direct access to all the security features used to keep the data safe.

Application developers also have a propensity for making too much information available. You use data hiding to keep manager-specific data hidden from other kinds of users. However, some data has no place in the application at all. If no one actually needs a piece of data to perform a task, then don't add the data to the application.

Many data items today are an aggregation of other data elements. It's possible for a hacker to learn a lot about your organization by detecting the form of aggregation used and taking the data item apart to discover the constituent parts. It's important to consider how the data is put together and to add safeguards that make it harder to discover the source of that data.

Interface

A big problem with software today is the inclusion of gratuitous features. An application is supposed to meet a specific set of goals or perform a specific set of tasks. Invariably, someone gets the idea that the software might be somehow better if it had certain features that have nothing to do with the core goals the software is supposed to meet. The term *feature bloat* has been around for a long time. You normally see it discussed in a monetary sense—as the source of application speed problems, the elevator of user training costs, and the wrecker of development schedules. However, application interface issues, those that are often most affected by feature bloat, have a significant impact on security in the form of increased attack surface. Every time you increase the attack surface, you provide more opportunities for a hacker to obtain access to your organization. Getting rid of gratuitous features or moving them to an entirely different application will reduce the attack surface—making your application a lot more secure. Of course, you'll save money too.

Another potential problem is the hint interface—one that actually gives the security features of the application away by providing a potential hacker with too much information or too many features. Although it's necessary to offer a way for the user retrieve a lost password, some implementations actually make it possible for a hacker to retrieve the user's password and become that user. The hacker might even lock the real user out of the account by changing the password (this action would, however, be counterproductive because an administrator could restore the user's access quite easily). A better system is to ensure that the user actually made the request before doing anything and then ensuring that the administrator sends the login information in a secure manner.

Constraint

A constraint is simply a method of ensuring that actions meet specific criteria before the action is allowed. For example, disallowing access to data elements unless the user has a right to access them is a kind of constraint. However, constraints have other forms that are more important. The most important constraint is determining how any given user can manage data. Most users only require read access to data, yet applications commonly provide read/write access, which opens a huge security hole.

Data has constraints to consider as well. When working with data, you must define precisely what makes the data unique and ensure the application doesn't break any rules regarding that uniqueness. With this in mind, you generally need to consider these kinds of constraints:

- Ensure the data is the right type
- Define the range of values the data can accept
- Specify the maximum and minimum data lengths
- List any unacceptable data values

Delving into Language-Specific Issues

The application environment is defined by the languages used to create the application. Just as every language has functionality that makes it perform certain tasks well, every language also has potential problems that make it a security risk. Even low-level languages, despite their flexibility, have problems induced by complexity. Of course, web-based applications commonly rely on three particular languages: HTML, CSS, and JavaScript. The following sections describe some of the language-specific issues related to these particular languages.

Defining the Key HTML Issues

HTML5 has become extremely popular because it supports an incredibly broad range of platforms. The same application can work well on a user's desktop, tablet, and smartphone without any special coding on the part of the developer. Often, libraries, APIs, and microservices provide content in a form that matches the host system automatically, without any developer intervention. However, the flexibility that HTML5 provides can also be problematic. The following list describes some key security issues you experience when working with HTML5:

Code injection
With HTML5, there are a large number of ways in which a hacker could inject malicious code, including sources you might not usually consider suspicious, such as a YouTube video or streamed music.

User tracking
Because your application uses code from multiple sources in most cases, you might find that a library, API, or microservice actually performs some type of

user tracking that a hacker could use to learn more about your organization. Every piece of information you give a hacker makes the process of overcoming your security easier.

Tainted inputs

Unless you provide your own input checking, HTML5 lets through any input the user wants to provide. You may only need a numeric value, but the user could provide a script instead. Trying to check inputs thoroughly to ensure you really are getting what you requested is nearly impossible on the client side, so you need to ensure you have robust server-side checking as well.

HTML5 Attack Surfaces

HTML5 adds a number of interesting features that hackers just love because they provide additional attack surfaces. For example, LocalStorage seems like a good idea until you consider how easy it is for malware to access a system's local storage. You can read the details about this attack surface (including some attack examples) at *http://www.slideshare.net/shreeraj/html5-localstorage-attack-vectors* and *https://blog.whitehatsec.com/web-storage-security/*.

Another problematic feature is WebSockets. This feature allows two-way communication between a client and a server. The only problem is that the client might be running untrusted code. You can read more about this particular feature's problems at *http://www.slideshare.net/SergeyShekyan/bay-threat-2012-websockets* and *http://blog.kotowicz.net/2011/03/html5-websockets-security-new-tool-for.html*, along with examples of how you can use WebSockets to overcome security protections and potential fixes for the problem.

Defining the Key CSS Issues

Applications rely heavily on CSS3 to create great-looking presentations without hard-coding the information for every device. Libraries of preexisting CSS3 code makes it easy to create professional-looking applications that a user can change to meet any need. For example, a user may need a different presentation for a particular device or require the presentation use a specific format to meet a special need. The following list describes some key security issues you experience when working with CSS3:

Overwhelming the design

A major reason that CSS3 code causes security issues is that the design is overwhelmed. The standards committee originally designed CSS to control the appearance of HTML elements, not to affect the presentation of an entire web page. As a result, the designers never thought to include security for certain issues because CSS wasn't supposed to work in those areas. The problem is that the cascade part of CSS doesn't allow CSS3 to know about anything other than its parent elements. As a result, a hacker can create a presentation that purports to do one thing, when it actually does another. Some libraries, such as jQuery, can actually help you overcome this issue.

Uploaded CSS

In some cases, an application designer will allow a user to upload a CSS file to achieve a particular application appearance or make it work better with a specific platform. However, the uploaded CSS can also contain code that makes it easier for a hacker to overwhelm any security you have in place or to hide dirty dealings from view. For example, a hacker could include URLs in the CSS that redirect the application to unsecure servers.

CSS shaders

A special use of CSS can present some extreme problems by allowing access to the user agent data and cross-domain data. Later chapters in the book will discuss this issue in greater detail, but you can get a quick overview of the topic at *http://www.w3.org/Graphics/fx/wiki/CSS_Shaders_Security*. The big thing is that sometimes the act of rendering data on screen opens potential security holes you might not have considered initially.

Defining the Key JavaScript Issues

The combination of JavaScript with HTML5 has created the whole web application phenomenon. Without the combination of the two languages, it wouldn't be possible to create applications that run well anywhere on any device. Users couldn't even think about asking for that sort of application in the past because it just wasn't possible to provide it. Today, a user can perform work anywhere using a device that's appropriate for the location. However, JavaScript is a scripted language that can have some serious security holes. The following list describes some key security issues you experience when working with JavaScript:

Cross-site scripting (XSS)

This issue appears earlier in the chapter because it's incredibly serious. Any time you run JavaScript outside a sandboxed environment, it becomes possible for a hacker to perform all sorts of nasty tricks on your application.

Cross-site request forgery (CSRF)

A script can use the user's credentials that are stored in a cookie to gain access to other sites. While on these sites, the hacker can perform all sorts of tasks that the application was never designed to perform. For example, a hacker can perform account tampering, data theft, fraud, any many other illegal activities, all in the user's name.

Browser and browser plug-in vulnerabilities

Many hackers rely on known browser and browser plug-in vulnerabilities to force an application to perform tasks that it wasn't designed to do. For example, a user's system could suddenly become a zombie transmitting virus code to other systems. The extent of what a hacker can do is limited by the vulnerabilities in question. In general, you want to ensure that you install any updates and that you remain aware of how vulnerabilities can affect your application's operation.

Considering Endpoint Defense Essentials

An endpoint is a destination for network traffic, such as a service or a browser. When packets reach the endpoint, the data they contain is unpacked and provided to the application for further processing. Endpoint security is essential because endpoints represent a major point of entry for networks. Unless the endpoint is secure, the network will receive bad data transmissions. In addition, broken endpoint security can cause harm to other nodes on the network. The following sections discuss three phases of endpoint security: prevention, detection, and remediation.

It's important not to underestimate the effect of endpoint security on applications and network infrastructure. Some endpoint scenarios become quite complex and their consequences hard to detect or even understand. For example, a recent article (*http://www.info world.com/article/2926221/security/large-scale-attack-hijacks-routers-through-users-browsers.html*) discusses a router attack that depends on the attacker directing an unsuspecting user to a special site. The attack focuses on the router that the user depends upon to make Domain Name System (DNS) requests. By obtaining full control over the router, the attacker can redirect the user to locations that the attacker controls.

Preventing Security Breaches

The first step in avoiding a trap is to admit the trap exists in the first place. The problem is that most companies today don't think that they'll experience a data breach—it always happens to the other company—the one with lax security. However, according to the Ponemon Institute's *2014 Global Report on the Cost of Cyber Crime* (*http://info.hpenterprisesecurity.com/LP_CP_424710_Ponemon_ALL*), the cost of cybercrime was $12.7 million in 2014, which is up from the $6.5 million in 2010. Obviously, all those break-ins don't just happen at someone else's company—they could easily happen at yours, so it's beneficial to assume that some hacker, somewhere, has targeted your organization. In fact, if you start out with the notion that a hacker will not only break into your organization, but also make off with the goods, you can actually start to prepare for the real-world scenario. Any application you build must be robust enough to:

- Withstand common attacks
- Report intrusions when your security fails to work as expected
- Avoid making assumptions about where breaches will occur
- Assume that, even with training, users will make mistakes causing a breach

 Don't assume that security breaches only happen on some platforms. A security breach can happen on any platform that runs anything other than custom software. The less prepared that the developers for a particular platform are, the more devastating the breach becomes. For example, many people would consider point-of-sale (POS) terminals safe from attack. However, hackers are currently attacking these devices vigorously (*http://www.computerworld.com/article/2925583/security/attackers-use-email-spam-to-infect-pos-terminals.html*) in order to obtain credit card information access. The interesting thing about this particular exploit is that it wouldn't work if employees weren't using the POS terminals incorrectly. This is an instance where training and strong policies could help keep the system safe. Of course, the applications should still be robust enough to thwart attacks.

As the book progresses, you find some useful techniques for making a breach less likely. The essentials of preventing a breach, once you admit a breach can (and probably will) occur, are to:

- Create applications that users understand and like to use (see Chapter 2)
- Choose external data sources carefully (see "Accessing External Data" on page 27 for details)
- Build applications that provide natural intrusion barriers (see Chapter 4)
- Test the reliability of the code you create, and carefully record both downtime and causes (see Chapter 5)
- Choose libraries, APIs, and microservices with care (see "Using External Code and Resources" on page 22 for details)
- Implement a comprehensive testing strategy for all application elements, even those you don't own (see Part III for details)
- Manage your application components to ensure application defenses don't languish after the application is released (see Part IV for details)

- Keep up to date on current security threats and strategies for overcoming them (see Chapter 16)
- Train your developers to think about security from beginning to end of every project (see Chapter 17)

Detecting Security Breaches

The last thing that any company wants to happen is to hear about a security breach second or third hand. Reading about your organization's inability to protect user data in the trade press is probably the most rotten way to start any day, yet this is how many organizations learn about security breaches. Companies that assume a data breach has already occurred are the least likely to suffer permanent damage from a data breach and most likely to save money in the end. Instead of wasting time and resources fixing a data breach after it has happened, your company can detect the data breach as it occurs and stop it before it becomes a problem. Detection means providing the required code as part of your application and then ensuring these detection methods are designed to work with the current security threats.

Your organization, as a whole, will need a breach response team. However, your development team also needs individuals in the right places to detect security breaches. Most development teams today will need experts in:

- Networking
- Database management
- Application design and development
- Mobile technology
- Cyber forensics
- Compliance

Each application needs such a team and the team should meet regularly to discuss application-specific security requirements and threats. In addition, it's important to review various threat scenarios and determine what you might do when a breach does occur. By being prepared, you make it more likely that you'll detect the breach early—possibly before someone in management comes thundering into your office asking for an explanation.

Remediating Broken Software

When a security breach does occur, whatever team your organization has in place must be ready to take charge and work through the remediation process. The organization, as a whole, needs to understand that not fixing the security breach and restoring the system as quickly as possible to its pre-breach state could cause the organization to fail. In other words, even if you're a great employee, you may well be looking for a new job.

The person in charge of security may ask the development team to help locate the attacker. Security information and event management (SIEM) software can help review logs that point to the source of the problem. Of course, this assumes your application actually creates appropriate logs. Part of the remediation process is to build logging and tracking functionality into the application in the first place. Without this information, trying to find the culprit so that your organization can stop the attack is often a lost cause.

Your procedures should include a strategy for checking for updates or patches for each component used by your application. Maintaining good application documentation is a must if you want to achieve this goal. It's too late to create a list of external resources at the time of a breach; you must have the list in hand before the breach occurs. Of course, the development team will need to test any updates that the application requires in order to ensure that the breach won't occur again. Finally, you need to ensure that the data has remained safe throughout the process and perform any data restoration your application requires.

Dealing with Cloud Storage

Cloud storage is a necessary evil in a world where employees demand access to data everywhere using any kind of device that happens to be handy. Users have all sorts of cloud storage solutions available, but one of the most popular now is Dropbox (*https://www.dropbox.com/*), which had amassed over 300 million users by the end of 2014. Dropbox (and most other cloud storage entities) have a checkered security history. For example, in 2011, Dropbox experienced a bug where anyone could access any account using any password for a period of four hours (see the article at InformationWeek (*http://www.darkreading.com/vulnerabilities-and-threats/dropbox-files-left-unprotected-open-to-all/d/d-id/1098442*)). Of course, all these vendors will tell you that your application data is safe now that it has improved security. It isn't a matter of if, but when, a hacker will find a way inside the cloud storage service or the service itself will drop the ball yet again.

A major problem with most cloud storage is that it's public in nature. For example, Dropbox for Business sounds like a great idea and it does provide additional security features, but the service is still public. A business can't host the service within its own private cloud.

In addition, most cloud services advertise that they encrypt the data on their servers, which is likely true. However, the service provider usually holds the encryption keys under the pretense of having to allow authorities with the proper warrants access to your data. Because you don't hold the keys to your encrypted data, you can't control access to it and the encryption is less useful than you might think.

Security of web applications is a big deal because most, if not all, applications will eventually have a web application basis. Users want their applications available everywhere and the browser is just about the only means of providing that sort of functionality on so many platforms in an efficient manner. In short, you have to think about the cloud storage issues from the outset. You have a number of options for dealing with cloud storage as part of your application strategy:

Block access

It's actually possible to block all access to cloud storage using a firewall, policy, or application feature. However, the ability to block access everywhere a user might want to access cloud storage is extremely hard and users are quite determined. In addition, blocking access can actually have negative effects on meeting business needs. For example, partners may choose to use cloud storage as a method for exchanging large files. A blocking strategy also incurs user wrath so that the users don't work with your application or find ways to circumvent the functionality you sought to provide. This is the best option to choose when your organization has to manage large amounts of sensitive data, has legal requirements for protecting data, or simply doesn't need the flexibility of using cloud storage.

Allow uncontrolled access

You could choose to ignore the issues involved in using cloud storage. However, such a policy opens your organization to data loss, data breaches, and all sorts of other problems. Unfortunately, many organizations currently use this approach because controlling user access has become so difficult and the organization lacks the means of using some other approach.

Relying on company-mandated security locations

If you require users to access cloud storage using a company account, you can at least monitor file usage and have the means to recover data when an employee leaves. However, the basic problems with cloud storage remain. A hacker with the right knowledge could still access the account and grab your data or simply choose to snoop on you in other ways. This option does work well if your organization doesn't manage data with legally required protections and you're willing to exchange some security for convenience.

Control access within the application

Many cloud services support an API that allows you to interact with the service in unique ways. Although this approach is quite time consuming, it does offer the advantage of letting you control where the user stores sensitive data, while still allowing the user the flexibility to use cloud storage for less sensitive data. You should consider this solution when your organization needs to interact with a large number of partners, yet also needs to manage large amounts of sensitive or critical data.

Rely on a third-party solution

You can find third-party solutions, such as Accellion (*http://www.accellion.com/*) that provide cloud storage connectors. The vendor provides a service that acts as an intermediary point between your application and the online data storage. The user is able to interact with data seamlessly, but the service controls access using policies that you set. The problem with this approach is that you now have an additional layer to consider when writing the application. In addition, you must trust the third party providing the connector. This particular solution works well when you need flexibility without the usual development costs and don't want to create your own solution that relies on API access.

Using External Code and Resources

Most organizations today don't have the time or resources needed to build applications completely from scratch. In addition, the costs of maintaining such an application would be enormous. In order to keep costs under control, organizations typically rely on third-party code in various forms. The code performs common tasks and developers use it to create applications in a Lego-like manner. However, third-party code doesn't come without security challenges. Effectively you're depending on someone else to write application code that not only works well and performs all the tasks you need, but does so securely. The following sections describe some of the issues surrounding the use of external code and resources.

Defining the Use of Libraries

A library is any code that you add into your application. Many people define libraries more broadly, but for this book, the essentials are that libraries contain code and that they become part of your application as you put the application in use. One commonly used library is jQuery (*https://jquery.com/*). It provides a wealth of functionality for performing common tasks in an application. The interesting thing about jQuery is that you find the terms *library* and *API* used interchangeably, as shown in Figure 1-2.

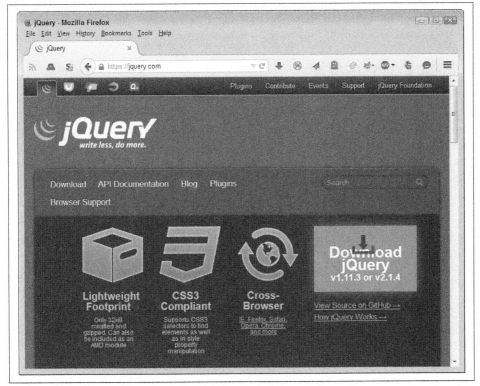

Figure 1-2. Many sites use library and API interchangeably

Looking at the jQuery site also tells you about optimal library configurations. In fact, the way in which jQuery presents itself is a good model for any library that you want to use. The library is fully documented and you can find multiple examples of each library call (to ensure you can find an example that is at least close to what you want to do). More importantly, the examples are live, so you can actually see the code in action using the same browsers that you plan to use for your own application.

 Like any other piece of software, jQuery has its faults too. As the book progresses, you're introduced to other libraries and to more details about each one so that you can start to see how features and security go hand in hand. Because jQuery is such a large, complex library, it has a lot to offer, but there is also more attack surface for hackers to exploit.

When working with libraries, the main focus of your security efforts is your application because you download the code used for the application from the host server. Library code is executed in-process, so you need to know that you can trust the source from which you get library code. Chapter 6 discusses the intricacies of using libraries as part of an application development strategy.

Defining the Use of APIs

An application programming interface (API) is any code you can call as an out-of-process service. You send a request to the API and the API responds with some resource that you request. The resource is normally data of some type, but APIs perform other sorts of tasks too. The idea is that the code resides on another system and that it doesn't become part of your application. Because APIs work with a request/response setup, they tend to offer broader platform support than libraries, but they also work slower than libraries do because the code isn't local to the system using it.

A good example of APIs is the services that Amazon offers for various developer needs (*https://developer.amazon.com/*). Figure 1-3 shows just a few of these services. You must sign up for each API you want to use and Amazon provides you with a special key to use in most cases. Because you're interacting with Amazon's servers and not simply downloading code to your own system, the security rules are different when using an API.

Each API tends to have a life of its own and relies on different approaches to issues such as managing data. Consequently, you can't make any assumption as to the security of one API when compared to another, even when both APIs come from the same host.

APIs also rely on an exchange of information. Any information exchange requires additional security because part of your data invariably ends up on the host system. You need to know that the host provides the means for properly securing the data you transmit as part of a request. Chapter 7 discusses how to work with APIs safely when using them as part of an application development strategy.

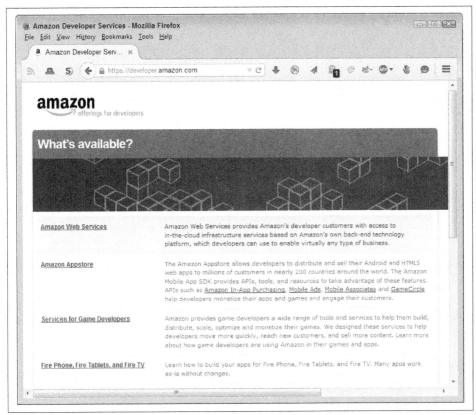

Figure 1-3. The Amazon API is an example of code that executes on a host server

Defining the Use of Microservices

Like an API, microservices execute on a host system. You make a request and the microservice responds with some sort of resource (usually data). However, microservices differ a great deal from APIs. The emphasis is on small tasks with microservices —a typical microservice performs one task well. In addition, microservices tend to focus heavily on platform independence. The idea is to provide a service that can interact with any platform of any size and of any capability. The difference in emphasis between APIs and microservices greatly affects the security landscape. For example, APIs tend to be more security conscious because the host can make more assumptions about the requesting platform and there is more to lose should something go wrong.

Current microservice offerings also tend to be homegrown because the technology is new. Look for some of the current API sites to begin offering microservices once the technology has grown. In the meantime, it pays to review precisely how microservices differ by looking at sites such as Microservice Architecture (*http://microservi*

ces.io/). The site provides example applications and a discussion of the various patterns in use for online code at the moment, as shown in Figure 1-4.

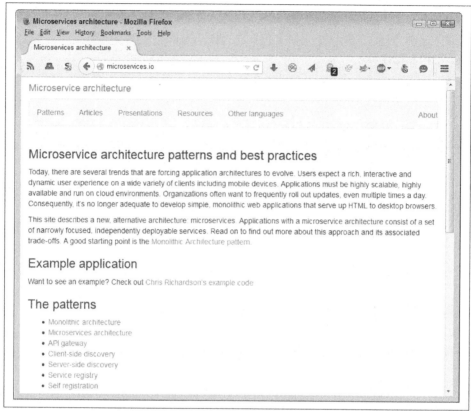

Figure 1-4. Microservices are new technology and it helps to see them in light of other usage patterns

When working with microservices, you need to ensure that the host is reliable and that the single task the microservice performs is clearly defined. It's also important to consider how the microservice interacts with any data you supply and not to assume that every microservice interacts with the data in the same fashion (even when the microservices exist on the same host). The use of microservices does mean efficiency and the ability to work with a broader range of platforms, but you also need to be aware of the requirement for additional security checks. Chapter 8 discusses how to use microservices safely as part of an application development strategy.

Accessing External Data

External data takes all sorts of forms. Any form of external data is suspect because someone could tamper with it in the mere act of accessing the data. However, it's helpful to categorize data by its visibility when thinking about security requirements.

You can normally consider private data sources relatively secure. You still need to check the data for potential harmful elements (such as scripts encrypted within database fields). However, for the most part, the data source isn't purposely trying to cause problems. Here are the most common sources of information storage as part of external private data sources:

- Data on hosts in your own organization
- Data on partner hosts
- Calculated sources created by applications running on servers
- Imported data from sensors or other sources supported by the organization

Paid data sources are also relatively secure. Anyone who provides access to paid data wants to maintain your relationship and reputation is everything in this area. As with local and private sources, you need to verify the data is free from corruption or potential threats, such as scripts. However, because the data also travels through a public network, you need to check for data manipulation and other potential problems from causes such as man-in-the-middle attacks.

 There are many interesting repositories online that you could find helpful when creating an application. Rather than generate the data yourself or rely on a paid source, you can often find a free source of the data. Sites such as the Registry of Research Data Repositories offer APIs now so that you can more accurately search for just the right data repository. In this case, you can find the API documentation at *http://service.re3data.org/api/doc.*

Data repositories can be problematic and the more public the repository, the more problematic it becomes. The use to which you put a data repository does make a difference, but ensuring you're actually getting data and not something else in disguise is essential. In many cases, you can download the data and scan it before you use it. For example, the World Health Organization (WHO) siteshown in Figure 1-5 provides the means to sift through its data repository to find precisely the data you require and then to download just that dataset, reducing the risk that you'll get something you really didn't want.

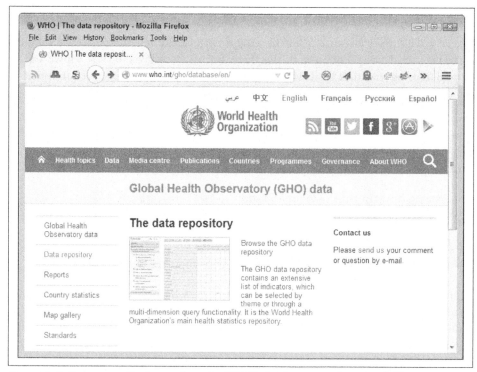

Figure 1-5. Some repositories, such as the WHO database, are downloadable

There are many kinds of data repositories and many ways to access the data they contain. The technique you use depends on the data repository interface and the requirements of your application. Make sure you read about data repositories in Chapter 3. Chapter 6, Chapter 7, and Chapter 8 all discuss the use of external data as it applies to libraries, APIs, and microservices. Each environment has different requirements, so it's important to understand precisely how your code affects the access method and therefore the security needed to use the data without harm.

Allowing Access by Others

The vast majority of this chapter discusses protection of your resources or your use of data and resources provided by someone else. Enterprises don't exist in a vacuum. When you create a data source, library, API, microservice, or other resource that someone else can use, the third party often requests access. As soon as you allow access to the resource by this third party, you open your network up to potential security threats that you might not ever imagine. The business partner or other entity is likely quite reliable and doesn't intend to cause problems. However, their virus becomes your virus. Any security threat they face becomes a security threat you face as well. If you have enough third parties using your resources, the chances are high that at least one of them has a security issue that could end up causing you problems as well.

Of course, before you can do anything, you need to ensure that your outside offering is as good as you think it is. Ensuring the safety of applications you support is essential. As a supplier of resources, you suddenly become a single point of failure for multiple outside entities. Keeping the environment secure means:

- Testing all resources regularly to ensure they remain viable
- Providing useful resource documentation
- Ensuring third-party developers abide by the rules (by doing things like building security requirements into the procurement language)
- Performing security testing as needed
- Keeping up with potential threats to your resource
- Updating host resources to avoid known vulnerabilities

Developers who offer their resources for outside use have other issues to consider as well, but these issues are common enough that they're a given for any outside access scenario. In addition, you must expect third parties to test the resources to ensure they act as advertised. For example, when offering a library, API, or microservice, you must expect that third parties will perform input and output testing and not simply take your word for it that the resource will behave as expected.

Once you get past the initial phase of offering a resource for third-party use, you must maintain the resource so applications continue to rely upon it. In addition, it's important to assume you face certain threats in making a resource offering. Here are some of the things you must consider:

- Hackers will attempt to use your resource to obtain access to your site
- Developers will misuse the resource and attempt to get it to perform tasks it wasn't designed to perform
- The resource will become compromised in some manner

CHAPTER 2

Embracing User Needs and Expectations

Security won't work unless you are able to convince the user to embrace it. Any Draconian device developers contrive to enforce security without the user's blessing will eventually fail because users are adept at finding ways around security. In situations where security truly is complete enough to thwart all but the hardiest user attempts, the user simply refuses to use the application. Long lists of failed applications attest to the fact that you can't enforce security without some level of user assistance, so it's best to ensure the user is on board with whatever decisions you make.

Users have two levels of requirements from an application, and security must address both of them. A user needs to have the freedom to perform work-required tasks. When an application fails to meet user needs, it simply fails as an application. User expectations are in addition to needs. Users expect that the application will work on their personal devices in addition to company-supplied devices. Depending on the application, ensuring the application and its security work on the broadest range of platforms creates goodwill, which makes it easier to sell security requirements to the user.

This chapter discusses both needs and expectations as they relate to security. For many developers, the goal of coding is to create an application that works well and meets all the requirements. However, the true goal of coding is to create an environment in which the user can interact with data successfully and securely. The data is the focus of the application, but the user is the means of making data-oriented modifications happen.

Developing a User View of the Application

Users and developers are often at loggerheads about security because they view applications in significantly different ways. Developers see carefully crafted code that does all sorts of interesting things; users see a means to an end. In fact, the user may not really see the application at all. All the user is concerned about is getting a report or other product put together by a certain deadline. For users, the best applications are invisible. When security gets in the way of making the application invisible, the security becomes a problem that the user wants to circumvent. In short, making both the application and its attendant security as close to invisible as possible is always desirable, and the better you achieve this goal, the more the user will like the application.

Current events really can put developers and users at loggerheads. Events such as the Ashley Madison hack (*http://www.computer world.com/article/2982959/cybercrime-hacking/ashley-madison-coding-blunder-made-11m-passwords-easy-to-crack.html*) have developers especially worried and less likely to make accommodations. In some cases, a user interface or user experience specialist can mediate a solution between the two groups that works to everyone's benefit. It pays to think outside the box when it comes to security issues where emotions might run high and good solutions might be less acceptable to one group or another.

The problem with developers is that they truly don't think like users. The cool factor of abstract technology just has too big of a pull for any developer to resist. A development team should include at least one user representative (one who truly is representative of typical users in your organization). In addition, you should include users as part of the testing process. Security that doesn't work, like any other bug in your application, is easier to fix when you find it early in the development process. When security is cumbersome, burdensome, obvious, or just plain annoying, it's broken, even if it really does protect application data.

Although this book doesn't discuss the DevOps development method, you should consider employing it as part of your application design and development strategy. DevOps (a portmanteau of *development* and *operations*) emphasizes communication, collaboration, integration, automation, and cooperation between the stakeholders of any application development process. You can find a lot of DevOps resources at *http://devops.com/*. A number of people have attempted to describe DevOps, but one of the clearer dissertations appears in the article at Patrick Debois' blog (*http://www.jedi.be/blog/2010/02/12/what-is-this-devops-thing-anyway/*). The article is a little old, but it still provides a great overview of what DevOps is, what problems it solves, and how you can employ it at your own organization.

Security is actually a problem that an entire organization has to solve. If you, as a developer, are the only one trying to create a solution, then the solution will almost certainly fail. The user view of the application is essential for bringing users on board with the security strategy you define for an application. However, you must also include:

- Management (to ensure organizational goals are met)
- Legal (to ensure data protection meets government requirements)
- Human resources (to ensure you aren't stepping on anyone's toes)
- Support (to ensure that any required training takes place)
- Every other stakeholder involved in defining business policies that control the management of data

After all, enforcing the data management rules is what security is all about. It's not just about ensuring that a hacker can't somehow find the hidden directory used to store the data. Security is the informed protection of data such that users can make responsible changes, but damaging changes are avoided.

Considering Bring Your Own Device (BYOD) Issues

Users will bring their own devices from home and they'll use them to access your application—get used to it. Theoretically, you could create methods of detecting which devices are accessing your application, but the fact is that users will find ways around the detection in many cases. Creating applications that work well in a BYOD environment is harder than working with a precise hardware configuration, but you can achieve good results. The main point is to assume users will rely on their own devices and to create application security with this goal in mind. The following sections describe the issues that you face when working with BYOD and provide you with potential solutions to these issues.

 Some organizations have actually embraced BYOD as a means to save money, which means that developers in these organizations have no standardized device to use for testing purposes. The organization simply assumes that the user will have a suitable device to use for both work and pleasure. If your organization is part of this trend, then you not only need to deal with BYOD devices as an alternative to company products, you need to deal with BYOD devices as the only option. It pays to know what sorts of devices your users have so that you have some basis on which to decide the kinds of devices to use for application testing and how to set device criteria for using the application.

Understanding Web-Based Application Security

The solution that is most likely to make BYOD possible is to create web-based applications for every need. A user could then rely on a smartphone, tablet, notebook, PC, or any other device that has an appropriate browser to access the application. However, web-based applications are also notoriously difficult to secure. Think about the requirements for providing anything other than password security for all of the devices out there. In fact, the password might not even be a password in the true sense of the word—you might find yourself limited to a personal identification number (PIN). The weakest security link for web-based applications in most cases is the mobile device. In order to make mobile devices more secure, you need to consider performing these steps:

1. Involve all the stakeholders for an application (including users, CIO, CISO, human resources, and other people outside the development team) in the decision-making process for application features. You need to make this the first step because these individuals will help you create a strategy that focuses on both user and business needs, yet lets you point out the issues surrounding unmet expectations (rather than needs).

2. Develop a mobile security strategy and put it in writing. The problem with creating agreements during meetings and not formalizing those agreements is that people tend to forget what was agreed upon and it becomes an issue later in the process. Once you do have a formalized strategy, make sure everyone is aware of it and has read it. This is especially important for the developers who are creating the application design.

3. Ensure that management understands the need to fund the security measures. Most companies today suffer from a lack of resources when it comes to security. If a development team lacks resources to create secure applications, then the applications will have openings that hackers will exploit. The finances for supporting the development effort must come before the development process begins.

4. Obtain the correct tools for creating secure applications. Your development team requires the proper tools from the outset or it's not possible to obtain the desired result. In many cases, developers fall short on security goals because they lack the proper tools to implement the security strategy. The tools you commonly require affect these solution areas:

    a. User or system authentication

    b. Data encryption

    c. Mobile device management

    d. Common antivirus protection

e. Virtual private network (VPN) support (when needed)

f. Data loss prevention

g. Host intrusion prevention

5. Create a partnership with an organization that has strong security expertise (if necessary). In many cases, your organization will lack development staff with the proper skills. Obtaining those skills from another organization that has already successfully deployed a number of web-based applications will save your organization time and effort.

6. Begin the development effort. Only after you have created a robust support system for your application should you start the development effort. When you follow these steps, you create an environment where security is part of the web application from the beginning, rather than being bolted on later.

 A 2014 IDG Research Services report based on surveys of IT and security professionals describes a number of issues surrounding mobile device usage. The top concern (voiced by 75% of the respondents) is data leakage—something the organization tasks developers with preventing through application constraints. Lost or stolen devices comes in at 71%, followed by unsecure network access (56%), malware (53%), and unsecure WiFi (41%).

Considering Native App Issues

The knee-jerk reaction to the issues surrounding web-based applications is to use native applications instead. After all, developers understand the technology well and it's possible to make use of operating system security features to ensure applications protect data as originally anticipated. However, the days of the native application are becoming numbered. Supporting native applications is becoming harder as code becomes more complex. In addition, providing access to your application from a plethora of platforms means that you gain these important benefits:

- Improved collaboration among workers

- Enhanced customer service

- Access to corporation information from any location

- Increased productivity

Of course, there are many other benefits to supporting multiple platforms, but this list points out the issue of using native applications. If you really want to use native applications to ensure better security, then you need to create a native application for each platform you want to support, which can become quite an undertaking. For most organizations, it simply isn't worth the time to create the required applications when viewed from the perspective of enhanced security and improved application control.

Some organizations try to get around the native/web-based application issue using kludges that don't work well in many cases. For example, using an iOS, Android, or web-based interface for your native application tends to be error prone, and introduces potential security issues. Using a pure web-based application is actually better.

Using Custom Browsers

In creating your web-based application, you can go the custom browser route. In some cases, that means writing a native application that actually includes browser functionality. The native application would provide additional features because it's possible to secure it better, yet having the web-based application available to smartphones with access to less sensitive features keeps users happy. Some languages, such as C#, provide relatively functional custom browser capability right out of the box. However, it's possible to create a custom browser using just about any application language.

It's a good idea to discuss the use of smartphone and tablet kill switches with your organization as part of the application development strategy. A kill switch makes it possible to turn a stolen smartphone into a useless piece of junk. According to a *USA Today* article (*http://www.usatoday.com/story/tech/2015/02/11/kill-switch-theft-down/23237959/*), the use of kill switches has dramatically reduced smartphone theft in several major cities. A recent *PC World* (*http://www.pcworld.com/article/2367480/10-things-to-know-about-the-smartphone-kill-switch.html*) article (*http://www.pcworld.com/article/2367480/10-things-to-know-about-the-smartphone-kill-switch.html*) arms you with the information needed to help management understand how kill switches work. In many cases, you must install software to make the kill switch available. Using a kill switch may sound drastic, but it's better than allowing hackers access to sensitive corporate data.

Besides direct security, the custom browser solution also makes indirect security options easier. Although the control used within an application to create the custom browser likely provides full functionality, the application developer can choose not to implement certain features. For example, you may choose not to allow a user to type

URLs or to rely on the history feature to move between pages. The application would still display pages just like any other browser, but the user won't have the ability to control the session in the same way that a standard browser allows. Having this additional level of control makes it possible to allow access to more sensitive information because the user will be unable to do some of the things that normally result in virus downloads, information disclosure, or contamination of the application environment. Of course, there are exceptions to every rule. If a virus that hooks the browser libraries and functions to steal information is already on the system, it's possible that the virus will still be able to read the content managed by a custom browser that uses that library.

A custom browser environment also affords the developer an opportunity to rely on programming techniques that might not ordinarily work. Developers experience constant problems making third-party libraries, frameworks, APIs, and microservices work properly because not every browser provides the requisite support. For example, in order to determine whether a particular browser actually supports the HTML5 features you want to use, you need to check it using a site such as HTML5test (*https://html5test.com/*) to obtain a listing of potential problem areas like the one shown in Figure 2-1.

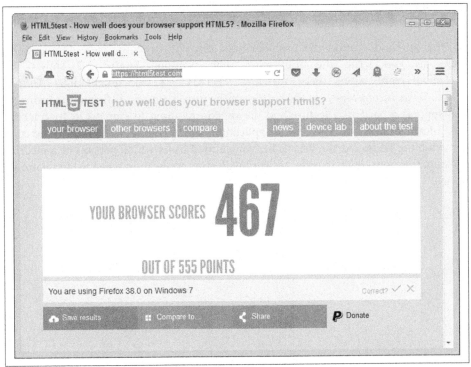

Figure 2-1. Using standard browsers means looking for potential support problems

The problem with the customer browser solution is that it introduces disparities in user support depending on the device the user chooses to rely upon. When these sorts of disparities exist, the developer normally hears about it. Users will want to access the organization's most sensitive data on the least secure device available in the most public place. Imagine working on patient records in a Starbucks using a smartphone. The data could end up anywhere, and a data breach will almost certainly occur. In some situations, the developer simply needs to work with everyone from managers on down to come up with a reasonable list of data-handling precautions, which may mean that using the custom browser solution won't be popular, but it will tend to enforce prudent data management policies.

Verifying Code Compatibility Issues

The BYOD phenomenon means that users will have all sorts of devices to use. Of course, that's a problem. However, a more significant problem is the fact that users will also have decrepit software on those devices because the older software is simply more comfortable to use. As a result of using this ancient software, your application may appear to have problems, but the issue isn't the application—it's a code compatibility problem caused by the really old software. With this in mind, you need to rely on solutions such as HTML5test (introduced in the previous section) to perform checks of a user's software to ensure it meets the minimum requirements.

Another method around the problem is to discover potential code compatibility issues as you write the application. For example, Figure 2-2 shows the W3Schools.com site that provides HTML 5 documentation (*http://www.w3schools.com/tags/*). At the bottom of the page, you see a listing of the browsers that support a particular feature and the version required to support it. By tracking this information as you write your application, you can potentially reduce the code compatibility issues. At the very least, you can tell users which version of a piece of software they must have in order to work with your application when using their own device.

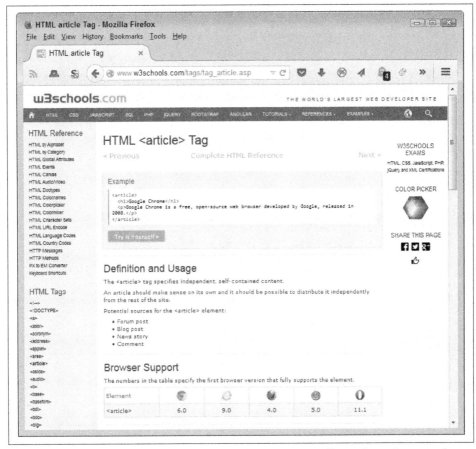

Figure 2-2. *Verify that the code feature you plan to use actually works with user software*

It's also important to note that some sites also tell you about compatibility issues in a succinct manner. The W3Schools.com site also provides this feature. Notice that the list of HTML tags shown in Figure 2-3 tells you which tags HTML5 supports, and which it doesn't. Having this information in hand can save considerable time during the coding process because you don't waste time trying to figure out why a particular feature doesn't work as it should on a user system.

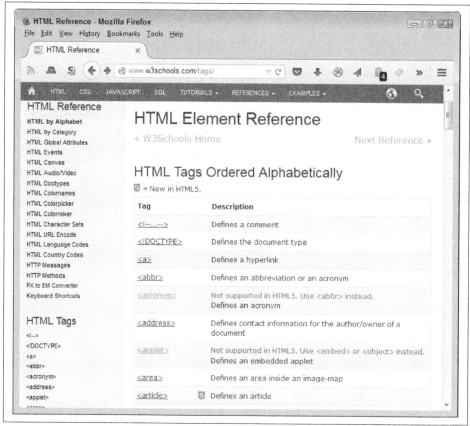

Figure 2-3. Finding documentation that tells you about version issues in a succinct way is important

A serious problem that most developers will experience with code compatibility is making HTML5 render properly with older browsers in the first place. Sites such as *http://www.w3schools.com/html/html5_browsers.asp* provide some answers you can use. For example, it shows how to use htm15shiv to make Internet Explorer support HTML5 elements. The cdnjs site (*https://cdnjs.com/*) contains a large assortment of these helpful JavaScript add-ins. You can find them at *https://cdnjs.com/libraries*. Figure 2-4 shows just a small listing of the available libraries. Unfortunately, you need to find examples for all of these libraries because the site doesn't provide much in the way of helpful information. The majority of the library documentation appears on GitHub. For example, you can find the *html5shiv.js* documentation at *https:// github.com/afarkas/html5shiv*.

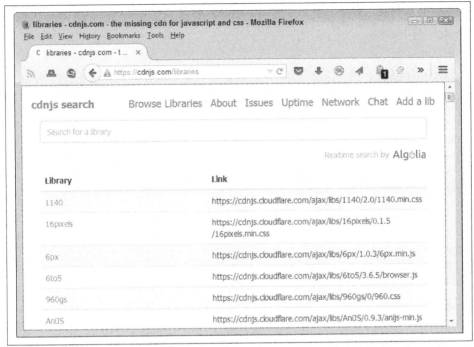

Figure 2-4. The cdnjs site provides you with a large number of helpful libraries

You see the abbreviation CDN used all over the place online. A content delivery network is a series of services that provides web content of various sorts. The main purpose of a CDN is to provide high availability and high-speed delivery. It also provides region-appropriate content when needed. Consequently, cdnjs is simply a CDN specifically designed to provide access to JavaScript code and make it available to a large number of developers, similar to the way that the Google CDN (*https://developers.google.com/speed/libra ries/*) performs the task.

Handling Nearly Continuous Device Updates

Your application will need to be flexible enough to handle all sorts of odd scenarios. One of the more common scenarios today is dealing with nearly continuous device updates. In this case, a user is perfectly happy using your application on a smartphone one day, but can't get anything to work the next. Common practice is for support to blame the user, but in many situations the user isn't at fault. At the bottom of the whole problem is that updates often take place without user permission or knowledge. Unfortunately, an update can introduce these sorts of issues:

- Code compatibility

- Security holes
- Lost settings
- Unbootable device
- Data damage

One of the ways around this issue is to make turning automatic updates off as part of the security policy for an application. Making the updates manually after you have tested the update as part of a rollout process is the best way to ensure that your application will continue to run. Unfortunately, this solution won't work. Users won't bring in their devices for testing unless something has already gone wrong. Even if users were willing to part with their devices, you likely won't have the resources needed to perform the required testing.

An alternative solution is to design applications such that they automatically check for updates during startup. If the version number of a product that the user relies on to work with the application changes, the application can send this information to an administrator as part of a potential solution reminder.

Creating flexible designs is also part of the methodology for handling constant updates. Although a fancy programming trick to aid in keeping data secure looks like a good idea, it probably isn't. Keep to best practices development strategies, use standard libraries when possible, and keep security at a reasonable level to help ensure the application continues to work after the mystery update occurs on the user's device. Otherwise, you may find yourself spending considerable time trying to fix the security issue that's preventing your application from working during those precious weekend hours.

Devising Password Alternatives

Passwords seem like the straightforward way to identify users. You can change them with relative ease, make them complex enough to reduce the potential for someone else guessing them, and they're completely portable. However, users see passwords as difficult to use, even harder to remember, and as a painful reminder about the security you have put in place. (Support personnel who have to continually reset forgotten passwords would tend to agree with the users in this particular situation.) Passwords make security obvious and bothersome. Users would rather not have to enter a password to access or to make specific application features available. Unfortunately, you still need some method of determining the user's identity. The following sections present you with some mature ideas (those you can implement today) that you might find helpful in searching for your perfect solution.

A Word About Near Field Communication (NFC)

One of the more interesting developments in technology has been the use of NFC for all sorts of needs. NFC is an extension of the radio frequency identification (RFID) technology used mainly in products. You find the passive tags in just about everything you buy. The RFID tag doubles as a security device, but its main purpose is to identify the product. Radio waves from a scanner power the tag and the tag returns the information it contains. NFC is a high-frequency subset of RFID that provides some special qualities you may find useful when creating security solutions for your application, including the following:

- The same device can act as a sender and tag.
- Devices exchange information securely.
- You can reprogram a device as needed.
- The device contains both intelligence and local memory, making it more flexible than RFID.

NFC offers the potential to eliminate passwords. A person could have a chip embedded in a credit card–sized ID badge. Tapping the badge on an NFC-enabled device would provide the required login. There are many NFC-enabled devices today, including PCs, tablets, and smartphones, so this solution could work everywhere.

The technology is also immature, so it's important to weigh your options carefully. Fortunately, the World Wide Web Consortium (W3C) is already working on standards for web development. You can see the working draft at *http://www.w3.org/TR/nfc/*. A library, API, or microservice that conforms to this standard can provide the resources needed to create robust applications that meet both organization and user needs, while reducing support costs and making the application significantly easier for the user to work with. Best of all, using an NFC solution lets you create a truly secure application.

Working with Passphrases

Passwords are hard to remember. Creating a password such as !jS2Zd5L8 makes it really hard for hackers to guess the password and does improve the chances that your application and its data will remain safe. However, the password is also impossible for anyone to memorize, so users often write it down somewhere. In fact, the user might just keep a file right on the hard drive to make access easy. Of course, hackers know this and look for such files. In short, complex passwords are a great idea from a security perspective, but they show terrible planning from the user's perspective. It's possible, however, to get nearly the same level of security using a passphrase that's actually easy to remember.

A passphrase is a semi-human readable phrase of some sort. You use letters, numbers, and special symbols in combination to make the password complex. For example, you could create a passphrase such as I luv fl0w3rs!. The passphrase contains upper- and lowercase letters, numbers, and special symbols. It's resistant to dictionary and other common brute force attacks. It's probably longer than most users will ever allow for a password. Yet, it's still easy to remember. A user won't have to write the passphrase down.

 Users do have reason to complain about the number of passwords that they're required to remember today. One of the technologies you might consider as part of solution is the password vault. A password vault makes it possible to store a number of user passwords in a way that's secure and continues to allow the use of complex passwords.

It's important to choose phrases that the user will remember, but that aren't associated with the application, the user's personal life, or the user's work environment. There isn't a good reason to let the hacker have advantages when it comes to guessing the passphrase. So, a passphrase such as I Work in R00m 23a. isn't a particularly good passphrase—it would be too easy to guess.

 Simply telling the user to rely on passphrases isn't going to work. In fact, users will still use passwords such as secret and master because they've used them for so long. Users tend to reject anything that makes them work even a little harder. As a consequence, you must still enforce complexity rules as part of your application code so that the user is forced to rely on something better than the usual suspects when it comes to passwords. If a user has to come up with a truly complex password, then the idea of using a passphrase instead becomes a lot more appealing.

Using Biometric Solutions

Biometric solutions rely on some unique characteristic of you as a person to generate a password. The idea behind biometrics is that a biometric password is unique to a particular person, isn't easy to steal, the user can't lose it, and the password is complex enough that hackers can't guess it (at least not easily). The three most common biometric solutions in use today are:

- Fingerprint

- Iris

- Voice print

All three of these solutions do have limitations, and hackers have ways to overcome them, so you might choose another biometric or combine a biometric with some other form of authentication. Vendors have a number of biometric alternatives in progress. The following list describes some of these alternatives:

Heartbeat
> One of the more interesting biometric alternatives is to combine a heartrate monitor with analysis algorithms. In fact, the solution already exists in the form of the Nymi wristband (*https://www.nymi.com/*). This solution relies on NFC to transmit the user's password to any NFC-enabled device. The same wristband could log on to a computer, enable an application feature, open a house door, or start a car.

Full facial recognition
> In the movie *Minority Report*, cameras scan people's faces and present them with ads as they walk down the street. The interesting thing is that the technology already exists in the form of Facebook's Deepface (*https://research.facebook.com/ publications/480567225376225/deepface-closing-the-gap-to-human-level-performance-in-face-verification/*). Simply by looking at your computer (webcam attached), you could log in to the system and have all the required application features in place. In fact, Facebook recently claimed (*http://money.cnn.com/ 2014/04/04/technology/innovation/facebook-facial-recognition/*) it could perform the scan from either the front or the side, which makes this solution relatively flexible when compared to other biometrics.

> Interestingly enough, all those selfies people are taking will make it quite easy for law enforcement and others to build a facial recognition database that will make it impossible for anyone to hide. Just think about the effect of every store camera being able to spot people based solely on their facial characteristics.

Ear shape
> You hold your smartphone up to your ear, just like you would when making a call. However, instead of hearing someone talk to you, you get logged in to an application. The solution already exists in the form of the Ergo Lock Screen App (*http://www.descartesbiometrics.com/ergo-app/*).

Typing technique
> Every person has a different way to type. The speed at which you type, the time you hold down the keys, even the pauses between letters, all identify you as a typ-

ist. By typing a specific phrase and monitoring how you type it, an application could create a two-factor authentication that's indistinguishable from just typing the password. However, now a hacker stealing the password still wouldn't be able to use it. One company that has already implemented such a solution is Coursera in the form of Signature Track (*http://blog.coursera.org/post/40080531667/signa turetrack*).

The promise of biometrics doesn't quite match the reality of biometrics. You already know from the descriptions that hackers have come up with methods for overcoming biometric passwords. If a user's password is compromised, you simply give the user a new password. However, if a user's fingerprint is compromised, it really isn't feasible to cut their finger off and sew a new finger on.

Why Use Two-Factor Authentication?

A problem with most single-factor authentication solutions is that they have a weakness that someone can exploit with relative ease. For example, a hacker could steal either a password or a passphrase using a social engineering attack or even brute force. By using two-factor authentication, it's possible to reduce the risk of someone overcoming the authentication process. Of course, it could be argued that three-factor or four-factor authentication would be even better, but there is a point at which no one could ever get onto their own account.

There are many types of two-factor authentication. For example, you could supply a user with both a password and a token. You could also combine passwords with biometric solutions. Many banks currently use two-factor authentication and you can optionally use it on sites such as Google, Facebook, and Twitter.

The problem with two-factor authentication is the same problem that occurs with single-factor authentication—users typically don't like authentication at all. The feeling is that it should be possible to use the application without doing anything extra at all. Of course, authentication is important, and you should use two-factor authentication for critical or sensitive data. However, it's important to consider the user's view of which authentication choices will work best. Creating a flexible solution is essential if you want this security solution to succeed.

Relying on Key Cards

Most people see key cards as an older-type technology that still sees wide usage. For example, go to a motel and it's likely the person behind the desk will give you a key card with a specially encoded magnetic strip. The key card replaces the key that you might have received in the past. Organizations also use key cards to meet various needs, including controlling access to areas such as parking lots. A combination of a key card and a PIN often provides access to sensitive areas. Suffice it to say that you have probably used more than one key card at some point in your life.

 Key card technology is constantly improving. Some modern key cards don't look like much of a card at all—they appear as part of a fob or other device that a user can put on a keychain or wear around the neck. By relying on RFID or NFC technology, it isn't even necessary for the user to slide the device; simply waving it in front of the lock works. The idea behind a key card hasn't changed, though. You have a physical device that contains security information that the user relies upon for access to resources instead of using a password.

PCs can also come with key card technology. You can use the key card to control access to the PC as a whole, or to control access to a specific application. When used for a specific application, the developer needs to provide code to read the card, determine its validity, and authenticate its user.

The main advantage of using a key card is that it can provide a complex password and potentially other details to help identify the user. The password can be as complex as is needed to thwart hackers. Depending on the technology used, you may even be able to change the key card information with relative ease, so a password change need not be a costly thing to do. Key cards also tend to be large enough that users won't routinely lose them (although you can count on users misplacing at least some of the key cards). Because the technology has been around so long, key cards can also be relatively low cost when compared to other security solutions. Users also tend to like key cards (except when lost) because they're fast and easy to use.

The main disadvantage of key card technology is that users do misplace them or leave them at home. A lost key card could provide a hacker with the sort of access needed to do real harm to your organization. Even if the user simply forgets the key card at home, providing a temporary key card is an additional support cost. Of course, there is also the matter of actually getting the temporary key card back when the user no longer needs it.

 An interesting place to look at various key card technologies is Secura Key (*http://www.securakey.com/*). This site shows you many of the key card options you have available. You can even find keyboards, such as the IOGEAR model (*http://www.iogear.com/product/GKBSR201/*), that provide the required key card reader as part of the keyboard. The point is to reduce the user interaction required to use your application in order to reduce potential user error and data leakage.

Relying on USB Keys

A USB key is essentially a flash drive that contains one or more passwords or tokens. You plug the USB key in to your computer, start it up, and the computer uses the data on the USB key to log you into the system. The same key could contain passwords used to access applications. The application would need to be aware that the password is on the key, but the technique makes it possible to log in to the application without actually providing a password or any other information. Google is currently working on a USB key setup (*http://www.technologyreview.com/view/510106/googles-alternative-to-the-password/*), and you can be sure other vendors will follow. USB keys have some significant advantages over key cards:

- It's possible to change the passwords without obtaining a new USB key.
- The USB key can hold multiple passwords.
- The overall cost of USB keys is lower than using key cards.
- It's possible to upgrade the sorts of credentials that a USB key provides.

Of course, the USB key shares many of the same failings as the key card as well. For example, whether a user loses a key card or a USB key, the result is the same—the user can no longer log in to the application and someone else could. In fact, given that USB keys are smaller than key cards, it's far more likely that a user will lose the USB key and compromise more than one password as a result.

Implementing a Token Strategy

You generally implement a token strategy using smartphones. A special site sends the user an SMS message, image, or sound that acts as the means to log in to a computer. For example, Illiri (*http://www.illiri.com/*) sends a sound to the user's smartphone that the user simply plays to the computer in order to log in. Likewise, Clef (*https://getclef.com/*) performs the same task using an image. In both cases, you can choose to send a different token every time the user logs in to the system, which means that even if a hacker steals the token, it's essentially useless.

In most cases, an application uses a token as a second authentication method in a two-factor authentication system. The first authentication method is still a key card, biometric source, password, or passphrase. However, it's theoretically possible to use a token as a primary authentication method should you wish to do so. As with any other method of authentication, this one comes with a number of issues you need to solve:

- The user would need to have a smartphone with them at all times.
- Losing a smartphone could potentially compromise the token system as a means for logging in to an application.

- This setup only works to log in to devices other than the smartphone, and many users today really do want to use their smartphone in place of a computing device whenever possible.
- The computer used to log the user in would need to have the requisite device for accepting the token.

Focusing on User Expectations

Up until this point of the chapter, you have focused on user needs. No user wants authentication, but every user needs authentication. Expectations fall into the "nice to have" category when it comes to development, but implementing them can create goodwill, which makes the user a little more open to actually using all those need-to-have items you added to the application.

Of course, some users have unrealistic expectations, such as an application that makes them look especially appealing to someone else or does all their work for them while they play solitaire and watch movies all day. Unfortunately, even the best developer in the world could never address expectations of that sort. The following sections describe some reasonable user expectations.

Making the Application Easy to Use

The chapter has made a point of emphasizing the need for ease-of-use. Users don't want to know the details about the security solution you implement. In fact, most users really don't want to know anything about the application other than it can provide the data needed to accomplish a task that matters to the user. In the long run, anything you can do to make security invisible to the end user increases the chances that the user will actually participate in the secure management of data and that the strategy will succeed in keeping data safe.

The counterpoint to the need for ease-of-use is creating a security scenario that works as advertised. Just one data breach can ruin a company's reputation and cost your organization buckets of money. According to a recent *Computerworld* article (*http:// www.computerworld.com/article/2926775/security0/data-breach-costs-now-average-154-per-record.html*), a data breach now costs $154.00 on average per record. The cost for each record lost will continue to increase, so the need for solutions that are safe continues to increase. The user expectation is ease-of-use, but the application reality is the need to keep data secure no matter what it takes to do so.

Making the Application Fast

Many developers don't understand the user's need for speed at all costs. Of course, part of the problem is that the user's attention span has decreased over the years.

According to an article on *The Guardian* website (*http://www.theguardian.com/media-network/media-network-blog/2012/mar/19/attention-span-internet-consumer*), you have between one and five seconds to grab the user's attention. Users want instant gratification and quick fixes. Deep thinking and in-depth analysis are no longer part of the user's repertoire. Unfortunately, the more security you add to an application, typically, the slower it becomes. If you were to ask most users how much time they want to spend on security, the answer would be zero. Users truly don't care about security—they want data fast.

The user expectation then is that there won't be any sort of wait for the data needed to perform a task. In addition, the data needs to be accurate and in a form the user needs at the outset. Anything less tends to breed frustration. The reality is that security will slow the application, but that you, as a developer, will need to concentrate on keeping delays to a minimum.

In addition, a secure environment means that not all data will be available all the time. You really can't permit a user to look at patient records while sitting at the local Starbucks sipping a latte. It's an unreasonable expectation on the part of the user to have this level of access (not that it will keep users from asking for it). So, a fast application is one that authenticates the user quickly and then presents the user with legal choices for data access. Hiding illegal options will often keep the user from looking for them in the first place, but you also need to provide help that specifies why certain data manipulation options are missing.

Creating a Reliable Environment

Above any other consideration, you must make the application reliable. The application can't behave in an unpredictable manner because the user will become frustrated and not use it. Even if the application is the tiniest bit slow, a user will complain less about speed than an application that truly is fast, but performs tasks incorrectly. It's also essential that the security and the data manipulation features work flawlessly. Chapter 5 discusses the various techniques you use to create a reliable application. Part III of this book is all about various kinds of testing. You need to take testing seriously to create a reliable application that generates few user complaints.

The user expectation in this case is that the application performs flawlessly in every situation. Again, it's a matter of making the application transparent so that all the user has to focus on is getting a task completed. In the real world, you can come close to flawless with proper coding techniques, testing techniques, threat analysis, and constant checks on issues such as device updates. So, in this one particular case, a user expectation comes quite close to being something you can provide in reality.

Keeping Security in Perspective

If you take nothing else away from this chapter, it's important to remember the fact that security is a balancing act. Unless you keep security in perspective, your application may not protect data enough or encumber the user to the breaking point by implementing Draconian features that don't really serve a useful purpose. Users are quick to spot not only functionality that they dislike but also functionality that doesn't serve a useful purpose.

Although it might appear that the user expectation is that applications don't need security, most users realize that security does have a place, especially if the user wants to keep the organization healthy. It's not really a matter of selling a user on the need for security, it's more a matter of selling the user on a specific level of security. When you keep security in perspective, it's a lot easier to close the deal and have the user on your side.

CHAPTER 3

Getting Third-Party Assistance

Reinventing the wheel is always a bad idea. It's entirely possible that someone else has already created a security solution that meets your needs well enough that you can use it instead of creating your own security solution. The third-party solution needs to appear as part of your security plan so that others know that you have a solution in mind. In addition, by having the third-party solution in your plan, you can include all sorts of information for it and invite discussion about the solution. This chapter discusses how you can add various kinds of third-party solutions to your security plan.

Of course, before you can do anything, you must discover the third-party solution you want to use. Fortunately, there are techniques you can use to reduce the time required to perform the process and then research the individual solutions to ensure they truly do meet your needs. Once you do discover the solutions you want to use, it's important to consider the pros and cons of each solution type. This chapter groups solutions into those that exist in the cloud and those that you add into your own application, such as a library or API. The following sections help you discover that third-party solutions really can meet your needs and reduce the time and effort to create a working solution.

 This chapter does discuss specific examples, but the information provided applies to a category as a whole. For example, although Capterra appears as a potential review site for products, other such sites exist, and you need to choose the site that best matches your philosophy of application design and development. The specific example simply helps illustrate the principle at hand.

Discovering Third-Party Security Solutions

Finding a third-party security solution can be difficult. Enter most search terms you can think of into a search engine and you get a list of individual security solutions back, many of which may not even relate to your particular problem. Search engines provide you with a haystack, not a needle. Unfortunately, they also remove the magnet, so that finding the needle is impossible. You really do need a better way to find the security solution of your dreams.

There is help in the form of review sites such as Capterra (*http://www.capterra.com/network-security-software/*), shown in Figure 3-1. This site provides help in the form of filtering that helps you make sense of the various vendors who are vying for your attention. Each of the entries has a short review that you can click to find out additional details. In many cases, the review also includes media that could provide a demo of the product or other useful information. The fact that the reviews are in one place, filtered by the criteria that you specify, and formatted in essentially the same way, makes the search process easier.

Figure 3-1. Search sites such as Capterra make looking for third-party resources easier

It pays to verify the information you find on Capterra and similar review sites. You can perform some level of verification by doing a web search for a product that interests you to determine if anyone else has provided a review of it. The insights provided by these additional reviews might help you make a better product selection.

Relying on magazine reviews can also be helpful, depending on the magazine you choose. For example, *SC Magazine* (*http://www.scmagazine.com/*) regularly reviews products that could be helpful to the security professional. In fact, you can get the reviews delivered to your inbox (*http://www.scmagazine.com/events/section/109/*). The magazine even sponsors competitions of a sort (*http://www.scmagazine.com/ 2014-sc-awards-us-finalists/section/3694/*) so that you can determine the most viable solutions available.

 Review sites of any sort are going to contain bias. Even if the site reviews products fairly, using criteria that you can examine and processes that you can verify, a review is still a matter of someone's opinion and you need to consider whether the person performing the review is informed enough to provide you with the information you need. Over time, you develop a sense that particular sites match your opinion of what really is a good product.

In some cases, you can find organizations that provide snapshots of their members that tend to provide you with consistent information. For example, the Cloud Security Alliance (CSA) (*https://cloudsecurityalliance.org/membership/solution-providers/*) falls into this category. By checking out these sites, you can get a quick overview of the players involved in specific security solutions. Of course, the problem is that the organizations provide the write-ups you read, so the information is biased. You can be sure that the vendors supporting the organization have left out any potentially negative aspects of their various products. You need to read these sorts of information sources carefully and then research the potential problems yourself.

 The good part about organizational sites is that you often find other helpful sorts of information because it's in the site's best interest to keep you involved. Some organizational sites also tell you about upcoming events where you can get additional information about potential solutions, meet with the vendors in person, and discover new techniques that you might not have known about before.

Some online magazine sites feature articles that can provide significant helpful information. For example, the *MIT Technology Review* article "Improving the Security of Cloud Computing" (*http://www.technologyreview.com/news/424298/improving-the-*

security-of-cloud-computing/) discusses techniques you can use to keep your data safe. The two solutions provided as part of the article point to issues you might not have considered. In the first case, you read about how computer scientists at the University of California, San Diego, and MIT demonstrated a need for each organization to have its own virtual server (as a result, Amazon changed the way it does things). In the second case, a new technology breaks your data into 16 pieces. You can then recover the data by using any 10 remaining pieces should some sort of failure occur. It's important to remember that articles normally have a goal, so you need to keep the goal in mind as you decide on the viability of the products featured in the article for meeting your organization's needs.

Considering Cloud Security Solutions

Organizations store a lot of data in the cloud today to keep costs under control and make the data easily accessible from any location the company may require. Cloud computing, which includes cloud data storage, is here to stay because it simply makes sense to use it instead of relying on custom solutions.

The problem with cloud computing is that it opens your organization to all sorts of problems. For example, you have no way of knowing that the hosting company will keep your data safe. There are way too many stories in the media about organizations that have had data hacked with devastating consequences. In fact, you can easily find stories about how easy it is to hack cloud-based storage, such as the *Tech Times* article "Cloud Hacking Isn't as Hard as Most Would Think" (*http://www.techtimes.com/arti cles/14800/20140903/cloud-hacking-isnt-hard-think.htm*). (One possible way around some of the data storage woes of the cloud is to encrypt the data before you send it there using strong encryption techniques. Of course, this solution would necessarily involve a speed penalty for your application due to the need to encrypt and decrypt data continuously.)

The following sections provide some ideas on how you can use third-party solutions to secure your online data. The sections consider three scenarios: data repositories, file sharing, and cloud storage. You may have to use combinations of solutions to create a complete package for your organization. However, these solutions provide you with a good start and will ultimately save time and effort on your part. Best of all, because someone else maintains the solutions, you save money in the long run as well because you aren't constantly fixing a custom solution.

A good rule of thumb to remember is that the best way to keep a secret is not to tell anyone. If you have storage requirements for data that simply can't see the light of day, storing it online is probably the worst possible solution. No matter how well you protect your data, if someone is certain they want to obtain access to it, they will. It's always easier to hack security than to build it. Consequently, if you have data you must legally keep secure under every potential scenario, then using local company storage that you control is the best idea. The article "Are My Files Really Safe If I Store Them in the Cloud?" (*http://computer.howstuffworks.com/cloud-computing/files-safe-in-the-cloud.htm*) tells you just how many different ways hackers can use to access your data and you can be certain that the hackers will come up with more.

Understanding Data Repositories

A data repository can be many things. Just try to find a consistent definition for one online and what you'll end up with is a new meaning for every site you try. The fact of the matter is that *data repository* means something slightly different to everyone that uses the term. However, most people will generally agree that a data repository is a centralized data storage location for information that an organization is maintaining as part of an organization's knowledge base. Using data mining techniques, the organization can probe this knowledge base and actually create new knowledge from it. Of course, there are many other implications of data repositories, but the bottom line is that you're talking about a lot of data in most cases; some of it maintained, some of it stored for historical reasons. Keeping data of this sort safe is a big job.

Data repositories abound. You can find a host of open data repositories on sites such as Open Access Directory (OAD) (*http://oad.simmons.edu/oadwiki/Data_reposito ries*), as shown in Figure 3-2. You might actually use some of these repositories in your application. So, security isn't simply a matter of keeping your private repository safe, but also ensuring that any public repository you use is also safe. After all, a hacker doesn't really care too much about the means used to access your application and ultimately your organization—all that matters is that the access happens.

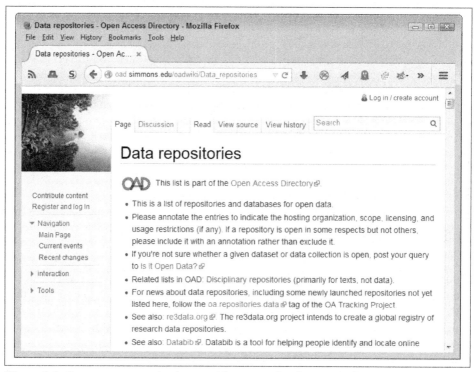

Figure 3-2. Open access repositories provide essential information for some organizations

Few data repositories contain data from just one project or affect just one project. In fact, there is little point to creating such a repository. Most data repositories contain data from a huge number of projects. For example, sourceforge.net contains 90,000+ projects that include every sort of programming project you can think of, including kernel mode software. Traditional approaches to keeping these data repositories secure, such as relying on the administrator to patch the server and manage access to it, don't work in this case because it's too easy for maintenance items to fall between the cracks.

A new type of protocol called Secure Untrusted Data Repository (SUNDR) from Secure Computer Systems Group (*https://www.yumpu.com/en/document/view/ 34269846/secure-untrusted-data-repository-sundr-usenix*) attacks the problem from the client perspective. A client can actually detect modifications to the file. Even if the server is untrusted or compromised in some way, the client can still detect the potential breach in security. The way in which this system works depends on logs maintained on a block server and a consistency server using methods that would be hard (but never impossible) to break. You can see a slideshow presentation of the technology at *http://slideplayer.com/slide/3389212/*.

It's important to remember that these new technologies will work hand in hand with existing technologies, such as the security provided by a database manager. They also don't dismiss your responsibility as a developer for including security as part of your solution. However, what technologies such as SUNDR do provide is another level of defense—this one at the server level and not dependent on the server or the administrator to maintain.

Dealing with File Sharing Issues

File sharing used to mean creating a cumbersome configuration that users hated to use, when it worked at all. In order to create a file sharing scenario, the organization needed to set up a special file server and create a VPN to access it. For a developer, it meant having to write tons of code to work around the problems associated with accessing the data in such an environment, along with an equally large amount of error-trapping code to reduce user frustration when the setup failed to work as planned. Moving data from private networks to cloud solutions maintained by third parties who have the deep pockets required to fund such a solution seems like an obvious solution. An organization can save 65% or more by moving data to a cloud provider instead of hosting the data on a private server.[1] Developers gain well-considered and documented APIs to make accessing the data easier. Users gain because there is a lot less frustration in using a publicly accessible file sharing solution and such solutions usually work with every device the user owns.

 It's essential to realize that any publicly available file sharing service is going to create potential security breaches. No matter how high the host builds the walls, a hacker will come along and dig under them to access your data. Using any sort of file sharing service incurs risks beyond what you might expect when using a VPN. Although many organizations use file sharing services successfully, keep in mind that a VPN is generally more secure and you may have to choose a VPN solution for some storage needs, despite the significantly higher costs.

When most people think about file sharing in the cloud today, they think about products such as Dropbox (*https://www.dropbox.com/business*). It's true that Dropbox does

1 "Moving Your Infrastructure to the Cloud: How to Maximize Benefits and Avoid Pitfalls" (*http://www.rack space.com/knowledge_center/whitepaper/moving-your-infrastructure-to-the-cloud-how-to-maximize-benefits-and-avoid-pitfalls*), "Cost Savings, Efficiencies Lead IT Pros to Cloud Computing" (*http://searchcloudcomputing.techtarget.com/feature/Cost-savings-efficiencies-lead-IT-pros-to-cloud-computing*), and "To Find Cloud Cost Savings, All You Need Is a Little Patience" (*http://searchcloudcomputing.techtarget.com/feature/To-find-cloud-cost-savings-all-you-need-is-a-little-patience*) provide additional insights into the whole savings picture.

have an API (*https://www.dropbox.com/developers*) that developers can use to create interfaces for their applications. The API provides full functionality and you can use it to meet a variety of needs, as shown in Figure 3-3. Of course, Dropbox has taken headlines for security issues as of late,[2] and *PCWorld* has even published an article (*http://www.pcworld.com/article/2918524/how-to-make-dropbox-more-secure-without-spending-a-cent.html*) that details solutions for fixing these problems.

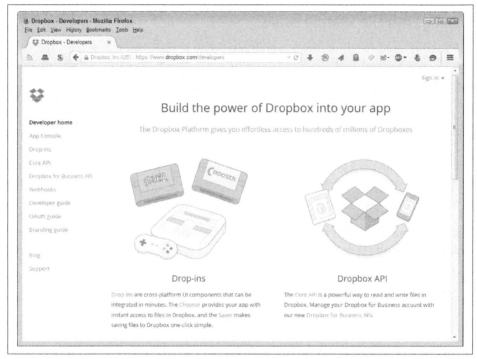

Figure 3-3. The Dropbox API makes online file sharing easy to add to your application

You actually have a number of solutions you can try when creating a file sharing solution for a small- to medium-sized business (SMB). They all come with security issues, so you need to research each one to determine which security issues you'd prefer to deal with. Some, like Dropbox, attract large headlines, but they also have good viable solutions for their security issues. Here is a list of the most common file sharing solutions (besides Dropbox) in use today:

- Acronis Business (*http://www.acronis.com/en-us/business/overview/*)

---

2 For example, see "Dropbox Drops the Security Notification Ball, Again" (*http://www.zdnet.com/article/dropbox-drops-the-security-notification-ball-again/*) and "Wary of Privacy Issues? Ditch Dropbox and Avoid Google, Says Edward Snowden" (*http://www.newsweek.com/wary-privacy-issues-ditch-dropbox-and-avoid-google-says-edward-snowden-276956*).

- Box (*https://www.box.com/*)
- Carbonite Business (*http://www.carbonite.com/online-backup/business/how-it-works*)
- Citrix ShareFile (*http://www.sharefile.com/*)
- CrashPlan Pro (*http://www.code42.com/business/*)
- Engnyte (*https://www.egnyte.com/*)
- Google Drive (*http://www.google.com/drive/start/index.html*)
- Hightail (*https://www.hightail.com/*) (Formerly YouSendIt)
- Microsoft OneDrive (*https://onedrive.live.com/about/en-us/*)
- MozyPro (*http://mozy.com/product/mozy/business*)
- SpiderOak (*https://spideroak.com/*)
- SugarSync for Business (*https://www.sugarsync.com/business/*)
- SyncPlicity (*https://www.syncplicity.com/*)

Choosing a third-party file sharing solution can be difficult. Your organization will have specific goals when choosing a file sharing solution, such as the cost/benefit ratio. However, as a developer, you have other concerns. Here are the sorts of things that you should consider when asking about a file sharing service:

Well-documented API
> In order to write custom code against the file sharing solution and make some types of access invisible, you need to have a well-documented API.

Security
> A cloud-based file sharing solution requires a number of unique security features to make it successful:

Cloud tiering
>> The most important of these features is cloud tiering, where you can define how the file is stored. Some files appear only on the file sharing service, some have a local copy in addition to the cloud copy, and some appear only on local drives, despite being available through the file sharing service.

File typing
>> Some file types may have special storage requirements. These files could contain sensitive data and you may need to store them locally or encrypt them even if they should appear in a different manner based on the file's tier.

Access frequency

Your application may only access files at a specific frequency. When something accesses the file at a different frequency, it could indicate a security breach. The file sharing service should alert you to this potential issue.

Global namespace

In some cases, a file sharing service will provide access in a manner that creates data silos, where accounting has its data completely separate from human resources. Data silos do serve a purpose, but sometimes it's necessary to store data in such a manner that anyone with rights to do so can access the data from any location using any device. To obtain this sort of access, you need a global namespace.

Redundancy

In order to keep writing code and not have to service user needs, you require a file sharing solution that has great redundancy. Otherwise, you can't ensure the data a user needs will be available at any given time. However, as part of data redundancy, you need to ensure the data is stored securely at each location using individual virtual servers (several types of shared file attacks depend on the attacker gaining access to the target's server—something that becomes harder when the file sharing service relies on virtual servers attached to individual clients).

Considering Cloud Storage

The term *cloud storage* encompasses a number of needs. Two of these needs have special mentions in the chapter: data repositories and file sharing services. However, your organization may have other cloud storage needs. It's usually easier if you can build an application to use a single host, but it may not always be possible. When choosing a host, you must also consider these additional cloud storage requirements:

Archiving

Data archiving is different from other sorts of cloud storage in that you need to ensure the data is safe, rather than necessarily accessible. If a major event occurs, you want to ensure that your data remains safe. Organizations previously relied on tapes and other media stored in an offsite location to ensure data security, but today cloud storage addresses this need. Any application you build may have to archive data and ensure that the archival occurs in a secure manner.

Settings storage

Your users will want to use all sorts of devices to access all sorts of data in all sorts of ways. Users have no clue that applications require settings to work well and that storing settings locally makes it impossible to create flexible applications that work everywhere. Unfortunately, settings stored in the cloud also make it easy for hackers to guess application features and potentially hack into your organization, so you need to ensure the settings storage is encrypted and is hosted in such a manner as to make any breaches obvious.

Media storage

Users require access to all sorts of media today, including video, audio, photographs, presentations, and more. Your application may need to manage the media as part of its purpose, which means relying on features such as tiering to ensure the application and cloud storage handles the data correctly. Your user should only have access to required media and not all the media the organization has to offer.

There are other types of cloud storage that aren't discussed in this book. For example, most developers don't have much of an interest in email unless they're writing an email application. The point is that storage encompasses a broad range of types and requirements that you need to consider as part of your security solution.

Choosing Between Product Types

As you read through this book, you discover how to use various product types to make your coding efforts significantly easier. It's important to understand that you can categorize coding products in three ways: libraries, APIs, and microservices. Each coding resource type has a specific purpose and helps you meet specific needs. It's possible to mix and match product types in a single application, but you need to ensure that the products are used in such a manner that they don't affect security in a negative way. The following sections discuss the different product types and help you understand how you can use them as part of an application strategy. More importantly, you get a glimpse of some of the security issues for each of the product types.

Using Other People's Code

Any time you use other people's code, you take a chance that some hacker is going to discover a way to overcome the security measures offered by that code. The benefits of doing so are huge. By creating a single security breach, the hacker can potentially gain access to the applications written by everyone who uses the library, API, or microservice to which the hacker has gained access. The same hack works everywhere, which means that the hacker can select which sites to invade and what data to acquire. Some hacks are so successful that a hacker gains complete control over a data source and does things like hold the data hostage unless the data owner pays up.

The benefit to using other people's code is that you can create an application in a fraction of the time it would normally take using fewer people. The costs of support and maintenance are also significantly lower. When someone discovers a problem in the library, API, or microservice, the owner of that code performs the fix, not you (assuming the owner is around to perform the fix; otherwise, you must move to a dif-

---

ferent library, API, or microservice). Without performing any work at all, you automatically gain all the benefits of the fix that the third party provides.

The third party also provides enhancements that make the code faster, more efficient, or more secure. When new technologies appear on the scene, the third party provides the updates needed to make your application work in new ways. If users start requiring access to a new device type, the third party will create the code needed to make that device function properly. In short, there are many good reasons to use other people's code, but you have to be wary when doing so.

Working with Libraries

Libraries are code that exists in separate files, but you load into your application. The library becomes part of your application. In most cases, you can download libraries to a local server, but in other cases you can't. Downloading a library to a local server has the benefit of not allowing others to see how you're using the library to create an application. This practice can also increase application speed by making the loading process faster and easier. In addition, downloading the library means that the library code remains stable, which makes it possible to create more reliable applications.

From a security perspective, it might seem as if downloading a library to a local drive is the best bet. You gain all the benefits of using someone else's code and don't have to expose your application to potential hacks based on seeing how you use the library. The downside, from a security perspective, is that using a local copy also means you don't get automatic updates. This means that your application could contain bugs that the library developer has already fixed and actually make it easier for a hacker to gain entry to your system.

 Whether someone can see what you're doing with a downloaded library depends on the library's source language. JavaScript is normally readable in a text editor. Many people obfuscate their JavaScript code (make the code virtually unreadable) in order to make it harder for others to determine what they're doing with the code. Products such as JScrambler (*https://jscrambler.com/en/*) and JavaScript Obfuscator/Encoder (*http://www.danstools.com/javascript-obfuscate/*) do make it quite hard to see what's going on, but a determined hacker could still do it. It's also possible to decompile many different types of code files used on the Internet. The point is that you can make things hard by downloading a library and making it unreadable, but you can't make it impossible to determine how your application works.

When working with libraries, you need to consider the originator's reputation, as well as the manner in which you use the library in your application. Because a library integrates directly into your application, you need to consider what type of access the library gains to your application internals. It's important to code defensively when using libraries because you don't want to tell others too much about how your application works. Some examples of libraries are:

- D3.js (*http://d3js.org/*)
- Google Web Toolkit (GWT) (*http://www.gwtproject.org/*)
- jQuery (*http://jquery.com/*)
- jQuery Mobile (*http://jquerymobile.com/*)
- jQuery UI (*http://jqueryui.com/*)
- MooTools (*http://mootools.net/*)
- PDF.js (*http://mozilla.github.io/pdf.js/*)
- QUnit (*http://qunitjs.com/*)
- SWFObject (*https://code.google.com/p/swfobject/*)
- YUI Library (*http://yuilibrary.com/*)

Accessing APIs

APIs are code that you access from your application by making calls to a central location. The APIs exist as a separate entity and you call on that entity from your application. The point is that APIs are completely separate from the other code of your application, so you need to create a reference to it and then make requests to the API. An API is normally attached to some type of service, such as data storage. You use APIs to create a client/server kind of connection, with all the security issues that such a connection implies.

Some APIs add secured access to help ensure hackers can't easily use certain exploits to gain control of the API or use it in ways that the creators never envisioned. A few APIs require a name and password combination to obtain access to the service, which is fine as long as the information is sent in encrypted form. However, even using encryption, the data isn't really safe. As an alternative, APIs can use keys to provide access. Unfortunately, when the keys are exposed, the API endpoints still happily give up information to whoever is requesting it. In short, security problems will occur with an API at some point, but you can employ methods to curtail hacker activity. It's still important to maintain vigilance and watch for hacker activity when using an API.

A potential problem with APIs is that they can be slow. Your application becomes less efficient and experiences delays. This is an important consideration because users aren't known for their patience and could end up doing something that will inadvertently break your application while waiting. Broken applications always present security issues that hackers are only too happy to exploit.

It's also possible for hackers to use man-in-the-middle attacks to access your data when using an API. A man-in-the-middle attack is especially hard to detect because the calls apparently work and you don't see any difference in the data when you retrieve it later. In the meantime, the hacker uses the data collected to do things like retrieve customer credit card numbers or obtain usable information about your organization. When working with an API, you have to pay close attention to issues such as data encryption to ensure your data remains safe. Some examples of APIs are:

- AccuWeather (*http://www.programmableweb.com/api/accuweather*)
- Amazon (*https://affiliate-program.amazon.com/gp/advertising/api/detail/main.html*)
- Box (*https://developers.box.com/*)
- Facebook (*https://developers.facebook.com/*)
- Flickr (*https://www.flickr.com/services/developer/*)
- Google (*https://developers.google.com/products/*)
- Pinterest (*http://www.programmableweb.com/api/pinterest*)
- Salesforce (*http://www.salesforce.com/us/developer/docs/api/index.htm*)
- Twitter (*https://dev.twitter.com/overview/documentation*)
- WordPress (*http://codex.wordpress.org/WordPress_APIs*)
- YouTube (*https://developers.google.com/youtube/*)

One of the differences between libraries and APIs is that most libraries offer free use, while many APIs cost money to use. In most cases, you can gain access to an API at a level sufficient for testing purposes, but to gain full API functionality you must obtain a key, which means paying for the level of access you require.

In addition, many API hosts require that you test your application in sandbox mode and obtain a certification for the resulting debugged application before the host allows the application to use the actual API. These requirements also add to the cost of using APIs, which can make them less popular than using libraries.

Considering Microservices

Microservices are a new technology that actually builds on existing technologies. A microservice is a sort of mix of web service, API, and library, but in a small package. In fact, microservices have the following list of features that you need to consider:

- Relies on a small, single-purpose, service-based application to create a fully functional application (each single-purpose application is a microservice)
- Uses the most appropriate programming language for the task
- Accesses application data using the most efficient data management technique for the particular microservice
- Develops lightweight communication between each microservice
- Depends on protocols such as REST to communicate, so that the pipe is dumb, but the microservice is smart
- Employs decentralized application management by monitoring each microservice separately
- Selects each microservice as needed to build any number of full-fledged applications (desktop, mobile browsers, native mobile apps, and even APIs)

Given the way microservices work, you need to consider some of the same issues that you do for both libraries and APIs. For example, a microservice could appear as part of your application code, so you need to consider just how the microservice interacts with the application. In addition, just like an API, you send and receive data when working with a microservice, so it's possible for man-in-the-middle attacks to cause problems.

From a security perspective, microservices tend to implement security differently than either libraries or APIs. Instead of offering a single solution for everyone and everything that uses the microservices on a site as a whole, each microservice offers individualized security based on that microservices' needs. As a result, microservices tend to provide better security, but the security is also uneven and harder to work with. Here are some examples of microservices (each of these sites provides access to a number of microservices—you'd choose which microservices you want to use in a particular application):

- Akana (*http://www.akana.com/solutions/microservices*)
- Archivematica (*https://ww.archivematica.org/en/*)
- Gilliam (*http://gilliam.github.io/*)
- LSQ.io (*https://angel.co/lsq-io*)
- Seneca (*http://senecajs.org/*)

Because microservices are so new, you'll find a lot of discussion on just what constitutes a microservice. For some authorities, the number of lines of code (LOC) matters. A service that uses between 200 and 500 LOC is in the microservice range, but a service above that range isn't. (Fewer than 200 LOC apparently doesn't provide a sufficient level of functionality.) Consequently, a microservice such as Cloner (*https://www.npmjs.com/package/app-cloner-heroku*) does meet the requirements (305 LOC), but a microservice such as Deploy Hooks (*https://devcenter.heroku.com/articles/deploy-hooks*) doesn't (1,240 LOC).

PART II

Applying Successful Coding Practices

In this part of the book, you begin looking at the techniques for coding secure applications. Each of the chapters that follow discusses a particular part of a typical web-based application. Chapter 4 begins with the user interface, which is potentially the most important part because security begins and ends with user cooperation. If the interface is flawed, the user simply won't cooperate (at least, not nearly as well) and your security solution will contain flaws. Chapter 5 goes hand in hand with Chapter 4. An application that is unreliable is frustrating for a user to interact with and tends to create still more security issues both directly and indirectly.

Modern applications don't exist in a vacuum. If a developer were to build every application from scratch, everyone would suffer. The use of libraries (Chapter 6), APIs (Chapter 7), and microservices (Chapter 8) makes the process of building an application much faster and easier. In addition, because the code provided by these third-party sources receives so much scrutiny, it tends to be safer than the standalone code you could build yourself and it usually receives updates faster than your organization could provide them for custom code.

CHAPTER 4

Developing Successful Interfaces

Applications rely on interfaces to interact with the user. When the interface is flawed, the user's opinion of the application diminishes and user satisfaction suffers. Every security solution you can conceive of depends on the goodwill of the user to make it a reality. Yes, you can attempt Draconian measures to force user participation, but often these measures result in the user constantly finding ways to overcome security, rather than work with it. In most cases, you receive the best results when the user is on your side, which means making an effort to create an interface the user can appreciate (in that it makes the application so easy to use that the application almost disappears from view). Of course, you do need to ensure the application enforces policies. Therefore, this chapter looks at both the carrot (user cooperating) and the stick (enforced policies) of application security from the interface perspective.

It's important to make the carrot part of the equation obvious. A user sees various kinds of eye candy, helpful tips, and a clear interface as signs that the developer really cares about the application and how the user views it. Making the user experience pleasant is essential.

The stick part of the equation is usually hidden and subtle. For example, instead of asking the user to type the name of a state, the application prevents unauthorized entries by creating a state list and having the user select from the list. Although the user's choices are constrained, what the user sees is ease-of-use.

Some interface decisions are mistakes before you even code them. For example, some validation techniques tell the user that the input is unacceptable without telling the user why the input won't work. More importantly, when the feedback lacks useful tips and examples, the user becomes frustrated. This chapter also discusses techniques you can use to refine the interface. It isn't a matter of some techniques working, while others don't—it's more a matter of some techniques creating less user angst.

It's important to understand that few people would handcode a website any longer. Fewer still would code a website without using libraries, APIs, frameworks, microservices, and any of a number of other third-party offerings. However, all of these third-party sources rely on the technologies described in this chapter. All that you're getting from a third-party source is prepackaged code that you could have created yourself. Viewing the code in the way shown in this chapter helps you understand the underlying techniques used by third-party sources so that you can better tell whether these sources are secure. With this in mind, the code in this chapter is designed to help you understand security principles, rather than something you'd actually employ on your website.

Assessing the User Interface

Most organizations need to spend time assessing the user interface of their applications because these interfaces create clear opportunities for hackers to gain access to your network. The section "Specifying Web Application Threats" on page 2 in Chapter 1 describes a number of common exploits that hackers use. A surprising number of those exploits rely on some user interface element to help things along. The tighter you can make your interface without inhibiting user interaction, the better. The following sections describe some of the techniques you can use to assess the user interface.

The best way to work with the examples described in this chapter is to use the downloadable source, rather than type it in by hand. Using the downloadable source reduces potential errors. You can find the examples for this chapter in the *\S4WD\Chapter04* folder of the downloadable source.

Creating a Clear Interface

An essential part of creating workable interfaces today is making them clear. The complex interfaces of old create security problems because the user isn't sure what to do or possibly has too much to do. The libraries available today make it possible to create clear interfaces that focus on one issue at a time in many situations. For example, the tabbed interface shown in Figure 4-1 provides an example of a clear interface that only does one thing at a time as part of the *Tabs.html* file.

Figure 4-1. A clear interface focuses on one issue in a manner the user can understand

This interface is quite clear. It asks a simple question, provides a limited number of responses, and makes it more difficult for the user to enter bad data. The user selects a color, clicks the button, and moves on to the next tab. A number of web applications now make use of this sort of interface. You often see it used for signup sheets. The example relies on the jQuery UI library (*https://jqueryui.com/*) to perform its task. Here's the source code for this example:

```
<!DOCTYPE html>

<html>
<head>
   <script
      src="https://code.jquery.com/jquery-latest.js">
   </script>
   <script
      src="https://code.jquery.com/ui/1.9.2/jquery-ui.js">
   </script>
   <link
      rel="stylesheet"
      href="https://code.jquery.com/ui/1.9.2/themes/base/jquery-ui.css" />
   <title>Using the Tabs Widget</title>
   <style>
      #Configuration
      {
         width: 90%;
```

```
                text-align: center;
            }
            #Configuration div
            {
                text-align: left;
            }
        </style>
        <script language="JavaScript">
            $(function()
            {
                $("#Configuration").tabs();
            });
        </script>
    </head>

    <body>
        <h1>Using the Tabs Widget</h1>
        <form id="ConfigForm" method="get" action="Tabs.html">
            <div id="Configuration">
                <ul>
                    <li><a href="#Tab1">Foreground Color</a></li>
                    <li><a href="#Tab2">Background Color</a></li>
                    <li><a href="#Tab3">Options</a></li>
                </ul>
                <div id="Tab1">
                    <input id="FGRed"
                            type="radio"
                            name="Foreground"
                            value="Red"
                            checked="checked" />
                    <label for="FGRed">Red</label><br />
                    <input id="FGOrange"
                            type="radio"
                            name="Foreground"
                            value="Orange" />
                    <label for="FGOrange">Orange</label><br />
                    <input id="FGGreen"
                            type="radio"
                            name="Foreground"
                            value="Green" />
                    <label for="FGGreen">Green</label><br />
                    <input id="FGBlue"
                            type="radio"
                            name="Foreground"
                            value="Blue" />
                    <label for="FGBlue">Blue</label>
                </div>
                <div id="Tab2">
                    <input id="BGRed"
                            type="radio"
                            name="Background"
                            value="Red"
```

```
                checked="checked" />
        <label for="BGRed">Red</label><br />
        <input id="BGOrange"
                type="radio"
                name="Background"
                value="Orange" />
        <label for="BGOrange">Orange</label><br />
        <input id="BGGreen"
                type="radio"
                name="Background"
                value="Green" />
        <label for="BGGreen">Green</label><br />
        <input id="BGBlue"
                type="radio"
                name="Background"
                value="Blue" />
        <label for="BGBlue">Blue</label>
    </div>
    <div id="Tab3">
        <input id="Sounds"
                type="checkbox"
                name="Sounds"
                value="SpecialSounds" />
        <label for="Sounds">Use Special Sounds</label><br />
        <input id="Effects"
                type="checkbox"
                name="Effects"
                value="SpecialEffects" />
        <label for="Effects">Use Special Effects</label>
    </div>
</div>
<input id="ChangeConfig"
        type="submit"
        value="Change Configuration" />
    </form>
</body>
</html>
```

In order to create this interface, you import the jQuery (*https://jquery.com/*) and jQuery UI libraries, and the associated jQuery UI stylesheet. The tab information appears in a <div> with an id of Configuration. The magic used to create the interface is the result of making the $("#Configuration").tabs() call.

Making Interfaces Flexible

Reducing the user's ability to enter invalid data, making the interface clear and concise, and keeping things simple all restrict the user in various ways. They're forms of constraints that help you keep data safe while making the user's task of interacting with the application simpler. However, interfaces also require flexibility. The user will use the application on a number of devices, not all of which will accept the initial organization you provide. The act of letting the user organize the screen as needed provides the user with a sense of power without leaving any security holes open. Whenever possible, an interface should let the user:

Drag

> Moving items around on screen can provide the user with a better view of the interface and potentially reduce errant inputs. At a minimum, reorganizing the interface lets a user interact with the application in a manner that best suits the user.

Resize

> There are many reasons the user may need to resize an interface element. Perhaps the text is too small. Combining the resize action with the ability provided by most browsers of making the text smaller or larger as needed helps the user see the information better.

Select

> Creating positive feedback for selections is essential. You should assume nothing about the user's ability to see. The selection should provide multiple means of feedback, such as using a thicker border, presenting the selection in a whiter (brighter) color, relying on changing textual attributes, and providing feedback in the form of color. This is one time where having someone on staff check the effects of selections using accessibility aids such as screen readers is important.

Sort

> The user should see the data in an order that makes sense to the user—not necessarily to you. With this in mind, provide multiple ways to sort data whenever possible so that the user can perform required analysis and make selections with greater ease.

The jQuery and jQuery UI libraries provide the means to perform all the essential interface flexibility tasks and a host of other tasks (such as allowing drag-and-drop data entry). Figure 4-2 shows an example of using these libraries to move items around on the screen.

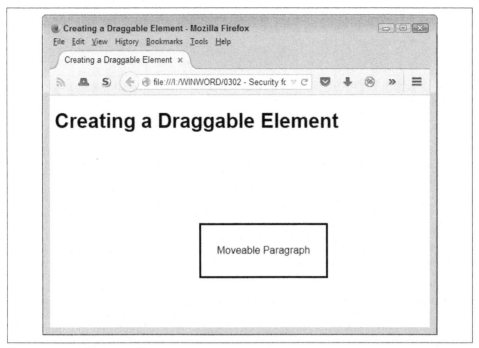

Figure 4-2. *Make it possible to move items around*

A library can help you create an appropriate environment for user data entry. However, it can't remove the need to validate every piece of data you receive. Hackers like it when developers make assumptions about inputs based on the interface. Always assume that a hacker will find a way around the interface aids you provide to honest users and validate every piece of data no matter what source it comes from.

Creating an interface with moveable elements is relatively easy. The following code shows you how (you can also see this code in the *DragContent.html* file):

```
<!DOCTYPE html>

<html>
<head>
   <script
      src="https://code.jquery.com/jquery-latest.js">
   </script>
   <script
      src="https://code.jquery.com/ui/1.9.2/jquery-ui.js">
   </script>
   <link
      rel="stylesheet"
```

```
        href="https://code.jquery.com/ui/1.9.2/themes/base/jquery-ui.css" />
    <style>
        #MoveMe
        {
            border: solid;
            width: 200px;
            height: 5em;
            text-align: center;
            line-height: 5em;
        }
    </style>
    <script language="JavaScript">
        $(function()
        {
            $("#MoveMe").draggable();
        });
    </script>
    <title>Creating a Draggable Element</title>
</head>

<body>
    <h1>Creating a Draggable Element</h1>
    <p id="MoveMe">
        Moveable Paragraph
    </p>
</body>
</html>
```

In this case, the MoveMe paragraph (<p> element) is the target. Notice that making the paragraph moveable doesn't affect the heading (<h1> element). All you need to do is call $("#MoveMe").draggable() when the form loads in order to make the paragraph element moveable.

Providing User Aids

Creating an environment in which even the least capable user is able to function well is hard for most developers because most developers can't even imagine not being able to relate well to a computer. Many of the people a developer supports with an application are quite smart—they simply aren't smart about computers or the way in which applications work, so it's important to give them a hand with various types of aids.

The one help item you should always provide is explanatory text. You add explanatory text as part of the HTML tag associated with an element. Here are the attributes most commonly used for explanatory text:

title

> The title attribute makes it possible to add explanatory information to just about any textual or control element on the page. When a user hovers the mouse

over the top of an element that has the `title` attribute defined, the browser displays the additional information in a text balloon. It's important not to make the text too long or to use anything but text within the `title` attribute because screen readers rely on these attributes to describe an element to someone with special visual needs.

`alt`

Use the `alt` attribute to provide a short description of an image element. When the browser can't display the image, it displays the description instead. In addition, when someone with special needs can't see the picture, the accessibility aid they use will typically use the `alt` attribute text to introduce the image. The point is that the `alt` attribute provides a description of the image and also acts as a substitute for it as needed.

`longdesc`

Many browsers ignore the `longdesc` attribute. This attribute provides a much longer description of an image than an `alt` attribute does. In most cases, you limit the description to about a paragraph of text. The point is to provide enough information so that someone with special needs can create a reasonable mental version of the image—at least the salient points of the image (rather than background).

User help information can appear in many other forms. A kind of help that most sites miss is to provide a sample of what you want as input for textboxes and other typed data as part of the input. You often see textboxes that contain a description of the desired content, rather than a sample of the desired content. (When the user types something in the textbox, the sample text disappears.) For example, instead of providing Last Name as the text within the textbox, provide an actual name, such as Doe (as in John Doe) or something along those lines.

Any input field should also provide a help link. When the user clicks the link, the application displays a help page with additional information. The point is to make it as easy as possible for the user to provide correct information. Any mistakes you can prevent at the outset will reduce user frustration, make data entry more accurate, and most importantly, avoid the mistakes that often lead to security issues.

Defining the Accessibility Issues

Accessibility can be a tricky issue to deal with, especially when working with modern tools. However, it's an important issue to consider because according to Web Accessibility In Mind (WebAIM), about 20% of the people visiting your site have a special need of some sort: visual, hearing, motor skills, or cognitive. As the world's population continues to age, the percentage will grow larger. In fact, you have a high likelihood of eventually needing some sort of assistance for a special need.

You may wonder what accessibility has to do with security. When people don't understand an interface, they make mistakes. However, training usually helps with this problem because you can instruct people on the proper use of the software (and sometimes they actually listen). When people can't understand an interface because of a special need, they still make mistakes, but no amount of training will ever solve the problem. Even if the user is positively motivated to use the software correctly, unmet accessibility needs will prevent them from doing so. Mistakes often translate into security holes of the worst sort. The unexpected input—the one you never imagined anyone would provide, often creates the biggest problems. An application that lacks accessibility features is more likely to create an environment where security busting mistakes occur on a regular basis.

Fortunately, many vendors design libraries, APIs, frameworks, and microservices with some level of accessibility in mind. They avoid uses of tables as a formatting aid, for example, which causes problems with the screen readers used by those who have visual needs. However, none of these tools is perfect and some of them are less perfect than others. Consequently, it's important to test your site to determine just what level of accessibility it provides. Most of these testing tools also provide tips on how to fix the accessibility issues found on your site. Table 4-1 provides a listing of testing tools and a description of how you can use them.

Table 4-1. Accessibility testing sites

Site	URL	Description
Lynx	*http://www.delori e.com/web/lynxvi ew.html*	This is a text-only browser that comes in versions for Linux, OS X, and Windows. It helps you check your site by displaying it in text only. This check helps you see your site as a screen reader will see it—making it possible to detect and correct problems with greater ease. Learn more about this product at *http://lynx.browser.org/*.
NIST Webmetrics Tool Suite	*http://zing.ncsl.nis t.gov/webmet*	A group of tools from the National Institute of Standards and Technology (NIST) helps you test the usability and accessibility of a site. For example, Web Static Analyzer Tool (WebSAT) ensures your page meets specific usability goals. The Web Variable Instrumenter Program (WebVIP) helps track user interaction so you know how well users are finding site features. There are more tools on this site and NIST updates them regularly.
Opera	*http://www.opera .com*	Like Lynx, this browser enables you to see your site as a screen reader will see it. However, unlike Lynx, this product also helps you turn certain features on and off as needed for comparison. For example, you can toggle images off so you can see how <ALT> tags will look (see the instructions at *http://help.opera.com/Windows/12.10/en/i mages.html*). Opera is available for a number of platforms including Windows, OS X, and Linux.

Site	URL	Description
O'Reilly XML.com	http://www.xml.com/pub/a/tools/ruwf/check.html	This site provides an XML syntax checker that also validates XHTML. You can provide the XML input directly or supply an URL containing the XML. The test run by this tool will check that the XML is well formed—it doesn't verify that the XML actually means anything. In most cases, you'll want to use the W3C HTML Validation Service for a final check of your web page. However, this website does perform fast checks of intermediate and test XML.
W3C HTML Validation Service	http://validator.w3.org	This site checks the HTML on your web page for conformance to World Wide Web Consortium (W3C) recommendations and standards. An error on this site means that the coding for your page is incorrect, even if most browsers will read it, so this tester goes beyond usability and accessibility requirements. Don't get the idea that passing the test on this site automatically makes your site accessible. Passing on this site means that your code is correct. However, making sure your code is correct is a good first step to ensuring you can add accessibility features.
Web Design Group HTML Validator	http://www.htmlhelp.com/tools/validator/	This site checks the HTML on your page or, as an alternative, on your computer. It also provides an option to validate a single page or the entire site. You may also find that this site is a little less picky than the W3C HTML Validation Service about which pages it will check and seems to output about the same information, but may not provide complete validation of your site.
WebAIM	http://webaim.org	You can find all sorts of interesting tools for verifying that your site is accessible on this site. For example, you can use the WAVE Web Accessibility Evaluation Tool (http://wave.webaim.org/) to determine whether your site has any major accessibility problems. A serious problem for many sites is the use of color. The Color Contrast Checker (http://webaim.org/resources/contrastchecker/) helps you verify that people with color deficiencies can actually see your site.

Testing tools are helpful in verifying that your development team has done a great job in creating an application that everyone can use. However, the actual development effort will often require a checklist of tasks to perform and issues to check. The Section 508 checklist at *http://webaim.org/standards/508/checklist* helps you create such a list for your application development efforts. Interestingly enough, as hard as this checklist might be to read, the government documentation at *http://www.section508.gov/* is a lot harder. The point of these requirements is to ensure that anyone, no matter what special needs they might have, can actually use your application as you intend. Without these features in place, you may find that up to 20% of your users have problems that they really shouldn't be having.

If you have worked through accessibility issues in applications long enough, you know about the Bobby Approved icon that used to appear on some sites. Unfortunately, Bobby isn't available any longer—at least, not as a free service. You can read the history of Bobby at *http://www.bobby-approved.com/*. The important thing to note is that accessibility is such an important issue and Bobby did such a terrific job at helping people add it to their sites that IBM eventually bought the product. Bobby is still around—it simply isn't free.

Providing Controlled Choices

Security is about exercising control. The application must maintain control over the manner in which it interacts with data. Managing data, without damaging it or causing a data leak, is the essential basis for creating a secure interface. One of the best ways to exercise control is to use techniques to ensure the user choices are limited to only the choices you expect. The use of specific entry controls limits user choices, but also makes the user more efficient because the user has to think less about the available options. Here are the common specific entry control choices:

Radio buttons

Lets the user choose one choice out of a number of choices. Selecting a new choice always deselects the previous choice. The most common error developers make is not setting one of the choices as a default. When the data is sent to the server after the user fails to select an option, the server encounters a blank data entry and could potentially experience problems.

Checkboxes

Lets the user choose anywhere between none and all of the available options by checking the desired options. The most common error developers make is allowing conflicting choices to occur. When working with checkboxes, each of the options is mutually exclusive.

List boxes

Depending on the configuration, a list box can act like a radio button or checkbox entry. An advantage of list boxes is that you can set them to hide the choices when the user hasn't selected the list box control. In addition to the issues that developers often experience with radio buttons and checkboxes, list boxes can suffer from issues in populating the list of choices. The user must have at least one choice available for the list box to act as a control. Inaccessible data sources can prove fatal for this control.

Menus

Depending on the configuration, menus can allow complex combinations of radio button and checkbox behavior. Of course, menus are also used to make client-side application choices. Many developers fail with menus by making them too complicated. A user won't search long for a particular option, so making the menu too complex leads to errors when the user becomes frustrated.

In addition to standard input types (including older types, such as password), you can also use special HTML5 functionality in creating a controlled choice environment. However, in this case, the alternative is to provide the user with a text input box, which means that these options aren't as secure as you might think they are. Here are the HTML5-specific controls:

color

Acts as a button with most supporting browsers. Clicking the button displays the platform's color picker. When the user chooses a new color, the color appears on the button so the user can see the current choice. Newer versions of Firefox, Chrome, and Opera all support this control.

date

Displays a date picker that the user can use to select a specific date. The min and max attributes let you set the range of allowable dates. Newer versions of Chrome, Safari, and Opera all support this control.

datetime

This input type isn't currently supported by any browser, so you shouldn't use it even though the specifications tell you that it's available.

datetime-local

Provides a combination of the date and time controls so that a user can choose both a date and a time (with the restrictions of those controls in place). When specifying the min and max attributes, supply both date and time values as input. Newer versions of Chrome, Safari, and Opera all support this control.

email

Displays a standard text input control. However, the control automatically validates the input to ensure the user supplies an email address. Newer versions of Internet Explorer, Firefox, Chrome, and Opera all support this control.

month

Displays a date picker that the user can use to select a specific month and year. The min and max attributes let you set the range of allowable dates (even though you're working with months, you must enter dates for these attributes). Newer versions of Chrome, Safari, and Opera all support this control.

number

Permits a user to type any numeric value, but not an alphabetic or special symbol value. Setting the min and max attribute values controls the range of input. Newer versions of Internet Explorer, Firefox, Chrome, Safari, and Opera all support this control.

range

Appears as a slider with most browsers. Setting the `min` and `max` attribute values controls the range of input. Use the `value` attribute to control the initial range setting. The `step` attribute controls the amount the slider moves for each change in position so that a user can only select specific values. Newer versions of Internet Explorer, Firefox, Chrome, Safari, and Opera all support this control.

search

There isn't much point in using this HTML5 control because it behaves like a standard `<input>` tag. Newer versions of Chrome and Safari support this control.

tel

Displays a standard text input control. However, the control automatically validates the input to ensure the user supplies a properly formatted telephone number. Newer versions of Safari support this control.

time

Displays a time picker that the user can use to select a specific time (but not a time zone). The `min` and `max` attributes let you set the range of allowable times. Newer versions of Chrome, Safari, and Opera all support this control.

url

Displays a standard text input control. However, the control automatically validates the input to ensure the user supplies a properly formatted URL. Newer versions of Internet Explorer, Firefox, Chrome, and Opera all support this control.

The `url` input control is the only control that currently provides special support on smartphones (not found on other computer types). On some smartphones, the browser adds a special `.com` key when it senses the `url` input control.

week

Displays a date picker that the user can use to select a specific week and year. The `min` and `max` attributes let you set the range of allowable dates (even though you're working with months, you must enter dates for these attributes). Newer versions of Chrome, Safari, and Opera all support this control.

It's important to remember that a hacker doesn't play by the rules or feel constrained by your forms in any way. It's possible to bypass the protections provided by these controls and submit data directly to the server in some other format. The ability to bypass protections is the reason that you must also range check and data type check any data received from the client at the server.

To use these controls, you use the `<input>` tag. For example, to create a number input type you might use (see the *InputTag.html* file for details):

```
<input id="NumberInput" type="number" min=1 max=5 value=1 />
```

In this case, the user sees a text input control, but this one includes an up/down arrow control as shown in Figure 4-3. In addition, the `value` attribute provides a default value. The user can easily change the value by typing a new value or simply using the up/down arrow control.

Figure 4-3. A number input features an up/down arrow control

The `number` input doesn't prevent the user from typing an unwanted value. However, it does perform automatic validation. Depending on the browser, an incorrect entry receives some form of highlight. For example, in the case of Firefox, the border becomes heavier and the box appears in red, as shown in Figure 4-4. The point is that HTML5 additions reduce the work you need to do for honest users, but it's possible for a determined hacker to overcome them.

Figure 4-4. HTML5 controls provide automatic validation

Some HTML5 controls are safer to use than others. For example, the range input type normally appears as a slider, so the user doesn't actually enter a value. You should never depend on any of the controls providing absolute safety, however.

Choosing a User Interface Solution Level

When working with web-based applications, you have a choice of which level to use for implementing the user interface. In fact, most web-based applications rely on multiple levels of interface controls. Some part of the page appears using HTML tags, another part is a manipulation of the interface using Cascading Style Sheets (CSS), and a third part relies on JavaScript. It's important to remember that you can use Java-Script both at the client and at the server, so really, there are four levels of solutions that you can exercise, as described in the following sections.

Implementing Standard HTML Controls

The section "Providing Controlled Choices" on page 82 tells you about the ways to control user choices. Many of those options appear as HTML controls. The advantage of HTML controls is that they work automatically for the most part. A browser does have to support the level of HTML that the control requires, but that's the only requirement.

Unlike most other control solutions, the browser doesn't have to support scripting in many cases to obtain an effect. Of course, if you want to perform detailed work, then you need some level of scripting support. As an example, if you want to use special controls to ensure a user fills out a form properly, you can actually perform that task and submit the form to the server for processing without using scripts. On the other hand, if you want to perform a client-side task, such as client-side validation, then you'll need scripting support in most cases (some HTML5 controls do provide rudimentary validation support).

There are a few disadvantages to using HTML controls. The most obvious is that HTML controls are rudimentary. If you want to add pizzazz to your site, then HTML controls will probably disappoint you. In addition, you can't go beyond the bare-bones basics. It's impossible to create a good tabbed interface (like the one shown in Figure 4-1) using just HTML controls.

Working with CSS Controls

The essential purpose of CSS is to format page content in such a manner that it doesn't rely on a specific browser, device, or platform. In addition, the formatting doesn't affect accessibility needs because the user can normally replace the fancy CSS formatting with simpler formatting that works better with accessibility devices. That said, it's possible to use CSS for all sorts of other tasks through clever programming techniques. One of those tasks is creating controls of various sorts using a combination of HTML, CSS, and JavaScript, with an emphasis on CSS. In other words, you create the actual control using CSS, rather than relying on either HTML or JavaScript to perform the task.

It helps to have tools available when using CSS to create controls. One place to look for the required tools is Dynamic Drive (*http://www.dynamicdrive.com/*). When you visit the site, you see it provides access to all sorts of tools, including the focus of this particular example, Button Maker (*http://tools.dynamicdrive.com/button/*). Figure 4-5 shows how Button Maker appears when you first access it. You use the settings on this page to generate the CSS needed to create a micro-button. However, you could just as easily create other sorts of controls using other tools.

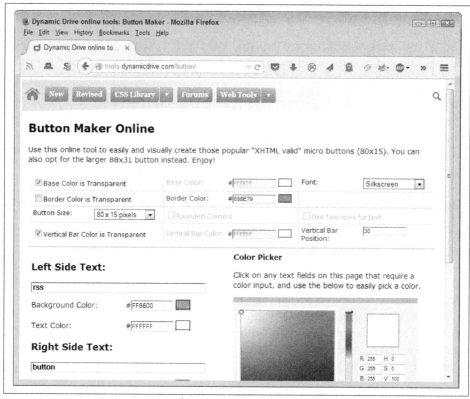

Figure 4-5. The Button Maker tool helps you create micro-buttons

The output of the process, for this example, is a bit of CSS and a Graphic Interchange Format (GIF) file named *MyButton.gif*. The example code (found in *TestButton.html*) is relatively simple, as shown here:

```
<!DOCTYPE html>

<html>
<head>
    <title>Testing a Micro Button</title>
    <style type="text/css">
        #MicroTest
        {
            border: none;
            background-color: transparent;
        }
    </style>
</head>

<body>
    <h1>Testing a Micro Button</h1>
    <button id="MicroTest"
```

```
            onclick="alert('Clicked!')">
        <img src="MyButton.GIF">
    </button>
</body>
</html>
```

Notice how the code uses HTML and JavaScript for support. The button itself is a GIF file. The CSS code performs the required formatting tasks. Of course, formatting would be more complex in a real application. The result of this experiment is a button like the one shown in Figure 4-6.

Figure 4-6. The micro-button is fully functional and nice to look at

The main advantage of creating CSS controls is that everything is generated locally, so they tend to look nice, but the application also performs well. In addition, CSS lets you create applications with pizzazz, so they're a lot more fun to use. The use of CSS can also provide visual hints to users, which means that you can use them to reduce mistakes—enhancing the security of your application.

CSS also presents some limitations when it comes to security. In order to obtain any level of validation, you must either employ HTML5 or JavaScript techniques. CSS doesn't offer any sort of validation potential because it was never designed to perform this sort of support. Remember that the designers of CSS meant it to provide basic page formatting and nothing more. Only through clever programming do you get some of the interesting effects that CSS can provide.

Creating Controls Using JavaScript

When it comes to controls, JavaScript provides the options that most developers use to create complex applications. Yes, the developer also relies on HTML5 for placement support and CSS3 for formatting support, but the essential tasks of defining the interface rests with JavaScript. You have access to two levels of JavaScript support when creating an interface, and may implement both levels in a single application. The following sections describe both client-side and server-side controls.

Relying on client controls

This chapter contains a number of examples of using JavaScript in various ways to create client-side control setups. Normally, you won't create the controls by hand, but will instead use a library setup such as jQuery and jQuery UI. When working with a client-side setup, the application loads the libraries from a local source or from a remote server, but once the libraries are loaded, everything happens locally. Later chapters in the book discuss the consequences of using in-process library support (see Chapter 6, Chapter 7, and Chapter 8 especially). The main benefit of client-side processing is that you gain a speed advantage and the application is more reliable in many cases because you have constant access to everything required to make the application run.

JavaScript offers the best opportunities for client-side control validation. You can configure the validation to work precisely as you want it to. The validation can also provide more functionality than other sorts of validation do. However, because a hacker can see your code, it's possible that the hacker will come up with a strategy to thwart whatever you have in place.

A significant security issue with using client-side controls is that you are incorporating someone else's code into your application. This means that you have a trust relationship between your application and code that you may never actually see. Yes, you can look at the content of libraries such as jQuery and jQuery UI, but few developers have the time to do so and certainly not the patience to review essentially undocumented code. Client-side controls have potential risks associated with them that you need to consider as part of your security strategy for the application.

Relying on server controls

Server-side controls often start with a PHP or other script on the server. In many cases, you can call the script directly, pass it the data it needs, and view just the script output in a browser. The processing all takes place on the server. Because the script is out-of-process, it's easier to keep your application separated from the third-party code, making your application more secure. However, you have reliability and speed issues to contend with when using server-side controls.

The client-side portion of this arrangement usually relies on JavaScript. In fact, you may embed the output from the server-side control in a page and update this content as needed using something like Asynchronous JavaScript and XML (AJAX). When using this setup, it's possible to speed the application by sending only the data to the server and only updating the portion of the page that the data affects.

Validating the Input

Of all the things you can do to ensure your application remains secure, the most important is to assume that all the input you receive is bad. When you assume that every input you receive contains a virus or some exploit that will cause damage to your system, you begin to view the input in a new way. Yes, it reeks of paranoia, but this viewpoint is essential to keeping your data secure. Validating data in a manner that reflects the corrupted input viewpoint is essential in today's application environment. Even with this viewpoint, you may find that you aren't paranoid enough (hackers are quite creative in finding new ways to make bad data look good) and need to hire someone to exercise even more paranoia on your behalf. The following sections give you some ideas on how you can protect your application and its associated data by validating absolutely every input in every way that you can think of.

Allowing Specific Input Only

The problem you read about most often when it comes to data validation is that the application didn't control input well enough. When you think about it, that's the underlying problem of many of the existing exploits. You should never allow a hacker to pass a script or other unwanted content through your application to the server. Of course, no one sets out to allow such content, but the content manages to get on the server anyway. The following list provides you with some ideas on the sorts of checks you should perform on any data passed from the application to the server (and then checked a second time on the server):

Type
> Always verify that the data type is correct. Strings are the hardest data type to check because they can contain anything by definition. Use stricter data types whenever possible. For example, when you need numeric input, use a number data type, rather than a string, to pass it.

Range
> Validate the range of any data type that supports it. Numbers are an obvious data type in this regard. However, you can check dates and times for range as well.

Regular expressions
> Determine that the form of the data is correct. In some cases, it's possible to check strings using regular expressions that match the input string pattern to an anticipated pattern. For example, when you want a telephone number as input, make sure you actually get a telephone number.

Special characters
> Users don't typically need to send any special characters to your application. A hacker employs special characters in a number of ways—none of them particu-

larly helpful to your application. So, weeding out content that includes special characters is a must.

The best possible input from the user is the kind of input that you expect at the outset. For example, if you want the user to choose between red, yellow, and green, then the only acceptable answers are red, yellow, and green. Any other choice is invalid and you should reject it. The more specific you can make input, the easier it is to keep your application and its associated data secure.

Looking for Sneaky Inputs

Hackers constantly look for ways of providing unexpected input data. The point of doing so is to cause the application to crash in specific ways or to force the application to react in an unexpected manner. For example, sneaky input is the root cause of SQL injection attacks. The hacker makes use of inputs on a form to create a situation where the application ends up behaving in an unexpected manner. The result of such an attack can range from corrupted data to executing scripts that shouldn't even appear as part of the data. You can find some additional information about this particular kind of attack at *http://blogs.msdn.com/b/raulga/archive/2007/01/04/dynamic-sql-sql-injection.aspx* and *https://www.owasp.org/index.php/SQL_Injection_Prevention_Cheat_Sheet*.

It may actually seem like a good idea at the time, but you should never allow the user to supply data used to create dynamic scripts. In fact, it's a good idea not to use dynamic scripts at all unless you can be sure of the source of the data used to create the dynamic script.

Requesting New Input

One of the favorite exploits that hackers employ is looking for situations where an application performs strict checks on input data during the first pass, but then relaxes those checks during subsequent passes. The situation is quite easy to create because of the way that many languages deal with loops. Only a careful developer will avoid the situation during second and subsequent input retries. Every code input pass should rely on the same code to check and verify the input. Whether the user is inputting data for the first or third time, the checks should provide equal protection.

However, the issue takes on new meaning when you begin to question user motivations during data entry. For example, you need to consider just why a user would need 10 retries to get their name right on a form. You can probably assume that the user does know their name—that it's not something they've suddenly forgotten. A constant need to resupply obvious data to the application may point to something other than a forgetful user. You need to question whether the form is clear enough.

When you're sure the form is clear and that you have the proper validation in place, you need to start looking at other sources for the issue, such as a hacker trying various methods to break your application. In short, most applications should allow a certain number of retries and then shut down pending an administrator's attention.

 Never assume that users are fully trained. Some users require a lot of training time and never really get the complete idea of precisely what it is that they're supposed to do. Unless you want to spend your days looking for hackers lurking in places where hackers never go, you need to consider user training as a primary security requirement. A large number of form retries may point to a need for more training time, rather than a potential hacker issue.

Using Both Client-Side and Server-Side Validation

Application speed is a primary concern when creating a web-based application. A user's focus can wander in as little as one to five seconds—not a long time to perform much in the way of validation. However, it's essential to perform validation and obtain the correct kind of input from the user. With this in mind, using client-side validation seems like the path to travel. A JavaScript routine can quickly check for errant input and tell the user about it before the data makes the round-trip to the server. The fact is that you really do want client-side validation.

However, client-side validation causes its own set of problems. The data must leave the host system at some point and travel to the server. Between the time the browser sends the data and the server receives that data, a hacker has all sorts of opportunities to intercept the data and change it. In order to ensure that the data really is of the right type and content, you need to perform a second validation check at the server. If no one has tampered with the data, the second validation will go quite quickly and the user will have a response within a reasonable timeframe.

Some people would consider the use of both client-side and server-side validation checks overkill. However, you really do need both. In fact, sometimes you get both whether you want them or not. For example, when using certain HTML5 controls, you get automatic validation. It's true that the validation isn't always the most precise or complete, but it does provide a certain level of safety for the user. Always remember that client-side validation is for the user's protection and you use it to keep the user happy. Anything you can do to reduce user frustration will also reduce application support costs and security concerns.

Server-side validation checks need to provide complete coverage of every input and output. It isn't enough to check data when it comes from the client and then assume that no one will tamper with the server. Hackers are motivated to attack the server because the server makes it possible to affect a lot of people with a single intrusion.

Consequently, you do need to provide validation checks for every input to every routine on the server to ensure that the application and its data remain secure.

The issue you fight most often with validation checks is application speed. It's not just users that can experience problems when an application runs slow—server loading increases as well. Therefore, you must maintain a balance with validation checks. Security is often a matter of defining how much risk you're willing to accept in the pursuit of specific goals. It's important that management understand that you have to maintain a balance as part of the application design and development process.

Some developers also falsely assume that throwing additional hardware at a problem will solve it. Adding hardware reduces the reliability of the system as a whole. A reduction in reliability is also a security risk. If a hacker has five servers to attack instead of just one, the probability of finding a server that lacks the proper patches or is loaded just enough to crash becomes greater. Increasing the amount of hardware used to serve an application is part of the solution, but you must balance it with increases in application speed without leaving major security holes in place.

Expecting the Unexpected

Users are amazing at times. They seem to find the one hole you didn't think to patch. A boring day might turn into a session of seeing just what it takes to break an application. In fact, the user might not even set out to break the application; perhaps it's all a matter of mindlessly doing things while talking on the phone. The point is that users will find problems with your application that you never expected to exist. These problems can lead to all sorts of issues in protecting the application and its associated data. Sometimes an issue can crash the application or perhaps even the server on which it's running. You may marvel at what users come up with, but in the real world, bored users spell unexpected events.

Hackers will also perform the unexpected with your application. However, in this case, the unexpected is more thoughtful and methodical. A hacker will continue probing your defenses looking for a way in until another target comes into view, the hacker gets bored, or the hacker finds the way in. In most cases, the hacker will find a way in when truly determined to do so. It's never a matter of if the hacker will gain access to your application, but the timing of when the hacker will succeed in the effort. The use of security measures slows hackers down and with proper monitoring, you can discover the hacker lurking about your system before it's possible to do any real damage.

Many of the unexpected things that users and hackers do are associated with inputs. For example, you might expect a string as input but receive a script instead. Users can click unexpected key combinations that result in a corrupted string that causes the application or server to crash. Sometimes it's simply a matter of assuming the user will do one thing, when quite another seems more appropriate. For example, a user might respond with a string when a number is required (or vice versa). Hackers, of course, are looking for all sorts of nefarious ways of providing input you didn't expect and will purposely provide the input you didn't expect.

CHAPTER 5

Building Reliable Code

You might wonder why this book contains a chapter about building reliable code when the topic is security. An interrelation exists between application speed, reliability, and security. Each of these elements has a role to play in turning a good application into a great application. You can't emphasize one over the other without diminishing your application in some way. Of course, companies do make the conscious decision to emphasize one element over another, but usually to gain specific goals. For example, you may have a legal requirement to protect applications at all costs, in which case you probably need to sacrifice some speed and reliability to achieve the goal. However, for most applications, the balance between the three elements is critical. Until you understand the interactions between speed, reliability, and security, it's nearly impossible to achieve an application with the maximum possible security in place, and it is impossible to create an application that performs well in an environment where all three elements are prized.

This chapter views reliability as it relates to security. In other words, it examines how you balance reliability in order to achieve specific security goals in your organization. It also considers reliability as a statistical science, although the chapter won't bore you with the specifics of reliability calculations. The point is to understand the concept of calculated risk with regard to the state of security in an application. Anyone who tells you that an application doesn't create risks with regard to both data and organizational integrity doesn't truly understand either reliability or security.

As part of dealing with reliability issues, the chapter explores reliability from several perspectives. For example, in order to create a reliable application, you must define team protocols that ensure everyone understands the required concepts. Reliability experts also learn from each iteration of the calculations they make—likewise, you must incorporate a feedback loop to make changes in the way in which your organization views reliability in its unique environment. There are also the issues of using packaged solutions. You won't build many applications from scratch, so it's important to know the effect that using a packaged solution will have on your application.

 The main thought to take away from this chapter is that the most reliable application in the world is one in which the application performs tasks without any sort of potential for disruption. This would exclude the use of any external processing, input, or resource because all three of these items have failure points. Such an application would have no users and would need to run on hardware with incredibly high reliability. However, even with all these factors in place, it's still impossible to create an application that is 100% reliable. Every application has the potential to fail, making it less than reliable.

Lack of Reliability Kills Businesses

The biggest headlines in the trade press are often about security failures. Hackers getting into supposedly secure health records or obtaining access to the Social Security numbers of thousands of credit card users tend to make for big news. It seems that you see reliability reported far less often. However, a lack of reliability can cause terrifying results—even business failures.

Consider the case of the Knight Capital Group (*http://dealbook.nytimes.com/ 2012/08/02/knight-capital-says-trading-mishap-cost-it-440-million/*). A glitch in the software it used to interact with the New York Stock Exchange caused it to buy nearly $7 billion of stock it didn't want. Quickly reselling the stock caused the company a net $440 million loss. However, the losses soon became greater. As people lost confidence in the Knight Capital Group, it began bleeding even more red ink. Eventually, another company, Getco, acquired the Knight Capital Group for pennies on the dollar (*http:// www.reuters.com/article/2012/12/19/us-knightcapital-getco- idUSBRE8BI0OF20121219*)—all because of a software glitch.

Differentiating Reliability and Security

Some people equate reliability with security. However, reliability and security are two completely different measures of application performance. Yes, the two measures do interact, but in ways that many people really don't understand well. A reliable application isn't necessarily secure and vice versa. The following sections examine the issue of the interaction between reliability and security in greater detail.

The best way to work with the example described in this chapter is to use the downloadable source, rather than type it in by hand. Using the downloadable source reduces potential errors. You can find the source code examples for this chapter in the \S4WD\Chapter05 folder of the downloadable source.

Defining the Roles of Reliability and Security

Reliability is a measure of how often an application breaks. It's a statistical measure. You use reliability to answer the question of how likely an application is to break given a certain set of circumstances. Reliability also tells you when the application environment is changing. For example, when you add staff and the load on the application increases, reliability may decrease unless you design the application to scale well. Even when the software is perfect, however, the hardware reaches a breaking point and reliability will still decrease. Therefore, reliability is a whole system measure. The hardware, user, platform, operating environment, management techniques, and myriad other things all affect reliability and change what you see as application faults or failures.

Security is a measure of how much effort it takes to break an application. Unlike reliability, there is no method available to measure security statistically. What you have instead is a potential for damage that can only be quantified by the determination of the hacker who is attempting to cause the damage. If hackers are sincerely determined to break into your application to cause damage, they will almost certainly find the means to do so. When dealing with security, you must also consider the effects of monitoring and the ability of a team to react quickly to breaches.

In both cases, an application breaks when the stress applied to the application becomes greater than the application's ability to resist. A broken application fails in its primary responsibility to manage data correctly. Just how this failure occurs depends on the application and the manner in which it's broken. Reliability faults tend to cause data damage—security faults, on the other hand, tend to cause data breaches or result in compromised system integrity.

It's important to demonstrate the difference between simply being secure and also being reliable. The following *RangeCheck1.html* example shows code that is secure from the client side (you would also check the data on the server side):

```
<!DOCTYPE html>

<html>
<head>
    <title>Performing a Range Check</title>
    <script language="javascript">
        function testValue()
        {
            value = document.getElementById("Data").value;
```

```
            if (value == "")
            {
                alert("Please type a number!");
                return;
            }
            if ((value < 0) || (value > 5))
            {
                alert("Value must be between 0 and 5!");
            }
            else
            {
                alert("Value = " + value);
            }
        }
    </script>
</head>

<body>
    <h1>Performing a Range Check</h1>
    <input id="Data" type="number" value="0" min=0 max=5 /><br />
    <button id="Test" onclick="testValue()">
        Test
    </button>
</body>
</html>
```

In this case, a casual user who uses the up and down arrows on the <input> tag will never provide data outside the range (as shown in Figure 5-1). However, the Java-Script code found in testValue() also ensures that the data will never appear outside the range even when typed. Using a number input type means that if someone types a value such as "Hello", what testValue() actually receives is an empty value. It's possible to test for this condition as well and provide the user with an appropriate response.

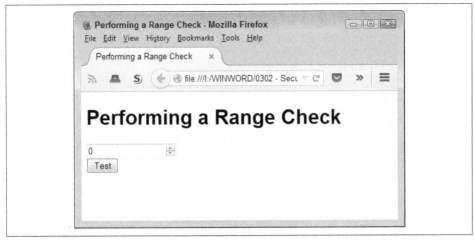

Figure 5-1. Range checks are made easier using the appropriate controls

The problem with this code is that it's secure, but it's not reliable. If conditions change, then the code will no longer function as it should. The following *RangeCheck2.html* example makes the code more reliable by tying the range check to the min and max attributes of the <input> tag:

```html
<!DOCTYPE html>

<html>
<head>
    <title>Performing a Range Check</title>
    <script language="javascript">
        function testValue()
        {
            inputObj = document.getElementById("Data");
            value = inputObj.value;
            if (value == "")
            {
                alert("Please type a number!");
                return;
            }
            if ((value < inputObj.getAttribute("min")) ||
                (value > inputObj.getAttribute("max")))
            {
                alert("Value must be between 0 and 5!");
            }
            else
            {
                alert("Value = " + value);
            }
        }
    </script>
</head>
```

```
<body>
    <h1>Performing a Range Check</h1>
    <input id="Data" type="number" value="0" min=0 max=5 /><br />
    <button id="Test" onclick="testValue()">
        Test
    </button>
</body>
</html>
```

The basic checks work as before. However, if someone chooses to change the min and max values accepted by the <input> tag, the code automatically responds by changing the conditions of the check. The failure points in this example are fewer.

However, to obtain code that is both secure and reliable, you must pay a price in speed. Notice the number of additional lines of code in the second example and the increased number of function calls. You won't likely notice a difference in the speed of this particular example, but when you start adding these sorts of checks to an entire application, you can see some serious speed degradation. The code is more reliable and secure, but the user may not be happy with the result.

Avoiding Security Holes in Reliable Code

Just as secure software isn't automatically reliable, reliable software isn't automatically secure. In fact, you may find that the more reliable the software, the greater the risk that it truly isn't secure. The problem is one of the divergent goals of reliability and security. A reliable application is always accessible, usable, and predictable, which causes more than a few security issues. Here are cases in which reliability has divergent goals from security:

- A complex password keeps software more secure, but it means that the software may not be available when the user forgets the password, making the software unreliable.

- Checks that ensure no one has tampered with application data can cause the software to become unavailable when the checks find tampering.

- False positives to security checks make the application's behavior unpredictable.

- Managing security settings increases application interface complexity and makes it less usable.

- Denial of access to required resources due to security restrictions (such as those created by a policy) makes the application less accessible and also makes it less predictable.

The results of security holes in reliable code really can be terrifying. In a recent InfoWorld listing of 10 extreme hacks (*http://www.info world.com/article/2933868/hacking/10-extreme-hacks-to-be-truly-paranoid-about.html*), medical devices came in at number 2. These devices are tested for 5 to 10 years to ensure they continue working no matter what else might happen. However, no one patches the software during the testing period (and patching would entail additional testing). In addition, medical devices must prove easy to use, so anything that even resembles comprehensive security is left out of the development process. As a result, it's quite easy to kill someone by hacking his or her medical device. Of all the examples of reliable software with serious security issues, medical devices are at the top of the heap. They also have the honor of being the software with the most devastating results when hacked.

In fact, there are many situations where security and reliability butt heads. You must choose some sort of balance between the two in order to ensure that application data remains reasonably safe and the application still runs reliably.

Using the examples in the previous section as a starting point, it's possible to see how a range check would interfere with the user's ability to enter values outside the predicted range. Of course, the range check makes the application more secure. However, it's important to consider what happens when the person configuring the application's range check performs the task incorrectly and now the user is unable to enter a perfectly valid value. The application is still secure, but it becomes unreliable.

In some situations, a designer may view the potential ramifications of such a limitation as unwanted and make the application more reliable by excluding the range check. After all, if the purpose of the software is to prevent a nuclear reactor from going critical, yet the software prevents the entry of a value that will keep the reactor from going critical, then the security of the software is no longer important because no one will be around to debate the issue.

A middle-ground fix for such a situation does exist, but it increases the complexity of the software and therefore affects reliability even more. In addition, because the fix requires added coding, application speed is also affected. However, by including the various security checks during normal operation and allowing an override by a manager or administrator to run the checks off during an emergency, the user can enter the correct value for saving the reactor, even though the software wouldn't normally allow it.

The point is that you can usually find a workaround for the security-only or reliability-only conundrum. It's usually a bad idea to focus on one or the other because the hackers (or the users) will make you pay at some point.

Focusing on Application Functionality

Making an application both secure and reliable fills a developer with joy, but the user won't care. Users always focus their attention on getting a task that the user cares about accomplished. The user's task might involve creating a report. (In reality, the report might not be the focus—the focus might involve getting money from investors. The report simply helps the user accomplish that goal.) If hand typing the report is easier and more transparent than using your application, the user will hand type the report. Users don't care what tool they use to accomplish a task, which is why you see users trying to create complex output using a smartphone. As a developer, you can secretly revel in the amazing strategies contained within your code, but the user won't care about it. The point is that a user won't come to you and say that the application is unreliable. The user's input will always involve the user's task—whatever that task might be. It's up to you to determine that the issue causing the user to fail is that the application you created isn't reliable in some important way.

The balance between reliability and security becomes more pronounced when you focus on application functionality. It isn't simply a matter of getting the task done, but getting the task done in the way that the user originally envisioned. In today's world, this means doing things like:

- Counting keystrokes—fewer is better
- Allowing the application to run on any platform
- Ensuring the application is always available
- Reducing the number of non-task-related steps to zero
- Making answers to questions obvious or avoiding the questions completely

Developing Team Protocols

Any effort made toward creating a reliable application has to consider the entire team. A development team needs to design and build the application with reliability in mind from the beginning. The team also needs to keep the matter of balance in mind during this process. It doesn't matter if an application is both reliable and secure if no one uses it because it runs slowly.

Team protocols can take in all sorts of issues. For example, in 1999, the Mars Climate Orbiter burned up on entry into the Martian atmosphere because one group working on the software used metric units and another group used English (imperial) units (*http://www.wired.com/2010/11/1110mars-climate-observer-report/*). The problem was a lack of communication—part of the protocol that you need to create for successful application development.

In order to create appropriate protocols for your organization, you need to break the tasks up in several ways. The team that creates an application must consider the issues of reliability from three separate levels:

Accidental design or implementation errors

When most people think about reliability problems, they think about glitches that cause the application to work in a manner other than the way in which the development team originally designed it to function. The application fails to perform tasks correctly. However, these errors could also be of the sort that open the application to access by hackers or simply don't provide the required flexibility. Development teams overcome this problem through the use of developer training and secure development practices, as well as the employment of tools designed to locate reliability issues of this sort.

Changing technology

An application becomes obsolete the day you finish working on it. In fact, sometimes the application is obsolete before you complete it. Technology changes act against software to make it unreliable. There are two levels of change you must consider:

Future-proofing

In order to create an environment in which an application can maintain its technical edge, you must future-proof it. The best way to accomplish this goal is to create the application as components that interact, but are also separate entities, to make it possible to upgrade one without necessarily upgrading the entire system. This is the reason that microservices have become so popular, but you can practice module coding strategies using monolithic designs as well.

Hacker improvements

Hackers do innovate and become better at their jobs. A security or reliability problem that wasn't an issue when you started a project may become quite problematic before you complete the application. You may not even know the issue exists until a hacker points it out. The best way to handle this problem is to ensure you keep your tools and techniques updated to counter hacker improvements.

Malicious intent

There is a good chance that someone on your development team isn't happy or has possibly taken a job with your organization with the goal of finding ways to exploit software glitches. This team member may even introduce the glitches or backdoors with the notion of exploiting them after leaving the organization. Of course, you don't want to create a Big Brother atmosphere, because doing so stifles innovation and tends to create more problems than it fixes; however, you also need to ensure any management staff actually does manage the development team.

Communication between members of the team is essential, but ensuring that the communication isn't misunderstood is even more important. Assumptions create all sorts of problems, and humans are especially good at filling in information gaps with assumptions. Of course, the assumptions of one team member may not be held by another member of the same team. Developing the sort of communication that teams require includes these best practices (you can find additional best practices, tools, and resources on the Cyber Security and Information Systems Information Analysis Center site (*https://sw.csiac.org/databases/url/key/2*)):

Reliability and security training

Team members can't communicate unless they speak the same language and understand reliability concerns at the same level. The only way to accomplish this goal is to ensure team members receive proper training. When creating a training program, ensure that the training is consistent, whether you use external or in-house trainers.

Reliability requirements

Creating an application without first defining what you want is a little like building a house without a blueprint. Just as you wouldn't even start digging the basement for a house without a blueprint in hand, you can't start any sort of coding effort without first establishing the roles that reliability and security will play in the overall operation of the application. Make sure any definition you create includes specific metrics and goals for each development phase. The definition should also outline the use of both security and reliability reviews, code audits, and testing.

Reliable design

Just as you begin any project by identifying the security threats an application will face, you must also identify the reliability issues and specify methods for overcoming them. The design process must include specifics on how to deal with reliability issues. Although many organizations are aware of the need for security experts to help solve security issues, few are aware that a similar capability exists with reliability experts such as Reliability Consulting Services (*http://www.relia soft.com/consulting/*).

Reliable coding

The coding process must keep both security and reliability in mind. It doesn't matter how much preparation you do unless you put what you've learned and designed into practice.

Secure source code handling

In order to handle threats such as malicious intent, your organization must practice secure source code handling. This means that only people with the proper training and credentials see the source code. In addition, it also means that you perform both design and code reviews to ensure the application remains faithful to the original design goals.

Reliability testing

It's essential to test the code to ensure it actually meets reliability goals that are part of the application requirements and design. Reliability testing can include all sorts of issues, such as how the application responds when a load is applied or when it loses access to a needed resource. The task is to test the failure points of the application and verify that the application handles each of them successfully.

 Blind testing (where you ask someone outside the group who has no experience with the application to try to use the application) can yield some interesting and useful information about potential application security holes. The test often demonstrates the kinds of keystroke combinations that hackers will try in an attempt to break the application. The testing can also demonstrate areas in which application features aren't self-explanatory and require rework, additional documentation, or additional training.

Reliability and security documentation

It's important to document the requirements, design, coding techniques, testing techniques, and other processes you have put into place to ensure the application is both reliable and secure. The documentation should express the balance issues that you found and explain how you handled them as part of the application requirements and design.

Reliability and security readiness

Just before application release, the development team needs to ensure no new threats have appeared on the scene that the application must address to work successfully. Reliability and security both deal with risk and this phase determines the risk posed by new threats. It may work just as well to handle low-risk threats as part of an update, rather than hold the application release.

Reliability and security response

After application release, the development team needs to respond to any new reliability and security threats in a timely manner. It's important to understand that sources outside the development team may report these issues and expect that the development team will provide a quick response.

Integrity checking

Ensuring the application continues to work as it should means securing the code using some type of signing technique (to ensure no one modifies it). In addition, the development team should continue testing the code against new threats and verify that the application manages data in a secure way. The idea is to keep looking for potential problems, even if you're certain that none exist. Hackers are hoping that your team will lack the diligence to detect new threats until it's too late.

Security and reliability research

It's important to task individuals with the requirement to find new threats as they appear and to come up with methods for handling them. Testing the application is fine, but knowing how to test it against the latest threats is the only way to ensure your testing is actually doing what it should.

Creating a Lessons Learned Feedback Loop

Reliability is based on statistical analysis of events over time. The more time that elapses and the more events recorded, the more accurate the prediction. The average time between failure events is the mean time between failures (MTBF). Most software texts don't seem to pursue the topic from this perspective, but software, like anything else, has failure patterns and it's possible to analyze those patterns to create a picture of when you can expect the software to fail. Of course, like any statistic, it's not possible to pin down precise moments—only the general course of activity for a given application in a specific environment.

 Some people view MTBF as an incorrect measure of software reliability because they feel it literally indicates the next time that a software bug, environmental issue, or other factor will cause the software to fail. The important thing to remember is that MTBF is based on a specific environment. Because software rarely operates in precisely the same environment from organization to organization, trying to create an MTBF for an application that works in any organization won't work. An MTBF for an application for a specific organization does work because the environment for that organization is unlikely to change significantly. When it does, the MTBF value is no longer valid.

The higher the MTBF of an application, the less time spent supporting it and the lower the maintenance costs. In addition, a high MTBF also signals a situation where security breaches due to application failures are less likely. Application failures don't occur just because of bugs in the software—they also occur due to usage failures, environmental issues (such as a lack of memory), unreproducible causes (such as cosmic rays causing a spike in power), and other sources. Because it's not possible to manage all of these failure sources, software can never be 100% reliable. At some point, even the best software will experience a failure.

 Cosmic rays really do affect computers. In fact, the higher the altitude of the computer's storage, the greater the effect experienced. The size of the transistors in the chips also affects the incidence of soft errors. You can discover more about this interesting effect in "Cosmic Rays and Computers" (*http://www.nature.com/news/1998/980730/full/news980730-7.html*), "Effect of Cosmic Rays on Computer Memories" (*http://www.ncbi.nlm.nih.gov/pubmed/17820742*), and "Should Every Computer Chip Have a Cosmic Ray Detector?" (*http://www.newscientist.com/blog/technology/2008/03/do-we-need-cosmic-ray-alerts-for.html*). The information is interesting and it may finally explain a few of those unreproducible errors you've seen in the past.

A feedback loop as to the cause of failures can help you increase MTBF within a given organization. By examining the causes of failure, you can create a plan to improve MTBF for the lowest possible cost. Here are some ideas to consider as part of analyzing the failure sources in software:

Quality
   As the quality of the software improves, the MTBF becomes higher. It's possible to improve the quality of software by finding and removing bugs, improving the user interface to make it less likely that a user will make a mistake, and adding checks to ensure needed resources are available before using them.

Failure points
   Reducing the number of failure points within an application improves MTBF. The best way to reduce failure points is to make the application less complex by streamlining routines and making them more efficient. However, you can also do things such as increase redundancy when possible. For example, having two sources for the same data makes it less likely that the loss of a single source will cause an application failure.

Training
   Better training reduces operational errors and improves MTBF. There is a point of diminishing returns for training, but most users today don't receive nearly enough training on the software that they're expected to use to perform useful work. In addition, training support personnel to handle errors more accurately and developers to spot the true sources of failures will help improve the feedback process.

Creating complete lists of failures, along with failure causes, is the best way to begin understanding the dynamics of your application. As the knowledge base for an application grows, it's possible to see predictive patterns and use those patterns as a means of determining where to spend time and resources making corrections. Of course, it's not possible to fix some failure sources. Yes, you could possibly shield all your hardware to get rid of those pesky cosmic rays, but the chances of any organization expending the money is incredibly small (and the returns are likely smaller still).

Considering Issues of Packaged Solutions

As mentioned in earlier chapters, most applications today rely on packaged solutions to perform common tasks. Trying to create an application completely from scratch would be too time intensive and financially prohibitive. There really isn't a good reason to reinvent the wheel. However, using these packaged solutions will affect your application's reliability. You're relying on code written by someone else to make your application work, so that code is also part of the reliability calculation. The following sections discuss some issues you need to consider when working with packaged solutions.

Dealing with External Libraries

External libraries create a number of interesting reliability problems. The most important issue is that the application will generally download a copy of the library each time it begins to run. If you keep the application running, this process doesn't happen often, but most web-based applications run on the client system, which means that the client will need to download the library every time it starts the application. Speed becomes a problem because of the library download. However, the application might not even start if something prevents the client download from succeeding. For example, consider the use of jQuery UI to create an accordion effect like the one shown in Figure 5-2.

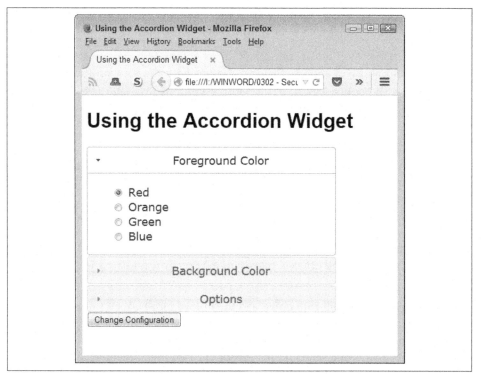

Figure 5-2. Even a simple jQuery UI example requires downloaded code

This example won't even start should the library files it depends on become inaccessible for some reason. The following code (found in the *Accordian.html* file) appears in the header to create the required connectivity:

```
<head>
   <script
      src="https://code.jquery.com/jquery-latest.js">
   </script>
   <script
      src="https://code.jquery.com/ui/1.9.2/jquery-ui.js">
   </script>
   <link
      rel="stylesheet"
      href="https://code.jquery.com/ui/1.9.2/themes/base/jquery-ui.css" />
```

If any of the three files shown in this example are missing, the application will fail to run. This example also shows two different approaches to selecting the libraries. Notice that the jQuery library relies on the latest version, which means that you automatically get bug fixes and other updates. However, the jQuery UI library (and its associated CSS file) both rely on a specific version of the library. You won't get updates in this case, but may get bug fixes that could still cause your application to crash if you've already included workaround code for the problem.

One of the best ways to improve the reliability of external library use is to download the library to local drives and use that copy, rather than the copy on the vendor site. This strategy ensures that you have the same version of the library at all times and that there is less of a chance that the library won't be available for use. Of course, you'll need to supply local hard drive space to store the library, but the increased use of local resources is a small price to pay for the stability you gain.

As with everything else, there is a price for using a localized copy of the library. The most important of these issues is the lack of upgrades. Most vendors provide upgrades relatively often that include bug fixes, improvements in reliability, and speed enhancements. Of course, the library will usually contain new features as well. Balancing the new features are deprecated features that you may need to make your application run. In order to achieve the reliability gains, you give up some potential security improvements and other updates you may really want to use in your application.

A middle-ground approach is to download the library locally, keep track of improvements in updates, and time your application updates to coincide with needed security and feature updates in the majority of the libraries you use. This would mean performing updates on your schedule instead of the vendor's schedule. Although this alternative might seem like the perfect solution, it isn't. Hackers often rely on zero-day exploits to do the maximum harm to the greatest number of applications. Because your application won't automatically receive the required updates, you still face the possibility of a devastating zero-day attack.

Dealing with External APIs

External APIs provide the means to access data and other resources using an external source. An API is usually a bundle of classes that you instantiate as objects and use for making calls. The code doesn't execute on the client system. Rather, it executes as an out-of-process (OOP) remote procedure call (RPC) on the server. A client/server request/response cycle takes place with the client making requests of the server. Creating a link to the API is much like creating a link to a library, except that you must normally provide a key of some sort to obtain access as shown here for the *GoogleAPI.html* file (see Chapter 7 for details on this example):

```
<head>
  <script type="text/javascript"
    src="https://maps.googleapis.com/maps/api/js?key=Your Key Here&sensor=false">
```

The query requires that the client build a request and send it to the server. When working with the Google API, you must provide items such as the longitude and latitude of the interface, along with the preferred map type. The API actually writes the data directly to the application location provided as part of the request, as shown here:

```
// This function actually displays the map on
// screen.
function GetMap()
{
    // Create a list of arguments to send to Google.
    var MapOptions =
    {
        center: new google.maps.LatLng(
                    Latitude.spinner("value"),
                    Longitude.spinner("value")),
        zoom: 8,
        mapTypeId: google.maps.MapTypeId.ROADMAP
    }

    // Provide the location to place the map and the
    // map options to Google.
    var map = new google.maps.Map(
        document.getElementById("MapCanvas"),
        MapOptions);
};
```

The result of the call is a map displayed on the client canvas. Figure 5-3 shows a typical example of the output from this application.

Using external APIs makes it possible to use someone else's code with fewer security concerns and potentially fewer speed issues (depending on whether it's faster to request the data or download the code). However, from a reliability perspective, external APIs present all sorts of risk. Any interruption of the connection means that the application stops working. Of course, it's relatively easy for a developer to create code that compensates for this issue and presents a message for the user. Less easy to fix is the issue of slow connections, data mangling, and other issues that could reflect the condition of the connection or hackers at work. In this case, user frustration becomes a problem because the user could add to the chaos by providing errant input in order to receive some sort of application response.

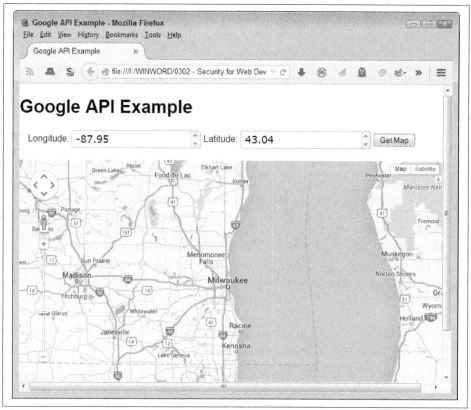

Figure 5-3. The Google API draws directly to the client canvas

A way around the reliability issue in this case is to time calls. When the application detects that the calls are taking longer than normal, it's possible to respond by telling the user about the slow connection, contacting an administrator, or reacting to the problem in some other way. The point is to ensure you track how long each call takes and act appropriately.

Working with Frameworks

Frameworks represent a middle ground of reliability between libraries and APIs. For the most part, frameworks are compressed code. One of the most commonly used frameworks is MooTools (*http://mootools.net/*). However, there are many other frameworks available out there, and you need to find the right one for your needs. In most cases, frameworks can run on the server, the client, or a combination of both. Depending on how you use the framework, you can see the same reliability issues found with libraries, APIs, or a combination of the two.

Differentiating Between Frameworks and Libraries

Although a framework like Dojo (*https://dojotoolkit.org*) and a library like jQuery look quite a bit alike—and you use them in the same manner, for the most part—Dojo is a framework and jQuery is a library. From a security, reliability, and speed perspective, the two entities are different.

A library is pure code that downloads and runs as part of your application. You call functions directly and the source for those functions is sometimes available so that you can change the function behavior.

Frameworks provide a means of interacting with a behavior, which means that some tasks aren't visible to the developer—the developer requests that the framework perform the task, and the framework determines how to accomplish it. Code still downloads from the vendor and still becomes part of your application, but the underlying technology is different. Some people define a framework as a packaged form of library that provides structure as well as code.

The interesting part about products such as MooTools is that you can perform many of the same tasks that you do when using libraries. For example, you can create a version of the accordion example using MooTools. The following code is much simplified, but it gets the point across:

```
<!DOCTYPE html>

<html>
<head>
   <title>MooTools Accordion Demo</title>
   <script src="MooTools-More-1.5.1.js"></script>

   <style>
     .toggler
     {

         color: #222;
         margin: 0;
         padding: 2px 5px;
         background: #eee;

         border-bottom: 1px solid #ddd;

         border-right: 1px solid #ddd;

         border-top: 1px solid #f5f5f5;
         border-left: 1px solid #f5f5f5;

     }
```

```
        </style>

        <script type="text/javascript">
            window.addEvent('domready', function()
            {
                var accordion = new Fx.Accordion('h3.atStart', 'div.atStart',
                    {
                        opacity: false,

                        onActive: function(toggler, element)
                        {
                            toggler.setStyle('color', '#ff3300');
                        },

                        onBackground: function(toggler, element)
                        {
                            toggler.setStyle('color', '#222');
                        }
                    }, $('accordion'));
            });
        </script>

<body>

    <h2>MooTools Accordion Demo</h2>
    <div id="accordion">

        <h3 class="toggler atStart">Section 1</h3>
        <div class="element atStart">
            <p>Section 1 Content</p>
        </div>

        <h3 class="toggler atStart">Section 2</h3>
        <div class="element atStart">
            <p>Section 2 Content</p>
        </div>

        <h3 class="toggler atStart">Section 3</h3>
        <div class="element atStart">
            <p>Section 3 Content</p>
        </div>
    </div>

</body>
</html>
```

You obtain the *MooTools-More-1.5.1.js* file from the Builder site at *http://mootools.net/more/builder*. Make sure you include the core libraries. Google does offer a hosted site at *https://developers.google.com/speed/libraries/*, but it doesn't include the additional features, such as Fx.Accordion.

The framework requires that you set up a series of headings and divisions to contain the content for the accordion, as shown in the HTML portion of the example. How these items appear when selected and deselected depends on the CSS you set up. The script defines two events: onActive (when the item is selected) and onBackground (when the item is deselected). In this particular case, MooTools behaves very much like a library and you see the output shown in Figure 5-4.

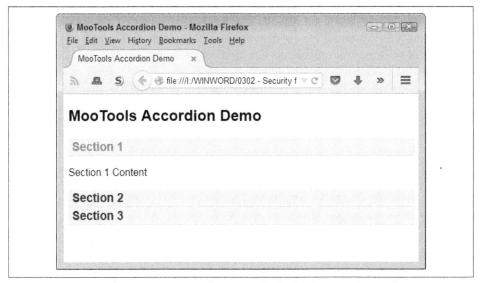

Figure 5-4. MooTools is a framework that provides both library and API functionality

Calling into Microservices

In many respects, a microservice is simply a finer grained API. The concept of using smaller bits of code so that it's possible to rely on whatever resources are needed to perform that one given task well makes sense. Because of the way in which microservices work, much of what you know about APIs from a reliability perspective also applies to microservices. For example, calls to a particular microservice may take longer than expected, fueling user frustration. The way around this problem is to provide application timeouts. However, in the case of a microservice, you can always try making the call using a secondary source when one is available.

However, microservices also differ from APIs in some respects simply because they are smaller and more customized. With this in mind, here are some reliability issues you need to consider when dealing with microservices:

- Using more microservices from different sources increases the potential for a lost connection and lowers application reliability.

- Choosing microservices that truly do optimize the service provided for the specific need you require will increase application reliability because there is less risk of major errors.

- Relying on a consistent interface for microservice calls reduces potential coding errors, enhancing application reliability.

- Having more than one source that can perform the same service reduces the number of single failure points, increasing application reliability.

- Keeping services small means that the loss of a single service doesn't mean all services become unavailable as it would when using an API, so reliability is higher in this case as well.

CHAPTER 6

Incorporating Libraries

It would be hard to find a web application that doesn't depend on a library—at least, not one of any consequence. Libraries are the epitome of not redefining the wheel. In fact, like wheels, there are libraries of every shape, size, and color out there. Yes, even color comes into play when you consider that many libraries include themes you can use to dress up your site. Consequently, it's likely that you've already spent a fair amount of time working with libraries in some way. In fact, a number of the book examples in earlier chapters relied on libraries simply because rewriting the code from scratch doesn't make sense.

This chapter doesn't try to persuade you about the value of using libraries. You've likely already sold yourself on their benefit. However, you might not have considered all the ramifications of using someone else's code in your application. There are always consequences to using libraries. The goal is to use libraries safely so that you get all the benefits of relying on someone else's code without creating any major security holes in your application. (Be assured, you do create some security holes; it's impossible to avoid it.)

Getting the Best Library Speed

You may find sites that tell you not to use libraries at all because they incur such speed penalties (for example, see *http://www.giftofspeed.com/dont-use-javascript-libraries/*). The fact is that libraries can slow your site down, especially when you don't use them wisely. The speed hit can be large enough to make people perform the click that takes them to the next site, which means that your site loses out on providing a service or offering some other resource to the people who visit it.

This book generally uses the uncompressed versions of the available libraries to make it easier for you to work with the examples and perform tasks such as using a debugger to examine the applications with greater ease. However, from a speed perspective, you normally want to use the compressed version of the library. The compressed version contains the same code, but it loads faster and sometimes you get a bit of a boost when making calls as well.

It's also important to realize that you won't use all of the library code. Many libraries, such as jQuery UI (*http://jqueryui.com/download/*), provide a builder that lets you create a personalized version of the library that loads. After you discover which parts of a library you actually will use, use a builder to create a version with just those parts in it. The library will load faster and you also reduce the library's attack surface, which means an improvement in security as well.

Considering Library Uses

How you use a library directly affects how secure it remains—at least, to an extent. For example, direct involvement of the library with your JavaScript code tends to open more potential security holes than using the library to format the page. Of course, any use of a library could open potential security gaps that will cost your organization time, effort, and resources. The following sections discuss how you might use libraries to perform various tasks and consider how the form of usage could create certain types of security holes.

 The best way to work with the examples described in this chapter is to use the downloadable source, rather than type it in by hand. Using the downloadable source reduces potential errors. You can find the source code examples for this chapter in the \S4WD\Chapter06 folder of the downloadable source.

Enhancing CSS with Libraries

CSS is all about formatting page content. Given the current state of CSS, it's amazing to see the sorts of pizzazz you can add to a site. Web developers use CSS to make a boring page pop out. Of course, there are mundane uses for CSS as well. For example, imagine trying to read multicolumned text without relying on CSS to format the content. What you'd end up with is a mess. Using just HTML tags to format the content would make the pages nearly impossible to use on the wide range of devices that people rely on today.

CSS alone could probably do everything you need to create fantastic pages. However, it's important to realize that even the best web developer doesn't have time to create all that CSS code by hand. There are a number of ways in which to pack CSS code into a library, but one of the more interesting is the `css()` function provided with jQuery UI, as found in the *Transform.html* file:

```
<!DOCTYPE html>

<html>
<head>
    <script
        src="https://code.jquery.com/jquery-latest.js">
    </script>
    <script
        src="https://code.jquery.com/ui/1.9.2/jquery-ui.js">
    </script>
    <script
        src="jquery.transform.js">
    </script>
    <link
        rel="stylesheet"
        href="https://code.jquery.com/ui/1.9.2/themes/base/jquery-ui.css" />
    <title>jquery.transform.js Demonstration</title>
    <style type="text/css">
        #TransformMe
        {
            border: double;
            border-color: Blue;
            border-width: thick;

            position: absolute;
            width: 120px;
            height: 40px;
            top: 90px;
            left: 75px;
        }

        #TransformMe p
        {
            margin: 0;
            padding: 0;
            height: 40px;
            font-family: "Comic Sans MS", cursive, sans-serif;
            font-size: large;
            color: Red;
            background-color: Yellow;
        }

        #Rotate
        {
            position: absolute;
            top: 190px;
            left: 75px;
        }
    </style>
    <script type="text/javascript">
        $(function()
        {
```

```
            $("#Rotate").click(function()
            {
                $("#TransformMe").css("transform", "rotate(45deg)");
            });
        })
    </script>
</head>

<body>
    <h1>jquery.transform.js Demonstration</h1>
    <div id="TransformMe">
        <p>Some Text</p>
    </div>
    <div>
        <input type="button"
               id="Rotate"
               value=" Rotate 45 Degrees " />
    </div>
</body>
</html>
```

The actual functionality found in this example relies on the *jquery.transform.js* script. However, before you get into the scripting, notice that the page does rely on standard CSS to place the content. In most cases, applications you create will rely on a combination of both local and library formatting sources. The content includes a paragraph formatted as a label and a button.

Clicking the button triggers the click event, which executes a single line of code. The CSS for TransformMe is modified to include a transform of 45deg. The text goes from being straight across to having an angle like the one shown in Figure 6-1.

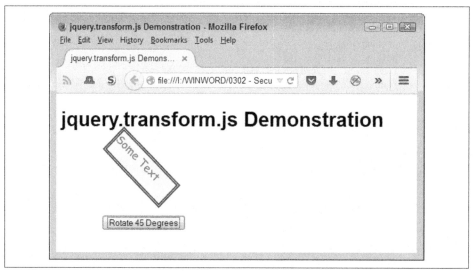

Figure 6-1. Using a transform can modify the appearance of text on screen

The problem with allowing a script to affect page formatting is that you can't be sure how the page will look once the script completes. The page could contain hidden elements or simply not present information as expected. Hidden elements could contain code to redirect the user to an infected site or perform other deeds that you don't want associated with your application.

Interacting with HTML Using Libraries

Some library functions interact directly with the HTML of your application in two common ways. The first is to interact with an existing element. In this case, content appears within the element based on the library function called. The second is to create new elements and attach them to the existing document. The new elements can contain any sort of content, including tags that could potentially cause problems for the end user.

A major concern when using a library to interact directly with the HTML on your site is that the library could fill various elements with misleading, incorrect, or outright contaminated data. For example, instead of creating the link you expected, it might actually redirect a user to another site—perhaps one that downloads a virus or other nasty piece of software to the user's machine. Libraries that work with HTML can cause subtle issues that you might not even know about immediately because everything will appear to work correctly. Unless a user complains about the misdirection (and given how URLs work today they probably won't), you won't know about the issue until enough machines are infected to cause severe problems.

The adding of new elements to a page is a common practice. The example found in *ViewJSON.html* adds new elements to the existing document based on the content of a JavaScript Object Notation (JSON) file named *Test.json*. The following code shows how the example performs this task:

```
<!DOCTYPE html>

<html>
<head>
   <title>Viewing JSON Files</title>
   <script
     src="https://code.jquery.com/jquery-latest.js">
   </script>
   <script language="JavaScript">
      function ViewData()
      {
         // Obtain the data from disk.
         $.getJSON("Test.json",
           function(data)
           {
              // Create an array to hold the data.
              var items = [];
```

```
            // Parse the data by looking at
            // each entry in the Users object.
            $.each(data.Users,
               function(key, value)
               {
                  items.push("<li>" +
                     value.Name + "<br />" +
                     value.Number + "<br />" +
                     (new Date(
                        parseInt(value.Birthday.substr(6)))
                     ).toDateString()
                     + "</li>");
               });

            // Place the result in an unordered list.
            $('<ul/>', {html: items.join("")}).
               appendTo('body');
         });
      }
   </script>
</head>

<body>
   <h1>Viewing JSON Files</h1>
   <input id="btnView"
          type="button"
          value="View JSON Data"
          onclick="ViewData()" />
</body>
</html>
```

In this case, the library opens the *Test.json* file and reads data from it. The code removes the JSON file formatting and adds HTML tag formatting. It then uses the join() function to add the new elements to the page. Figure 6-2 shows the output from this example.

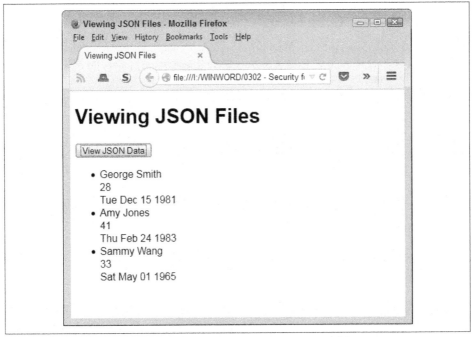

Figure 6-2. Injecting data from an external source is always problematic

Notice that the example avoids the use of the `document.write()` call, which could expose users to all sorts of unwanted content. Using the `join()` function instead provides a safer alternative that should keep the page free of security issues.

Extending JavaScript with Libraries

Most people think about the ways in which libraries extend either CSS or HTML. The presentation of information is at the forefront. However, libraries can affect the underlying scripting as well. For example, most people are familiar with how to use `alert()` to display simple messages. Most libraries contain alternatives that a hacker could use to display other sorts of information on screen or affect the application in other ways. For example, the *DialogBox.html* file contains an example of creating a custom dialog box like the one shown here:

```
<!DOCTYPE html>

<html>
<head>
    <title>Creating a Simple Dialog Box</title>
    <script
        src="https://code.jquery.com/jquery-latest.js">
    </script>
    <script
```

```
            src="https://code.jquery.com/ui/1.9.2/jquery-ui.js">
    </script>
    <link
        rel="stylesheet"
        href="https://code.jquery.com/ui/1.9.2/themes/base/jquery-ui.css" />
    <style type="text/css">
     .Normal
     {
         font-family: Arial, Helvetica, sans-serif;
         color: SaddleBrown;
         background-color: Bisque;
     }
     .Emphasize
     {
         color: Maroon;
         font-style: italic;
         font-size: larger;
     }
    </style>
</head>

<body>
    <h1>Creating a Simple Dialog Box</h1>
    <div id="DialogContent"
         title="Simple Dialog Example"
         hidden>
        <p class="Normal">
            This is some
            <span class="Emphasize">interesting</span>
            text for the dialog box!
        </p>
    </div>
    <script type="text/javascript">
        $("#DialogContent").dialog();
    </script>
</body>
</html>
```

In this case, the example displays the dialog box immediately when you open the application, as shown in Figure 6-3. The threat offered by such functionality is that a user could open your application expecting one experience and get something completely different. Because the dialog box appears as part of the application, the user will provide any sort of information the dialog box requests or do anything it wants the user to do.

Figure 6-3. The dialog box functionality of jQuery UI could be used to create a security hole

A hacker could enable such functionality by using something like script (code) injection. For example, the hacker could hide the code as a comment on a blog page (which is why manual moderation of comments is such a good idea). The underlying attack is one of social engineering—putting the user at ease by presenting the dialog box as part of the application and then using that situation to do something nasty.

Differentiating Between Internally Stored and Externally Stored Libraries

You may get the idea that all JavaScript libraries appear on a third-party site. It's true that many popular JavaScript libraries, such as jQuery, do appear on someone else's site. However, many organizations have their own personal libraries as well. The factors that affect internally stored libraries are:

- They reside on systems owned and maintained by the organization.
- The organization controls the source code and can modify it as needed to address issues that developers encounter or are brought to the organization's attention by others.
- Outside parties can't access the library without the organization's permission.

- The connectivity to the library relies on internal lines, rather than access through the Internet.

Internally stored libraries have many advantages not found in those stored externally on a third-party site. For the most part, given the same level of coding, an internally stored library is faster, more reliable, and more secure than an externally stored library. (For example, a hacker can easily download a copy of a library stored on an external site, but is less likely to do so for an internally stored library.) In addition, because the library contains only the code an organization actually needs, it's quite possible that the internally stored library will use fewer resources because it will be smaller than its generic counterpart will. Of course, these statements make a lot of assumptions about the internally stored library that might not be true. Here are the counterpoints you need to consider:

- Internally stored libraries are expensive to build and maintain, so the organization may not keep them updated as required to keep them secure.
- Few organizations can field a development team equivalent in skills to a third-party vendor, so the quality of the library will likely suffer.
- Third-party libraries receive testing from a substantial number of testers, so that even small errors come out. Internally stored libraries generally receive a modicum of testing that may not even weed out some major flaws.

The bottom line is that internally stored libraries are successful when they target special functionality not provided by third-party counterparts and the team putting them together takes the care required to do the job well. When putting your application design together, you must weigh the benefits that internally stored libraries provide against the risks they present. In addition, you must further define the risks presented by third-party libraries.

Defining the Security Threats Posed by Libraries

Any JavaScript code you create is likely to contain some error that a hacker can exploit for various purposes. Libraries aren't special in this regard. However, because you're incorporating code that your organization didn't create into an application your organization did create, there is a chance that code that would normally behave correctly will end up having a security flaw due to assumptions on both sides. With this in mind, the two tools that every developer needs to know about when it comes to libraries are testing tools specifically designed for security needs and a good security expert.

It isn't ever possible to say that the library you maintain is completely secure. You can say that you've written the code to meet security best practices and that a security expert has reviewed the code, but even with the best intentions and robust tools, it simply isn't possible to guarantee that a library (or any other code for that matter) is secure. This issue comes up relatively often when speaking with nonprogrammers—especially management staff of an organization that wants to use your library for development purposes. It's important that everyone understand that you have taken every appropriate security measure, but that no one can guarantee any code is completely secure.

Even after testing, you have to realize that there is a potential for security flaws in a library, the application it supports, or as a result of combining the two. With this in mind, here is a list of the most common sorts of threats that you could encounter when working with libraries (with no emphasis on the actual source of the flaw):

Cross-site scripting (XSS)

The most common security problem that developers face is XSS. There are three easy ways to get past XSS:

- Never transmit untrusted data in the same HTTP response as HTML or JavaScript. In fact, it's best if the main HTML document remains static.

 You might wonder how your server would even end up sending untrusted data to anyone. It's easier than you think. "ScriptGard: Automatic Context-Sensitive Sanitization for Large-Scale Legacy Web Applications" (*http://www.cs.berkeley.edu/~prateeks/papers/scriptgard-ccs11.pdf*) describes just how hard it is to ensure data integrity even if you use the right sanitizers. The safe assumption is that any data you didn't personally create is untrusted.

- When you must transmit untrusted data from the server to the client, make sure you encode it in JSON and that the data has a `Content-Type` of `applica tion/json`.

- Once the data is ready for display, use the `Node.textContent()`, `docu ment.createTextNode()`, or `Element.setAttribute()` (second parameter only) calls to ensure the page presents it properly.

Dangerous function calls

Just because JavaScript supports a particular call, doesn't mean the call is safe. Using `setInnerHtml()` or `.innerHtml` = can inject unwanted script code. Rely on the `setInnerText()` call instead.

Modifying the document directly

Although you may see `document.write()` appear a few times in the book for the sake of expediency, using this call in a production environment is an invitation to disaster. The code could write anything, anywhere. Use calls that add, remove, or update Document Object Model (DOM) elements instead.

Creating scripts on the fly

Any time you turn a string into a script, you're inviting a hacker to provide the string. Using calls such as `eval()`, `setTimeout()` with a string argument, `setInterval()` with a string argument, or `new Function()` makes your code significantly less secure.

Code that executes, but causes security flaws

Some JavaScript calls give you all sorts of rope to hang yourself with. In order to avoid this situation, use JavaScript strict mode to ensure that only safe calls will actually work.

Content that purports to be something it isn't

Hackers love to send you content that isn't quite what you think it is. The best way to avoid this problem is to follow a Content Security Policy, which means including the appropriate content tags, such as `script-src 'self'` and `object-src 'self'`.

Scanning a library using a product such as JSLint (*http:// www.jslint.com/*) can help you ensure the quality of your code. High-quality code is less likely to contain errors that will cause security issues. However, it's important to realize that JSLint (and tools like it) don't scan specifically for security issues. In fact, you can't scan for security issues in your code. In order to check for security issues, you must begin by testing your code specifically for security issues. If the code requires a higher level of confidence than testing will provide, then you must also employ the services of a security expert to check the code for potential problems manually.

Enabling Strict Mode

Newer browsers provide support for ECMAScript 5, which includes the JavaScript strict mode. In order to use this security feature, you need to ensure that your users aren't hanging on to that fossil of a browser that's been on their machine from the first time they used it. For example, IE 9 doesn't support this feature, but IE 10 does. You can find which browsers support strict mode at *http://kangax.github.io/compat-table/es5/*. It's essential that you develop an organizational policy that requires users have certain browsers in order to work with the application.

Strict mode makes many obvious and subtle changes to the way JavaScript operates. The important thing is that it makes it easier to debug JavaScript applications because instead of silently failing or acting oddly, your JavaScript application will now raise errors when it encounters a problem. This means that those odd library calls that used to die without doing anything will now tell you something about the problems. Here are the major problems that strict mode helps you deal with:

Eliminates the use of `with`

Using the `with` statement can open security problems in your application. The latest versions of JavaScript have deprecated this feature because it's so dangerous. Strict mode will raise an error whenever you try to use `with` in your code.

Prevents unwanted variables

A major problem in JavaScript is that you can accidentally create new variables by assigning a value to a variable with a mistyped name. In some cases, this error can create unwanted global variables that can result in security holes. Strict mode forces you to declare every variable before you use it, so it's not possible to create variables accidentally any longer.

Disallows coercion using `this`

Some existing code coerces local variables to the global state by assigning a value to them when they're in the unassigned or null state. For example, you can't assign a value to a variable within a constructor without first instantiating an object by calling `new`.

Precludes duplicates

It's quite easy to create duplicates of properties in objects or named arguments in functions. Strict mode throws an error if you try to create a duplication in either situation.

Notifies of immutable value change attempts

It isn't possible to change an immutable value in JavaScript. However, in the past, the attempt would fail silently, so it was possible to assume the code was in one state when it was really in another. Strict mode throws an error after any attempt to change an immutable value.

Strict mode comes with ECMAScript 5 and above. You don't have to install anything special to get strict mode support. However, you do have to include the `"use strict";` string. Older versions of JavaScript ignore the string, so you won't see any changes in how older code runs. The *StrictMode.html* file contains the following example:

```html
<!DOCTYPE html>

<html>
<head>
    <title>Working with Strict Mode</title>
    <script language="javascript">
        function testStrict(Name)
        {
            "use strict";

            try
            {
                this.Name = Name;
                alert(this.Name);
            }
            catch (e)
            {
                alert(e);
            }
        }
    </script>
</head>

<body>
    <h1>Working with Strict Mode</h1>
    <button id="Test" onclick="testStrict('George')">
        Test
    </button>
</body>
</html>
```

Without strict mode checking (you can simply comment the statement out to try it), the code displays the value erroneously assigned to this.Name of George. However, with strict mode checking in place, you see the error message shown in Figure 6-4.

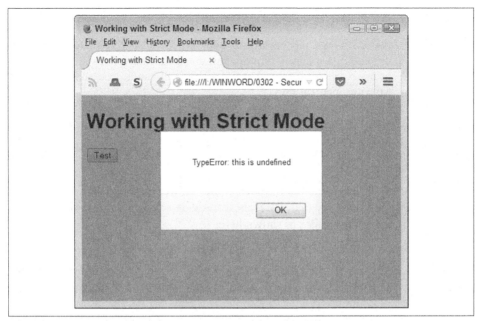

Figure 6-4. Strict mode checking prevents errant assignments

 Never use strict mode globally. It might seem like a good idea at first, but you'll quickly find that some library code will fail. The idea behind strict mode is to ensure you have firm control over the code you create. Using validation checks, you can monitor the behavior of libraries that you use.

Developing a Content Security Policy (CSP)

One of the biggest problems that developers face is creating applications that aren't susceptible to various kinds of script and content injection attacks such as XSS. The problem defies easy resolution because of the way in which browsers work. Browsers effectively trust any content coming from a specific origin, so that the browser trusts anything injected at the same level as the original data. CSP seeks to remedy this problem by creating a whitelisting facility of a sort.

For browsers that support CSP (see the table at *http://caniuse.com/contentsecuritypo licy* for a listing of compatible browsers), CSP provides the means for keeping browsers from recognizing scripts and contents from unsupported sites. The policy appears as a series of headings that you add to the top of the page. When a browser sees the headings, it uses them to determine which scripts and content are safe to load.

When a browser doesn't provide support for CSP, it ignores the headings you provide and acts as it normally would. This means that users must rely on browsers that support CSP if you want to use CSP as a means of blocking unwanted content. Otherwise, the browser will work as it always has and continue to load content from unsupported sites.

A header consists of three basic elements: policy name, data type, and data source. Here is an example of a CSP heading that contains just one data type:

```
Content-Security-Policy: script-src 'self'
```

In this case, the CSP states that the browser should only execute scripts found embedded within the page. Let's say that you want to provide support for jQuery as well. In this case, you'd extend the policy as shown here:

```
Content-Security-Policy: script-src 'self' 'https://code.jquery.com'
```

You don't need to provide the specific location of the source code file, just the host site information. Each entry is separated from the next using a space. A CSP can define all sorts of content types. For example, you may decide that you want to support scripts found on the local page, but you don't want to support objects at all. In this case, you use the following CSP header:

```
Content-Security-Policy: script-src 'self'; object-src 'none'
```

Notice that the content types appear separated by a semicolon (;). CSP supports a number of different content type directives. You can find a quick reference guide containing a list of these directives, sample values, and descriptions at *http://content-security-policy.com/*. The important thing to remember is that using CSP can save you from that subtle hole in your code that a hacker could otherwise exploit.

Incorporating Libraries Safely

Some organizations simply add a library to their toolbox because it provides some functionality that the organization needs without much thought about how that library is put together or even if it's a good idea to use it. In at least some cases, organizations that don't put a lot of thought into the use of a library end up regretting it later because the library will contain a lot of security holes, run unreliably or slowly, or actually end up costing the organization more time than if it had simply created its own library in the first place. The following sections will help you determine whether incorporating that interesting library you found into your application is actually a good idea.

Embracing the Sandbox Solution

It's quite likely that even if you check the third-party JavaScript and clean the data you use thoroughly that something will still try to sneak by. Remember that it's easier to overcome the walls you build than to build them in the first place. When it comes to JavaScript security threats, you must consider that hackers will simply come up with new ways of circumventing your security every time you have a new bulletproof strategy in your arsenal.

A potential way around this problem is to rely on sandboxing. Essentially this means that the third-party library runs at a lower privilege level than your code does. Using sandboxing doesn't guarantee that your application will remain safe, but it does reduce the potential for security breaches. You can read about sandboxing techniques at *http://www.slideshare.net/phungphu/a-twotier-sandbox-architecture-for-untrusted-javascript*. The techniques described in the slideshow are complex, but they do work. As with everything, it comes down to determining what level of risk you're willing to tolerate when running an application. Chapter 10 discusses the use of sandboxes in detail.

Researching the Library Fully

Whenever you choose to add a library to your application, you're expressing trust in the creator of that library. Even with the help of a competent security expert, taking a library apart and examining every bit of code it contains (assuming the code is even fully available) will prove more time consuming than creating the library from scratch. (Make sure you don't get the minimized version of the library, which is hard to review because the vendor removes the whitespace characters.) Consequently, you must consider whether the library poses few enough risks to be part of an application solution that you create. When researching a library, consider these questions as part of your research:

- Are there any trade press stories that discuss the library in a negative way? (If the library is already known to have unpatched security holes, you may want to reconsider using it for your application.)
- Are other organizations using the library without problem?
- Is the company that created the library proactive in answering questions about library integrity?
- Does the company that created the library provide consistent bug fixes and updates?
- What sorts of questions are people asking as part of the online support provided for the library?

- How long has the library been around? (Libraries with long lives tend to have fewer problems and the longevity speaks of good support on the part of the creator.)

Defining the Precise Library Uses

No one uses every feature provided by every library found in an application. Some research sites state outright that many developers use a library for just one or two of the features it contains. Documenting how you use a particular library helps you mitigate risks associated with using the library by focusing your attention on those areas. More importantly, keeping track of specific usage areas tells you when you must perform an update and how you can decrease the size of a library by removing unused features from it. The more you know about how you use a library to perform specific application tasks, the more you reduce the risk of using it.

Keeping Library Size Small and Content Focused

It's essential to keep third-party libraries small and focused on specific needs whenever possible. This means removing code that you won't ever use because such code tends to:

- Slow download times
- Increase security issues
- Reduce reliability
- Cause unnecessary updates

Fortunately, the best third-party libraries are on your side. They want you to create a custom version of the library to use on your site. For example, when you use jQuery UI, you can create a customized version using the special builder shown in Figure 6-5.

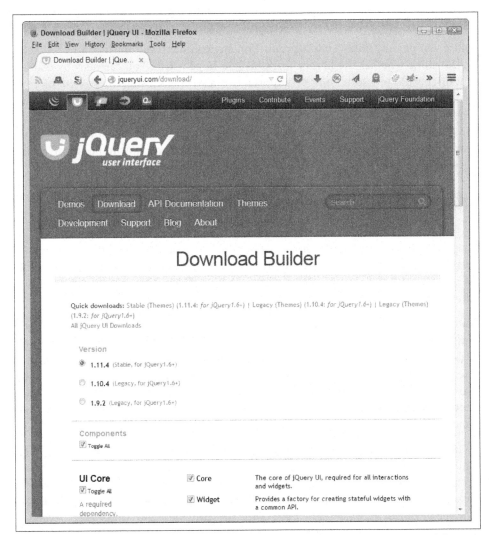

Figure 6-5. Using the jQuery UI builder helps you create a customized version of the library

Using a builder means that the library you create will contain only the library elements you actually need. Of course, the downside is that you must provide hosting for the library, which means you won't get automatic updates as the creator makes them available. If you use an option like this, it's essential to check for the need to update your copy of the library on a regular basis.

Performing the Required Testing

Before you put any library into a production environment, you must build a test suite to determine whether the library works as you hope it will. You can start by using a vendor-specific test suite, but it's important to also check using a test suite of your own design that mimics how your application will use the library. The testing process should include both valid and invalid data input checks. It's important to ensure that you get the expected output with valid inputs and some sort of exception when using invalid inputs. Chapter 11 and Chapter 12 provide details on how to perform various levels of testing on your application and the libraries it uses.

Differentiating Between Libraries and Frameworks

The sidebar "Differentiating Between Frameworks and Libraries" on page 115 in Chapter 5 gives you a brief overview of how libraries and frameworks differ from a reliability perspective. Of course, there is more to the difference than simply reliability concerns. It's important to have a better understanding of precisely how the two differ and why you should care.

Frameworks provide templating for a site in a manner that libraries don't. When using a library, an application is simply relying on another source for code. Framework usage implies another level of participation, where the application now uses external sources for additional support. Because a framework integrates more fully into an application and provides more resources, you must also hold it to a higher standard than when working with a library (although you should hold both to a high standard anyway).

Trying to figure out whether a framework is safe to use can be quite hard. In fact, testing can become nearly impossible. With this in mind, third-party security experts are attempting to quantify the safety level of frameworks and templating libraries. One of the better places to look for information is mustache-security (*https://code.google.com/p/mustache-security/*). This site provides you with seven levels of checks for frameworks, as shown in Figure 6-6.

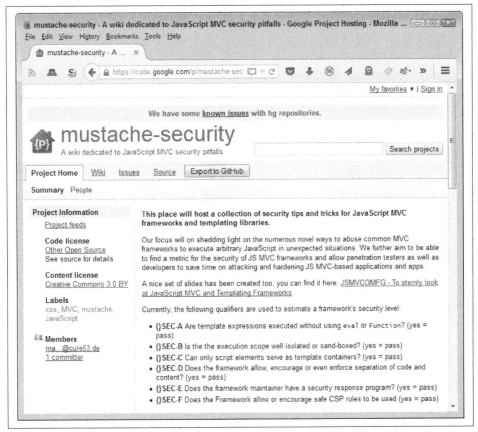

Figure 6-6. Sites such as mustache-security provide seven levels of checks for frameworks

Looking a bit further down the page, you can see that the security news for frameworks isn't good. Most frameworks today contain serious security problems that you need to consider before using them for application development. Figure 6-7 shows the results for some of the most popular frameworks and templating libraries available today.

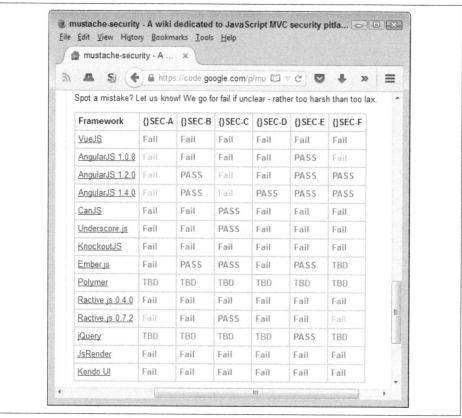

Figure 6-7. Most frameworks and templating libraries today have a long way to go before they become secure

The interesting thing about sites like these is that they often provide specific examples of how the framework fails. For example, click the AngularJS link in the table shown in Figure 6-7 and you see specifics on how the framework failed in the security area, as shown in Figure 6-8. The information also includes workarounds you can use to help mitigate the problems, which is the main reason you want to spend some time researching the frameworks and ensuring you understand precisely where they fall short.

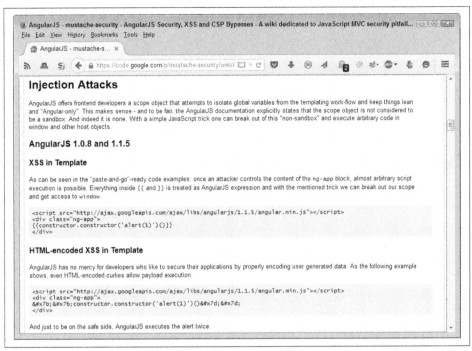

Figure 6-8. Some security sites provide example code demonstrating security issues in frameworks

CHAPTER 7

Using APIs with Care

APIs provide a means of using full-blown applications on someone else's server to meet your specific needs. Working with an API means sending a request to a black box and receiving a response of some sort back. The request can be as simple as a function call, but often requires that you supply data. The response can be in the form of data, but could also be some other service. For example, there are APIs for performing physical tasks such as opening doors. In fact, APIs can likely meet any generic need you might require. This chapter discusses the security implications of using APIs, including how APIs differ from libraries.

Part of discovering the security threats that APIs represent is viewing coded examples. This chapter uses a simple example as part of the explanation process. Although you could use the target API for a significant number of application tasks, the point is to create some to use for discussion purposes and then look at how the use of an API could create problems for any application. View the example in this chapter as a point of discussion, rather than an actual programming technique.

 Although this chapter does discuss specific APIs in both coded examples and as examples of where APIs can go wrong, the intent isn't to single out any particular API. Every API you use could have serious flaws that enable a hacker to gain access to your system or cause other sorts of problems for your application. The specific examples help you understand how all APIs can go wrong in general. In short, you shouldn't see the specific examples in this chapter as an indication of particular APIs to avoid using.

Of course, the result of all this exploration is to determine how you can use APIs safely as part of your application development strategy. Because APIs are so beneficial, you won't see them go away anytime soon, even though they can be a bad idea from a security perspective. In fact, you can count on the use of APIs to expand because developers have constant time-crunch issues that APIs solve. As more people use web-based applications and those applications become more complex, you can count on the use of APIs to expand to meet specific needs. As usage increases, so does the appeal for creating exploits by hackers who want to access your data and use it in ways you never intended. In short, if anything, the security footprint of APIs will increase, so your diligence in using them must increase as well.

Differentiating Between APIs and Libraries

Some developers think that all sources of outside code are the same. However, APIs and libraries differ in some significant ways. For example, APIs represent an out-of-process call because they run on another server, while libraries represent an in-process call because you include them as part of your application. Just the matter of out-of-process versus in-process significantly changes the way in which you must view security issues. The following sections help define the differences between APIs and libraries more fully so that you get a better understanding of the security implications of using one over the other.

Some people use *library* and *API* interchangeably, but the two have specific meanings in this book. Chapter 6 defines libraries in detail, but essentially, a library is external code you incorporate into an application using whatever technique the host language requires. You use libraries directly in your code as part of the application. As a result, a library is always an in-process coding technique, even when the library source resides on a third-party server. In order to use the library, the code on the third-party server downloads onto your server and becomes part of the application, running in the same process as the application.

This book also differentiates between APIs used to perform tasks and those used as part of an application development effort. For example, the JavaScript web APIs described at *http://www.w3.org/standards/webdesign/script* define the JavaScript language elements. This sort of API defines a language used for scripting purposes. Yes, this is a legitimate API, but not in the context used in this book. The book context is more along the lines of a web service, rather than a language-specific specification.

Considering the Differences in Popularity

Libraries and APIs both provide benefits to the developer by saving development time. In fact, most web-based applications today use a combination of libraries and

---

APIs to perform tasks. However, APIs appear to be gaining in popularity faster than libraries for some good reasons:

Reduced resource usage

APIs run on someone else's server, so you don't need to worry about obtaining the required resources. However, the fact that the code runs on someone else's server also means that you lose control of your data at some point and never see the actual API code so that you can assess the security threats it represents.

Decreased coding requirements

Using an API is often easier and requires less code than using a library. Of course, you also have less control over an API. The trade-off is flexibility and the price is complexity. Given that developers are increasingly overloaded, the reduced coding requirements of APIs can make them quite attractive. However, the reduced flexibility also represents a potential source of security issues because you can no longer tailor code usage to meet your particular requirements.

Smaller learning curve

It's usually easier to learn how to use an API than it is a library because the API is generally in a client/server form. The biggest issue is determining how to format the data so that the API understands what you want it to do. It's in the data formatting that the greatest security issue exists. A hacker could cause malformation of your query that causes the server to crash or force the server to respond in unexpected ways. Because the query source is traced to your application, the host will blame your application, rather than the hacker that caused the problem.

Defining the Differences in Usage

It isn't possible to use APIs in every case that you use a library (and vice versa). Some situations call for an integrated approach. For example, you can't easily code a user interface using an API—it really does call for a library. (You can obtain the data for the user interface, as described for the Google API example later, but this is different from actually creating the interface elements.) The following list describes typical uses for APIs and their security implications:

Data query

The most common use for APIs is to make a request and obtain data as a result. The request commonly contains the parameters of the requested data. A data source can include databases, sensors, calculations, and analyses. Whenever you deal with data, man-in-the-middle attacks are common. However, a hacker could simply choose to modify the data in order to mislead you or to use the received data as a method for gaining access to your network.

Supervisory control and data acquisition (SCADA)

The Internet of Things (IoT) relies on web interfaces to perform a number of SCADA tasks. For example, with the right thermostat, it's relatively easy to adjust the temperature of your house using a web application from your smartphone, wherever you might be. A hacker could easily plug into the same interface and lower your house temperature until the pipes freeze or make it so hot that you need to open the doors when you get home. Of course, SCADA encompasses all sorts of things, including industrial controls. In this case, a breach of security not only affects data, but has physical effects as well.

Monitoring

A middle ground between data query and SCADA is the act of monitoring systems. For example, the police may want to monitor certain street cameras during a protest or other event. APIs make it possible to create applications that can monitor any camera, anywhere, as needed to provide protection for the general populace. A hacker could trick the same API into providing false information.

 It would be easy to think that an application you or your organization uses doesn't actually qualify as a monitoring system. However, home security, baby monitors, health care devices, and all sorts of other applications act as monitors. Consequently, the domain for monitoring software may be much larger than you initially think.

Multimedia

An API need not work only with textual or other abstract data. It can also perform tasks related to the other senses, with visual and audio being the most common. The control and manipulation of multimedia creates an environment in which users interact with applications in nontraditional ways and the results are often surprising. By combining multimedia with data science, it's possible to recognize new patterns and objects in everyday situations, enhancing a user's ability to perform tasks, such as visualizing scenes in ultraviolet, which might otherwise be impossible. However, it's important to realize that multimedia is simply another form of data and data of all sorts is easy for hackers to intercept, corrupt, and otherwise manipulate in unwanted ways.

Location

Although geolocation is the most common form of location acquisition, query, and manipulation, it's important to understand that APIs exist to work with all sorts of location information. Location, like multimedia, is a special kind of data. In this case, it provides a two- or three-dimensional point in space relative to a particular target space, such as the earth. For that matter, some APIs add a fourth dimension to the equation: time. Imagine what would happen if hackers chose to modify location data such that two objects, such as cars, attempted to occupy the same space at the same time (resulting in a crash).

Extending JavaScript Using APIs

It's important to consider security from a real-world perspective. The following sections describe some issues in locating appropriate APIs for testing and application development purposes. We then look at an example for the Google Maps API in action. This simple application demonstrates the need to consider issues such as malformed requests, server errors, and errant data return. The example is interesting because it does demonstrate how to create an application that works with the browser canvas to draw part of the user interface based on API return data.

 The best way to work with the example described in this section is to use the downloadable source, rather than type it in by hand. Using the downloadable source reduces potential errors. You can find the Google Maps API example in the *\S4WD\Chapter07\GoogleAPI* folder of the downloadable source.

Locating Appropriate APIs

JavaScript provides an extensible programming environment that supports both APIs and libraries. Developers have taken advantage of both forms of extensibility to create some astounding sharable code that performs tasks that you might not think possible. For example, it's possible to use a JavaScript application to interact with the vibrate feature of a mobile device to create special effects (check out the technique at *https://developer.mozilla.org/en-US/docs/Web/Guide/API/Vibration*). With the right resource, you can find an API to perform just about any task you can think of. The following list provides you with some ideas of where to look for that API of your dreams:

- {API}Search (*http://apis.io/*)
- 40 useful APIs for web designers and developers (*http://www.webdesignerdepot.com/2011/07/40-useful-apis-for-web-designers-and-developers/*)
- API Directory (*http://www.programmableweb.com/apis/directory*)
- API For That (*http://www.apiforthat.com/*)
- APIs Dashboard (*http://www.programmableweb.com/apis*)
- APIs Data.gov (*https://www.data.gov/developers/apis*) (click the "browse the current catalog for APIs" link)
- Guide to Web APIs (*https://developer.mozilla.org/en-US/docs/Web/Guide/API*)
- MashApe (*https://www.mashape.com/*)

- Public APIs (*https://www.publicapis.com/*)
- Web API Interfaces (*https://developer.mozilla.org/en-US/docs/Web/API*)

This is just a sampling of the API search sites online. Most of them provide write-ups on the APIs; some sites also provide reviews. Before you select a particular API, make sure you read as much as you can about it. Perform tests with the API on a test system. Make sure you verify the sorts of data that the API actually transfers between your test system and the host by using a packet sniffer. It might sound a little paranoid to test APIs in this way (see "Accessing APIs Safely from JavaScript" on page 157 of this chapter for additional details), but performing the tests helps reduce your risk. Remember that security is always a balance between risk and the benefits you obtain from taking the risk.

 Some API providers have so many APIs that they provide their own listing. For example, Google provides a wealth of APIs and you can find them listed in the *GData API Directory* (*https://developers.google.com/gdata/docs/directory*). It's important to realize that many host-specific listings contain biased information and reading about the capabilities and deficiencies of the API on another site is always recommended.

Creating a Simple Example

Creating a secure application that relies on APIs is harder than you might think because even the best APIs rely on a certain amount of trust. You trade the risk of trusting the host for the data or other resources the host provides. To see how the security issues come into play, this section works through a simple example that uses the Google Maps API. In order to make the API usable, it also relies on the jQuery (*http://jquery.com/*) and jQuery UI (*http://jqueryui.com/*) libraries to display the data and associated user interface. Rarely will you use an API without also relying on libraries to interact with the data in some way.

 In order to use this example, you must obtain a developer key. Google provides two kinds of keys: paid and free. You only need the free key for this example. The paid key does provide considerably more flexibility and you'll likely need it for any full-fledged application you create. However, for experimentation purposes, the free key works just fine. You can obtain this key at *https://developers.google.com/maps/licensing*. Make sure you understand the terms of service fully before you begin working with the Google Maps API. You can also find some additional assistance in using the Google Maps API with JavaScript at *https://developers.google.com/maps/documentation/javascript/tutorial*.

It's best to create the code for this example in several steps. The first is to add the required jQuery references shown here:

```
<script
    src="https://code.jquery.com/jquery-latest.js">
</script>
<script
    src="https://code.jquery.com/ui/1.9.2/jquery-ui.js">
</script>
<link
    rel="stylesheet"
    href="https://code.jquery.com/ui/1.9.2/themes/base/jquery-ui.css" />
```

Although the code makes a reference to an external library, the code from the library is included as part of the application as an in-process element. Chapter 6 describes all of the security issues regarding library use. In addition, you also need to add a reference to the Google Maps API, as shown here:

```
<script type="text/javascript"
    src="https://maps.googleapis.com/maps/api/js?key=Your Key Here&sensor=false">
</script>
```

 This example won't work at all unless you replace the words "Your Key Here" with the key that you receive from Google. Consequently, this particular step is important because it's the one step that you must perform even if you're using the code downloaded from the book's site.

Both the library and the API references rely on the <script> tag, but the manner in which they use the tag is different. Notice that the library accesses a file without any additional information. The API requires additional information in the form of a key and a sensor configuration option in this case. As the section progresses, you'll see other differences.

Now that you have all of the required references in place, it's time to create a canvas to draw the map. The canvas is simply a <div>, as shown here:

```
</div>
    <div id="MapCanvas">
</div>
```

You must provide style information that gives the <div> size or else the map won't appear on screen, even when Google sends it to you. The example uses the following style information:

```
#MapCanvas
{
    height: 90%;
    width:100%;
}
```

In addition to the canvas, the example provides two textboxes for input and a button you can use to request a new map. There isn't anything too complex about the interface, but it gets the job done (the example is preset to show the location of Milwaukee, Wisconsin, in the center of the map—you can change the longitude and latitude to any other location you wish):

```
<div id="Input">
    <label for="longitude">
        Longitude:
    </label>
    <input id="longitude"
           value="-87.95"
           type="text" />
    <label for="latitude">
        Latitude:
    </label>
    <input id="latitude"
           value="43.04"
           type="text" />
    <input id="submit"
           value="Get Map"
           type="button" />
</div>
```

The code for this example uses many of the jQuery and jQuery UI tricks you've seen in other applications. For example, the application creates a spinner for the longitude and latitude controls to make it easier to move the center of the map incrementally. Moving an entire degree at a time wouldn't make the application very useful, so the two spinners change the inputs by a tenth of a degree at a time (even this setting may be too large and you might want to change it). Notice the use of the `step` option to perform this task. Of the code that follows, the `GetMap()` function is the most important because it actually displays the map on screen:

```
$(function()
  {
      // Track the current latitude using a
      // spinner control.
      var Latitude = $("#latitude").spinner(
        {
            min: -90,
            max: 90,
            step: .1,

            change: function(event, ui)
            {
                if (Latitude.spinner("value") < -90)
                    Latitude.spinner("value", -90);
                if (Latitude.spinner("value") > 90)
                    Latitude.spinner("value", 90);
            }
```

```
    });

// Track the current longitude using a
// spinner control.
var Longitude = $("#longitude").spinner(
    {
        min: -180,
        max: 180,
        step: .1,

        change: function(event, ui)
        {
            if (Longitude.spinner("value") < -180)
                Longitude.spinner("value", -180);
            if (Longitude.spinner("value") > 180)
                Longitude.spinner("value", 180);
        }
    });

// This function actually displays the map on
// screen.
function GetMap()
{
    // Create a list of arguments to send to Google.
    var MapOptions =
    {
        center: new google.maps.LatLng(
                    Latitude.spinner("value"),
                    Longitude.spinner("value")),
        zoom: 8,
        mapTypeId: google.maps.MapTypeId.ROADMAP
    }

    // Provide the location to place the map and the
    // map options to Google.
    var map = new google.maps.Map(
        document.getElementById("MapCanvas"),
        MapOptions);
};

// The example provides two methods of getting a
// map: during page loading or by clicking Get Map.
$(window).load(
    function()
    {
        GetMap();
    });

$("#submit").click(
    function()
    {
        GetMap();
```

```
        });
    })
```

 Latitudes range from 90 degrees north to –90 degrees south, so the example reflects this requirement. Likewise, longitudes range from 180 degrees west to –180 degrees east of Greenwich, England. You can read more about latitude and longitude at *http://geogra phy.about.com/cs/latitudelongitude/a/latlong.htm.*

The GetMap() function performs the actual task of obtaining the map. To do this, your application must create a list of map options. The example shows a simple, but typical list. The most important of these options is where to center the map. In this case, the map automatically centers itself on Milwaukee, Wisconsin, but you can change the settings to any location you want. The example uses a zoom factor of 8, and you'll see a road map. The Google Maps API actually provides a number of map types that you can try.

There are two times when GetMap() is called. When the application loads, you see Milwaukee, Wisconsin (unless you change the default settings). After you change the inputs, you can also click Get Map to display a new location. Figure 7-1 shows typical output from this application.

 This chapter doesn't provide a detailed look at the Google Maps API, which is relatively complex. What it does provide is a simple look at something you could easily expand into a full-fledged application later. Many organizations today use maps for all sorts of interesting purposes. The article at *http://blog.smartbear.com/ software-quality/bid/242126/using-the-google-maps-api-to-add-cool-stuff-to-your-applications* provides some additional ideas on how you can use the Google Maps API with your browser-based application.

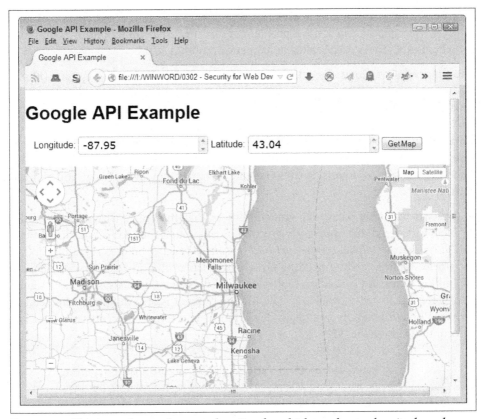

Figure 7-1. The example can show any location for which you have a longitude and latitude

Defining the Security Threats Posed by APIs

It's important to know what sorts of API threats you might face as a developer. Although the following sections may not contain the most recent of API threats, they do represent various kinds of API threats and provide you with the kind of information needed to help research the latest threats to your application. These real-world examples make it possible for you to understand what sorts problems you'll encounter.

Ruining Your Good Name with MailPoet

Blogging represents a major investment of time for many people. I use my blog (*http://blog.johnmuellerbooks.com/*) to communicate with my readers and tell people about my latest self-sufficiency efforts. You can find a blog for just about any purpose and on just about any topic. People place their reputations in their blogs as a way to help the world as a whole. So, when a blogging software plug-in, such as MailPoet (*http://www.mailpoet.com/*), has a problem, it can affect the reputations of every blogger who uses it. That's precisely what happened on July 1, 2014.

The vulnerability allows the attacker to place any PHP file on the system (*http://blog.sucuri.net/2014/07/remote-file-upload-vulnerability-on-mailpoet-wysija-newsletters.html*) using a remote upload, which means that your blog may now serve up phishing attacks (*http://wptavern.com/wordpress-mailpoet-plugin-security-vulnerability-immediate-update-recommended*) with the information it used to provide. At first the hack would cause the site to crash in some cases, but this flaw has since been fixed, so unless you're vigilant, you may not even know you've been hacked.

A problem with this particular vulnerability is that the entity that discovered the problem (Sucuri) didn't apparently give MailPoet enough time to fix and distribute a fix (*http://www.mailpoet.com/sucuri-hack-lessons-learned/*) before revealing it, so there is lots of finger pointing going on. This particular plug-in has been downloaded 1.7 million times, but is used on multiple blogs by some individuals, so it has a significant potential to cause problems. The MailPoet threat is an example of the need to verify API security before you begin development and to perform constant checks as you continue to use the API.

A significant problem exists now with security issue reporting. Some white hat hackers are overanxious to make names for themselves by reporting a major issue and don't give the API host time to fix problems before releasing the information—resulting in zero-day exploits that other hackers love to learn about. Likewise, some API hosts are slow to repair bugs that could cause security issues, which means that a black hat hacker discovers them before the problem is fixed (again, resulting in a zero-day exploit). The white hat hackers that provided notification are now left pointing fingers and telling everyone that they made the vendor aware of the issue. A potential fix for this problem would be to create a standardized method of handling security issue reporting and fixes so that everyone can work together to keep software safer. Unfortunately, no such fix is even in the discussion phase as of this writing.

Developing a Picture of the Snappening

Snapchat (*https://www.snapchat.com/*) is a great way to exchange photos with other people in a way that isn't permanent. The purpose of the service is to allow a freer flow of information in an environment with fewer risks. It actually does work when everyone plays by the rules, but not everyone does (as explained in Security Lessons

Courtesy of Snapchat (*http://blog.smartbear.com/apis/readyapi/security-lessons-courtesy-of-snapchat/*)).

The API is extremely easy to hack because of a flaw in a third-party library. Instead of actually fixing the problem, Snapchat has responded recently by admonishing users (*http://www.computerworld.com/article/2846038/snapchat-to-ask-users-to-stop-using-unauthorized-apps.html*) not to download third-party programs that allow them to overcome the built-in rules. The result of not providing a solid API in this case is the leaking of 90,000+ pictures that are likely more revealing than anyone cares to know. Talk about a loss of reputation! Of course, the usual amount of extortion will take place and it's unlikely that anyone will ever be able to track down the monetary implications because no one will be willing to talk about it.

The short take on this particular API hack is that it just doesn't pay to use some services—no matter how appealing they might be. This particular threat demonstrates the need to check vendor reputation before you begin development using the API. In addition, it shows that you need to research the API before using it because many hackers knew of this flaw before the trade press started making an issue of it.

Losing Your Device with Find My iPhone

The Find My iPhone (*https://www.apple.com/icloud/find-my-iphone.html*) service is supposed to protect your iPhone in case it gets lost. You can locate your iPhone, see where it has been, and lock it to keep prying eyes away. However, Apple didn't secure access to iCloud, the service that supports Find My iPhone, very well. It's vulnerable to a brute force attack—one in which the attacker keeps trying passwords until one is successful.

Some hackers discovered this flaw and used it to lock people's iPhones (*http://ifwnewsletters.newsletters.infoworld.com/t/9545692/122348447/801278/52/*). For a small sum of $100, the victim could get their iPhone unlocked. If the victim resisted, the hackers promised to erase all their data. The only way around the problem without paying is to restore the device to factory settings. Fortunately, this story does have a happy ending: the hackers have been arrested (*http://www.computerworld.com/article/2490607/cybercrime-hacking/the-hackers-behind-those-iphone-ransom-attacks-have-been-arrested-in-russia.html*). No one is saying just how many people paid the fee, how many lost their data, or just how many phones were hacked, but to create this much press, it has to be more than a few.

This particular threat is an example of the need to test inputs and outputs. By thinking through how the API worked, it's possible that developers could have figured out the brute force approach sooner than later and avoided potential problems.

Leaking Your Most Important Information with Heartbleed

You depend on Secure Sockets Layer (SSL) to provide secure communication between client and server. Unfortunately, like any other piece of software, SSL can contain vulnerabilities. In this case, the use of a feature called a heartbeat in OpenSSL (*https://www.openssl.org/*) versions 1.0.1 through 1.0.1f allows an attacker to gain access to user passwords and long-term private keys used to encrypt communication.

According to InfoWorld (*http://www.infoworld.com/article/2608736/data-security/heartbleed-to-blame-for-community-health-systems-breach.html*), Heartbleed was to blame for the Community Health Systems (*http://www.chs.net/media-notice/*) breach that released patient records for 4.5 million patients. The price tag for just this one breach could cost up to $150 million (*http://venturebeat.com/2014/08/25/community-health-systems-breach-could-cost-up-to-150-million/*). The interesting thing about Heartbleed is that it has serious staying power. According to ComputerWorld (*http://cwonline.computerworld.com/t/8953013/1084055737/677451/17/*), as of June 24, 2014, there were still 300,000 servers that were susceptible to Heartbleed (which is a long time for applying a patch given that the vulnerability was discovered in April). The Heartbleed vulnerability is so serious that it has spawned its own information site (*http://heartbleed.com/*).

You should see this threat as a wakeup call not to trust any particular API to remain secure. Hackers are constantly testing the waters to see just what they can get by with. In this case, constant testing of the API might have yielded information about the vulnerability before it became a problem. Certainly, relying on just one means of securing information is probably not the smartest thing to do.

Suffering from Shellshock

Some pundits are calling Shellshock (*http://www.troyhunt.com/2014/09/everything-you-need-to-know-about.html*) worse than Heartbleed (*http://www.eweek.com/news/why-shellshock-bug-is-way-nastier-than-heartbleed.html*). It's hard to say that one is worse than the other when both are incredibly bad and affect a large number of servers. In this case, a bug in the bash utility used by Linux administrators can be hacked by creating a malformed environment variable and then running a bash script. Access to this functionality can be provided through the Common Gateway Interface (CGI) or PHP.

The biggest limiting factor for this hack is that it isn't automatically exploitable (*http://www.infoworld.com/article/2687975/security/four-no-bull-facts-to-know-about-the-shellshock-bash-bug.html*)—there has to be an outside interface to access the server. There are reports that larger organizations, such as Yahoo! (*http://www.businessweek.com/news/2014-10-06/yahoo-says-no-data-stolen-in-shellshock-hack*) and WinZIP (*http://arstechnica.com/security/2014/10/white-hat-claims-yahoo-and-winzip-hacked-by-shellshock-exploiters/*) have been hacked using Shellshock. The potential for

Shellshock hacks is huge because the number of affected servers is larger than those affected by Heartbleed. In addition, a viable patch was longer in coming (*http://www.infoworld.com/article/2687750/security/attacks-against-shellshock-continue-as-updated-patches-hit-the-web.html*); although, one is in place now (*http://www.eweek.com/security/shellshock-vulnerability-finally-patched-as-exploits-emerge.html*).

This is an example of keeping your data localized under lock and key. By providing an outside interface to critical data, organizations open themselves up to data loss. Keeping sensitive data under wraps is the only way to ensure that it actually remains secure. Of course, you need to make some data accessible, but doing so should be the option of last resort and you should make only the required data available.

Accessing APIs Safely from JavaScript

It's possible to access APIs safely using JavaScript if you perform some testing first. Of course, testing takes time and you may encounter resistance to spending the time to ensure the API works as advertised. All you really need to do is ask about the value of the organization's data compared to the time required for testing. The answer is usually obvious, and the data is always worth the testing time. With this in mind, the following sections describe some measures you can take in using APIs safely.

Verifying API Security

The section "Defining the Security Threats Posed by APIs" on page 153 describes some of the threats that APIs can present to the developer. Unfortunately, the trade press often exposes these threats after you implement a solution using the API, making it hard to change the API you're using without incurring a huge cost. However, verifying that the API is currently clean by looking for stories about it is always a good place to start.

It also pays to look at the vendor's reputation for security. New vendors are untested and therefore, unreliable. You use them at a much greater risk than a known vendor, one who has had products on the market and tested for some amount of time. Partially offsetting the new versus experienced vendor is the fact that hackers also target vendors with a larger market share in order to improve the odds of getting something truly useful in exchange for their efforts.

The manner in which the API is constructed, the documentation provided, and the amount of input requested for calls all point to the level of security provided. It may be a nuisance to sign up for a service provided by Google, but the fact that you must use a special key to access the API can reduce the API's attack surface at least a little. In addition, the Google APIs don't ask you to provide sensitive data; although, an attacker could possibly derive some data by simply looking at your requests. For example, asking for maps at specific longitudes and latitudes could mean a new business venture in the area or some other reason for the increased attention.

The Google API is a good choice for the example in this chapter because Google has a relatively good reputation for security. In addition, it's easy to verify that you actually are interacting with Google in most cases and that the results you receive are of the right type. Google's documentation helps you perform the sorts of checks that make it easier to verify that the API is secure.

 Don't forget to keep communication needs in mind when reviewing API security. It's important to ensure that the vendor provides SSL data encryption and that both parties ensure they know whom they're talking to by employing mutual SSL authentication.

However, don't let secure communication become a potential security issue in its own right. Hackers can and do steal certificates so that they can provide the sort of secret information required to verify a secure communication. You never really know who is at the other end of the line. All you can do is provide the required security and then hope the security is strong enough to keep most hackers at bay.

Testing Inputs and Outputs

A simple way to verify the usefulness and security of an API is simply to test known quantities. Check known inputs and outputs to ensure the API works as advertised. It may surprise you to discover that some APIs really don't work as advertised. In some cases, the problem isn't one of actual coding errors, but one of not understanding how the API works.

Of course, many organizations perform an input/output test during the initial design and development phase for an application. However, creating a test harness lets you perform the tests at random. The benefit of this approach is that the tests can help you detect potential data corruption or other potential security problems. Running tests at intervals helps you ensure that the API remains viable. The tests also tend to trash any conclusions eavesdroppers may make about the queries you make against the API.

The Google Maps API example in this chapter should have also included code to verify both the input and output data. These checks were left out in order to make the application easier to understand. However, in a real application, you need to test the data before you submit it and verify that you get the kind of information you expected as a return value. Of course, it's not possible to check the data specifically because the map will change with each call.

It's important to verify that the APIs you use remain consistent over time. In some cases, a vendor will release an API update that introduces breaking changes. The change may be so subtle that you don't notice it at first, but a hacker may notice it while looking for potential security holes to exploit. Performing input and output testing regularly will help mitigate this sort of issue by verifying that the API continues to work as expected, even when the vendor performs those unexpected updates.

Keeping Data Localized and Secure

The more data you send to an API, the higher the probability that someone will intercept that data. The data need not be intercepted en route to present a problem. If the data ends up residing on the host's server, then anyone accessing the server can likely access the data as well. The best way to keep a secret is not to tell anyone. Sharing as little data as possible with an API is a good idea.

The use of an encoded key with the Google API is a good security measure because it positively identifies your organization. However, the key is important for another reason. In some cases, other APIs use identifiers that a hacker could track back to your organization. Anyone intercepting the Google key won't know anything more about your organization than before.

One example of an API that used to require input that a hacker could track back to an organization was Amazon.com. Some APIs used to rely on the associate identifier that an organization also attaches to links for buying products. A hacker could discover this identifier with relative ease and could begin tracking an organization's API calls as well.

Coding Defensively

When writing your application, always assume the inputs and outputs are wrong, that the user is going to handle everything incorrectly, and that there is a hacker looking over your shoulder. Yes, developers need to develop a sense of true paranoia in order to avoid some of the problems prevalent in applications today. As the book progresses, you see the usefulness of techniques such as API sandboxing in order to determine just how bad bad can be when it comes to interacting with the API. The important thing is to assume nothing about code—even the code you create.

CHAPTER 8

Considering the Use of Microservices

Microservices are a relatively new technology that breaks huge monolithic applications into small components. Each of these small components acts independently and performs just one task well. Because of the technologies that microservices rely on and the way in which they're employed, microservices tend to provide better security than some of the other technologies described so far in the book. However, just like any other technology, microservices do present opportunities for hackers to cause problems. It's important to remember that any technology has gaps that hackers will exploit to accomplish tasks. The goal of the developer is to minimize these gaps and then ensure as many safeguards as possible are in place to help in the monitoring process.

Because microservices are so new, the chapter begins by spending a little more than the usual time explaining them. This book doesn't provide you with a complete look at microservices, but you should have enough information to understand the security implications of using microservices, rather than older technologies you used in the past. In addition, it's important to consider the role that people will play in this case. A hostile attitude toward microservice deployment can actually cause security issues that you need to consider during the development stage.

The chapter discusses how you might create a microservice of your own (but doesn't actually provide source code because this is a book about security and not about writing microservices). The example focuses on a combination of Node.js and Seneca to create a simple microservice, and then access that microservice from a page. The point of the example is to discuss how microservices work so that you can better understand the security information that follows in the next section. The reason for using the combination of Node.js and Seneca is that these applications run on the Mac, Windows, and Linux platforms. Other microservice products, such as Docker, only run on Linux systems at present.

The chapter finishes by reviewing the importance of having multiple paths for microservice access. One of the advantages of using microservices is that you can employ multiple copies of the same microservice to reduce the risk of an application failing. In short, microservices can be both more secure and more reliable than the monolithic applications they replace.

 The best way to work with the examples described in this chapter is to use the downloadable source, rather than type it in by hand. Using the downloadable source reduces potential errors. You can find the source code examples for this chapter in the \S4WD\Chapter08 folder of the downloadable source.

Defining Microservices

Applications that work on a single platform will eventually go away for most users. Yes, they'll continue to exist for special needs, but the common applications that most users rely on every day won't worry about platform, programming language requirements, or any of the other things that applications need to consider today. Microservices work well in today's programming environment because they define a new way of looking at code. Instead of worrying how to create the code, where to put it, or what language to use, the developer instead thinks of just one task that the code needs to perform. That task might not necessarily even fit in the application at the moment —it may simply represent something interesting that the application may need to do when working with the data. In the new world of application development, applications will run anywhere at any time because of technologies such as microservices. The following sections provide you with a good overview of precisely what microservices are and why you should care about them.

Specifying Microservice Characteristics

Many developers are used to dealing with monolithic designs that rely heavily on object-oriented programming (OOP) techniques. Creating any application begins by defining all sorts of objects and considering all sorts of issues. Current application design techniques require a lot of up front time just to get started and they're tied to specific platforms. Microservices are different. Instead of a huge chunk of code, you write extremely small pieces of code and make many decisions as you go along, rather than at the beginning of the process. Microservices have these characteristics:

Small
    Each microservice performs just one task.

Language independent
    Every microservice relies on the language that best suits the task it performs without any consideration for the needs of any other microservice.

Data transfer independence

Although most microservices currently rely on JavaScript Object Notation (JSON) to transfer data, you can use any method of data transfer that works best for the microservice.

Queued messages

Communication typically occurs using an asynchronous messaging system so that no one microservice can cause delays in the application as a whole.

Dumb pipe

A problem with many methods of communication today is that the intelligence resides in the pipe. Microservices rely on a dumb pipe and intelligent services. Most microservices rely on Representational State Transfer (REST) for communication purposes.

Decentralized

Each microservice is separate from every other microservice and from the application as a whole. A failure of one microservice typically won't affect application operation. Each microservice receives separate monitoring.

Platform independence

Any application can make use of any microservice no matter what platform the application is running on and regardless of which platform the microservice uses.

You might wonder about the size of microservices—what performing just one task well really means. Think about a string for a second. When working with a monolithic application, you have a single object that can capitalize, reverse, and turn the string into a number. When working with a microservice, you create a single microservice to perform each task. For example, one microservice would capitalize the string, another reverse it, and still another turn it into a number. When you think about microservices, think focused and small.

From a developer perspective, microservices represent the ultimate in flexibility and modularity. It's possible to work on a single function at a time without disturbing any other part of the configuration. In addition, because updates are so small, it's not like an API where you have a huge investment in time and effort. When you make a mistake, correcting it is a much smaller problem.

Differentiating Microservices and Libraries

It's important to realize that microservices don't execute in-process like libraries do. A microservice executes on a server like an API. This means that you don't have the security risks with microservices that you do with libraries. It's possible to separate your application code from the microservice completely.

The calling syntax for a microservice also differs from a library in that you create a JSON request and send it to the server. The response is also in JSON format. The use of JSON makes it possible to work with data in a rich way without resorting to XML. Working with JSON is much easier than working with XML because JSON is native to JavaScript and it provides a more lightweight syntax. You see how this works later in the chapter. For now, just know that microservices work differently than library calls do for the most part.

From a security perspective, microservices tend to be safer than libraries because they don't execute in-process and you can guard against most forms of errant data input using best practices approaches to working with JSON. Of course, hackers can thwart any effort to make things more secure and microservices are no exception.

Differentiating Microservices and APIs

APIs often require that you create an object and then execute calls against that object. Requests can take a number of forms such as REST, HTML request headers, or XML. Responses could involve direct manipulation of objects on the page (as in the case of the Google Maps API example shown in Chapter 7). The process is cumbersome because you're working with a large chunk of monolithic code that could contain all sorts of inconsistencies.

Like APIs, microservices do execute out of process. However, unlike APIs, microservices aren't huge chunks of monolithic code. Each microservice is small and could execute in its own process, making it possible to isolate one function from another with complete assurance. Data exchanges occur using just one approach, JSON, which is likely the best approach to use today because it's simpler than working with XML.

Considering Microservice Politics

Now you know that microservices have a lot to offer the developer, IT in general, and the organization as a whole. Using microservices makes sense because the technology makes it possible to create applications that work on any device in any location without causing hardship on the developer. Unfortunately, monolithic application development scenarios tend to create fiefdoms where a hierarchy of managers rule their own particular set of resources. Because microservices are small, easily used for all sorts of purposes, and tend not to care about where needed data comes from, they break down the walls between organizational groups—upsetting the fiefdoms that ruled in the past. As in any situation of this sort, some level of fighting and even sabotage is bound to happen.

The sabotage part of the equation is what you need to consider as a developer. It's unlikely that anyone will purposely spend time trying to kill a microservices project, but the subtle reluctance to get tasks done or to do them correctly can kill it just as easily. All organizations have a "we've never done it that way here before" attitude when it comes to new technologies—inertia has a role to play in every human endeavor, so it shouldn't surprise you to find that you have to overcome inertia before you can start your first project.

From a security perspective, flaws induced in the project during this early stage leave openings that hackers are fully aware of and will almost certainly exploit if your organization becomes a target (or sometimes by pure random chance). With all this in mind, it often helps to follow a process when incorporating microservice strategies into your programming toolbox (you won't always follow these steps in precisely the order listed, but they do help you overcome some of the reluctance involved in working with microservices):

1. Form a development team that is responsible for microservices development that's separate from the team that currently maintains the monolithic application.

2. Create a few coarse-grained microservices for new application features to start.

3. Develop microservices that provide self-contained business features at the outset so that you don't have to worry about interactions as much.

4. Provide enough time for existing teams to discover how to use microservices and begin incorporating them into existing applications. However, don't move existing applications completely to microservices until you have enough successes so that everyone agrees that making the move is a good idea.

5. As development progresses with the initial microservices and you can see where changes need to be made, create finer-grained microservices to produce better results.

6. Standardize service templates so that it's possible to create microservices with a minimum of chatter between groups. A standardized template also tends to reduce security issues because no one has to make any assumptions.

7. Create enough fine-grained microservices to develop a complete application, but don't focus on the needs of an existing application—consider creating a new application instead.

8. Obtain the tools required to perform granular monitoring, log aggregation, application metrics, automated deployment, and status dashboards for data such as system status and log reporting.

9. Build a small application based solely on microservice development techniques. The idea is to create a complete application that demonstrates microservices really can do the job. Developing a small application tends to reduce the potential for failure for a development group that is just learning the ropes.

10. Slowly cross-train individuals so that the sharp divisions between skill sets diminishes.

11. Break down the silos between various groups. Start creating microservices that make code, resources, and data from every group available to every other group without consideration of the group that originated the item.

12. Slide development from the existing monolithic application to one designed around microservices.

13. Beginning with a small monolithic project, move the monolithic project entirely to a microservices environment if possible. Perform the task slowly and use metrics after the addition of each microservice to ensure that the application truly does work faster, run more reliably, and stay more secure.

14. Prune older microservices from the system as you replace them with finer-grained and more functional replacements.

Making Microservice Calls Using JavaScript

The previous section helped you understand what a microservice is, but it doesn't show you how a microservice works. The following sections provide you with a simple example of how you might put a microservice together and use it in an application. Of course, you need a lot of microservices to create a fully functional application, but this example is a good way to get started.

Creating a Microservice Setup for JavaScript

Before you can begin working with microservices, you need a setup that supports them. Of course, you have all sorts of options for creating a usable installation, but one path is a whole lot easier than the rest—using a combination of Node.js and Seneca.

You begin by installing a copy of Node.js on your system if you don't have one installed. The download you need for the installation is at *https://nodejs.org/down load/*. It helps to have installation instructions. You can find instructions for a Mac install at *http://blog.teamtreehouse.com/install-node-js-npm-mac*, a Windows install at *http://blog.teamtreehouse.com/install-node-js-npm-windows*, and a Linux install at *http://blog.teamtreehouse.com/install-node-js-npm-linux*. Make sure the folder you use allows developer access, which means not using the *C:\Program Files* folder on Windows systems, for example. (Install the product to *C:\nodejs* on Windows systems if possible.) Make sure you run the suggested tests after installation to ensure your Node.js setup is working properly.

This book uses Seneca for microservices because it works well on Mac, Windows, and Linux systems. Of course, you can use any API gateway that suits your needs. Once you have Node.js installed, you can use the Node Package Manager (NPM) to install Seneca using the instructions found at *http://senecajs.org/install.html*. Make sure you are in the folder you plan to use to create your code when you install Seneca so that the Seneca files are in the right location. The downloadable source code includes the Seneca files for you.

Using NPM (*https://www.npmjs.com/*) makes it easy to install all sorts of packages for Node.js and reduces the complexity of creating applications of all sorts. It's important to note that the Seneca installation instructions show a $ prompt. When working with platforms other than Linux, you'll see another sort of prompt, but the command, npm install Seneca, is the same across all platforms. Interestingly enough, the prompt will simply display a busy indicator during the installation process—you won't see any sort of output that indicates anything is really happening until the end when you see the Seneca directory structure. (If you absolutely can't get the standard NPM install to work, you can always get the source directly from *https://github.com/rjrodger/seneca* and install it that way, but the manual installation is definitely much harder.)

Understanding the Role of REST in Communication

Microservices rely on REST, which is an architectural style of communication, because it's more lightweight than protocols such as the Simple Object Access Protocol (SOAP). Using SOAP does have advantages in some situations, but it presents problems in Internet scenarios such as significant use of bandwidth and the need for a more formal level of communication between client and server. Applications that rely on REST for communication are called RESTful applications. Using REST for microservices provides the following advantages:

- Decouples consumers from producers
- Provides stateless communication
- Allows use of a cache
- Allows use of a layered system
- Provides a uniform interface

You have a number of options for using REST with microservices. However, the easiest method (and the method used for the example) is to rely on a specially formatted URL. For example, *http://localhost:10101/act?say=hello* is the URL used for the example. In this case, you contact the localhost using a special port, 10101. You send a message using act. The message is interpreted as a JSON name/value pair, {say:"hello"}. The example demonstrates how this all works, but the idea is that you send a request and then get back a JSON response. Using REST for communication makes things simple.

Transmitting Data Using JSON

Microservices rely on JSON for transferring both requests and responses. Yes, you can also send data using REST, but the information ultimately ends up in JSON format. There are three main reasons that you want to use JSON to transfer data:

Clean data

The data format for JSON is straightforward. The data appears in two forms: name/value pairs or as a list of values. Because the data format is so strict and simple, there is less chance for error when transferring data and therefore, fewer reliability and security issues.

Efficiency

Because JSON avoids the whole tagged appearance of both HTML and XML, it tends to be smaller than other sorts of data transfers. The information is still in text form, but the format itself is quite efficient, which means you waste fewer resources transferring the data.

Scalability

The strict data format used by JSON means that data transfers are standardized, which makes it easier to expand your application as needed. Using a single data structure means that you can plug in your code anywhere that you need it.

JSON typically uses five distinct data forms. Unlike XML, you don't create complex data hierarchies that can follow just about any form imaginable. Here are the five forms that you rely on to transmit data:

Object

An object is a name/value pair. The pair appears within curly braces ({}) and is separated by a colon (:). You can create complex objects by separating several name/value pairs using a comma. For example, {say:"hello"} is a name/value pair.

Array

An array consists of one or more values contained within square brackets ([]). For example, ["One", "Two", "Three"] is an array containing three string values.

Value

A value is a single item. JSON recognizes string, number, object, array, true, false, and null as values.

String

A series of characters within quotes (most texts say you should use double quotes). JSON recognizes control characters preceded by the backslash (\). These characters are: backspace (\b), formfeed (\f), newline (\n), carriage return (\r), and horizontal tab (\t). You can also specify Unicode characters using \u and a four-digit hexadecimal value. For example, \u00BC is the one quarter (¼) symbol.

Number

A number is an unquoted series of numeric characters with or without a decimal point. The plus and minus signs show positive and negative values. You can also specify numbers using scientific notation by adding an e or an E. For example, -123e20 is a perfectly acceptable presentation of a value.

Creating a Microservice Using Node.js and Seneca

You can find a number of examples for using Node.js and Seneca to create a microservice online. Unfortunately, most of them are convoluted and difficult to use. Some are simply outdated. The best example appears at *http://senecajs.org/*. The source for the server works precisely as shown. However, an even simpler example is the one found in *service.js*, as shown here:

```
require('seneca')()
    .add(
      { say:"hello"},
      function( message, done )
      {
        done( null, {message:'hello'} )
        })
    .listen()
```

In this example, require('seneca') loads the Seneca library into memory. The code then adds a match pattern of { say:"hello"} as a JSON object. The function() associated with the match pattern outputs another JSON object, {message:'hello'}. The example purposely uses both single and double quotes when creating JSON objects to show that it is possible, even if the official specifications don't seem to say so. The final step is to tell the service to listen(). You can add a port number to the listen() function. If you don't provide a port number, the service listens at the default port of 10101. To start the service, you type node server.js and press Enter at the command prompt. You see startup messages like the ones shown in Figure 8-1.

Figure 8-1. The microservice is listening for requests

The startup process logs two steps. The first is the initialization process for Seneca (where Seneca says "hello" on the third line of the output in Figure 8-1). The second is placing the microservice in listen mode (as shown on the fifth line). Whenever the microservice makes a call or performs some other task (other than simple output), you see one or more log entries added to the window. From a security perspective, this makes it possible for you to track the microservice functionality and detect whether anyone is attempting to do something unwanted with it.

Of course, you'll want to test the microservice. Open your browser window and type *http://localhost:10101/act?say=hello* as an address. The microservice outputs a simple JSON object, as shown in Figure 8-2.

Figure 8-2. This simple example outputs a JSON object

When you look back at the console window, you don't see anything. That's because the function outputs a simple JSON object and didn't make any calls outside the environment. However, try typing *http://localhost:10101/act?say=goodbye* as a request. Now you see some activity in the console window, as shown in Figure 8-3.

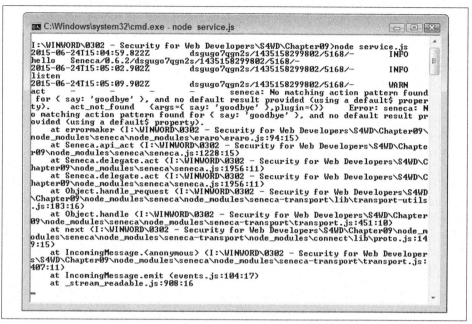

Figure 8-3. Errors produce copious output text

The output includes a stack trace, which you can ignore in this case, but could prove helpful when working with complex microservices. The most important information appears at the top in this case. You see a warning that there is no matching pattern for { say: 'goodbye' }. Notice that the REST request is translated into a JSON object. The error output tells you precisely what happened, so it's harder for someone to get by with an invalid request.

This is actually a good example for experimentation because you can see the results of trying to fool the REST communication part of the microservice functionality without worrying about other elements covering up the results. When you finish working with the example, press Ctrl–C or Ctrl–Break to stop the service. The service will stop and you'll see the command prompt reappear.

Defining the Security Threats Posed by Microservices

In many respects, microservices mirror APIs when it comes to security concerns. For example, it's possible that a microservice could suffer from a man-in-the-middle attack. The ability of a hacker to truly benefit from such an attack is less than with an API because a microservice is small, self-contained, and only performs one task.

However, the threat is still there and a hacker really only needs one avenue of attack to ruin your day. Although you may see all sorts of articles telling you about the natural security that microservices provide, they do have security issues and you need to know about them too. The following sections provide a mix of benefits and problems that you need to consider when it comes to microservice security.

Lack of Consistency

The biggest potential threat posed by microservices is the lack of consistency that appears to haunt just about every library and API ever created. The library and API developers begin with the simple idea of creating an easy-to-use and consistent interface, but over time the library or API becomes a mishmash of conflicting strategies that makes a Gordian knot easy to untangle by comparison. Trying to fix either code base is incredibly difficult because developers use libraries and APIs as a single piece of code. These inconsistencies cause security issues because developers using the code bases think the calls should work one way when they really work another. The result is that a mismatch occurs between the code base and the application that relies on it. Hackers seize such errors as a means for gaining access to the application, its data, or the system it runs on.

Microservices can also suffer from a lack of consistency. It's essential that you create a template for describing precisely how to call microservices as early as possible in the development process. Just like libraries and APIs, hackers could use inconsistencies as a means for overcoming any security you have in place. Unlike libraries and APIs, the inconsistency would affect just one microservice, rather than the entire code base. Fixing the microservice would also prove easier because you're looking at just one call, rather than an entire API. Publishing a new microservice is also easier than publishing an entirely new library or API. Consequently, overcoming a microservice inconsistency is relatively easy.

Considering the Role of the Virtual Machine

Each microservice typically runs in its own virtual machine (VM) environment. This means that one microservice can't typically corrupt another. Even if a hacker does gain access to one microservice, the amount of damage the hacker can do is typically minimal. However, it's quite possible to run multiple microservices in the same virtual machine—at which point it would become possible for a hacker to try various techniques to obtain access to the entire API. To maximize security, you want to avoid stacking microservices as shown by the *service2.js* example here (to access this example, you must use port 999, such as *http://localhost:999/act?say=goodbye*):

```
require('seneca')()
  .add(
    { say:"hello"},
    function( message, done )
```

```
    {
      done( null, {message:'hello'} )
      })
  .add(
    { say:"goodbye"},
    function( message, done )
    {
      done( null, {message:'goodbye'} )
      })
  .listen(999)
```

Best practice is to run each service in a separate virtual machine to ensure each service has its own address space and process. Separating each microservice presents fewer opportunities for error and also for issues resulting from code tricks hackers could employ.

Using JSON for Data Transfers

There are no perfect data transfer methodologies. Yes, JSON is lightweight, easy to use, and less susceptible to security issues than other technologies such as XML. However, hackers still have a number of methods for causing problems with JSON. The following sections describe the more prevalent issues.

Considering the dangers of eval()

It's possible that someone could send a response to the client that contains a `<script>` tag with a script that could do just about anything (in some cases, you don't even need the tag—passing just the script instead). Fortunately, most browsers now detect such attempts and refuse to transfer the information. For example, try *http://localhost: 999/act?<script>alert('Hello');</script>=goodbye* and you may see something like the output shown in Figure 8-4. In addition, the microservice itself refused to process the request. However, this particular script is simplistic in nature—a more advanced attempt could succeed.

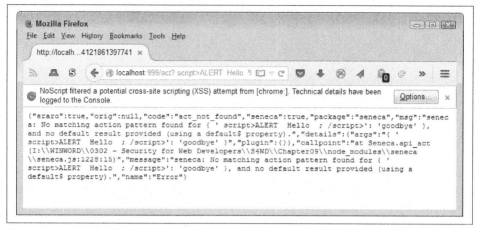

Figure 8-4. Scripting issues can plague microservices just as they do APIs

Defending against cross-site request forgery

A cross-site request forgery (CSRF or XSRF) is an attempt by an attacker to get a user to execute code unwittingly or unknowingly. The code executes at the user's privilege level and under the user's credentials, so it appears that the user has executed the code, rather than someone else. In most cases, this particular attack works against microservices when the following series of events occur:

1. A user logs in to an application that relies on microservices.

2. The user performs various tasks, each of which relies on REST for communication in the background.

3. An attacker sends the user an URL that is specially formatted to look just like the other REST messages, but does something the attacker wants the user to do. The URL could appear as part of an email message or some other communication, or even as a link on a website.

4. The user initiates the request by sending the URL to the microservice just like normal.

5. The malicious request executes and the user may not even realize it has happened.

A real-world example of this exploit occurred in 2008 as a µTorrent exploit. The reason this particular exploit is so important to microservice developers is that it works on a system where a web server runs in the background. When the exploit occurs, it compromises the entire system, which is why you want to keep those microservices separated in their own VMs. You can read about it at *http://xs-sniper.com/blog/2008/04/21/csrf-pwns-your-box/*.

Because of the way in which this exploit works, what you really need to do is ensure that the application automatically logs the user out after a period of inactivity. In addition, you need to look for odd usage patterns and set limits on what a user can do without approval. For example, a user can transfer $1,000 at a bank, but transferring $10,000 requires a manager's approval. Using multistep workflows, where an attacker would need to interact more with the user to make the exploit work, can sometimes prevent this sort of exploit as well, but then you face the user's wrath for having to perform more steps to accomplish a given task.

Defining Transport Layer Security

The Achilles' heel of both microservices and APIs is that both function by sending messages back and forth, rather than performing processing on a single machine. The cornerstone of developing a fix for this issue is Transport Layer Security (TLS). It's essential to ensure the transport layer between client and server remains secure throughout the messaging process. This means using technologies such as HTTPS and REST to ensure that the communications remain as secure as possible.

An issue with wrapping absolutely every call and response in HTTPS and REST is that the application can slow to a crawl. The best method of overcoming this problem is to rely on load balancing to terminate client communications, while also keeping a channel open to backend processing needs. Keeping the backend processing channel open reduces overhead and helps reduce the effects of using HTTPS and REST.

 One of the issues with using HTTPS with public-facing networks is that you must have a certificate from a Certificate Authority (CA) —an expensive proposition that may keep some organizations from using HTTPS. When you control both ends of the communication channel, it's possible to create your own certificate to achieve the same goal at a significantly reduced cost.

The use of HTTPS and bidirectional TLS ensures that both client and server establish each other's identity during each request/response cycle. Authentication reduces the chance that someone can successfully implement a man-in-the-middle attack to obtain unauthorized access to data. Most communication today takes place using unidirectional TLS where the client verifies the server's identity, but the server just assumes the client isn't compromised. Given the nature of microservice communication, you really do need to implement bidirectional TLS to verify the identity of both client and server.

Creating Alternate Microservice Paths

Something that many developers will have a problem understanding is the decentralized nature of microservices. Each microservice is separate. You don't have to think about the platform a microservice needs, what language it uses, or where it resides physically. It's possible to have two microservices written in two different languages residing on two different platforms in two different locations perform the same task. Because the environments used by the two microservices are so different, it's unlikely that an issue that affects one microservice will also affect the other microservice. Consequently, it's a good idea to keep both of them around so that you can switch between them as needed to keep your application running. That's what this section is all about—considering the implications of having multiple paths to access multiple microservices.

When thinking about microservices and the paths they employ, also consider things like ports. You can create microservices that work on different ports. Normally, you might rely on the microservice on port 999 to perform the work required by an application. However, if the microservice on port 999 becomes overloaded, compromised, or simply doesn't work, you can switch to the same microservice on a different port. Your code remains the same—only the port changes. Using this approach gives your application resilience, reliability, and flexibility. It also means that you have options should something like a distributed denial-of-service (DDOS) attack occur.

PART III

Creating Useful and Efficient Testing Strategies

It isn't likely that you'll escape potential security problems with your application, but you can reduce them by ensuring you take time to think things through and perform proper testing techniques. This part of the book is all about helping you reduce the risk that someone will find your application inviting enough to try to break into it. Chapter 9 starts out by helping you think like a hacker, which is an important exercise if you actually want to see the security holes in your application. It isn't as if someone marks security holes in red with a big sign that says "Fix Me!", so this thought process is incredibly important.

Chapter 10 discusses sandboxing techniques. Keeping code in a sandbox doesn't actually force it to behave, but it does reduce the damage that the code can do. Sandboxes make your system and its resources far less accessible and could make all the difference when it comes to security.

Chapter 11 and Chapter 12 discuss testing of various sorts. Chapter 11 focuses on in-house testing, which often helps in locating major problems, but may not be enough to find subtle problems that could cost you later. Chapter 12 discusses third-party testing, which is an especially important option for smaller businesses that may lack a security expert. No matter where you perform testing, ensuring you test fully is essential to knowing what the risks are of using a particular product with your application.

CHAPTER 9

Thinking Like a Hacker

Most developers spend their time in a world where it's important to consider how things should work (i.e., they focus on how things will work when the code is correct). The whole idea of thinking about things as they shouldn't work (i.e., trying to determine ways things could break when the code is errant) is somewhat alien. Yes, developers deal with bugs all the time, but the line of thought is different. When you think like a hacker, you might actually use code that is perfectly acceptable as written —it may not have a bug, but it may have a security hole.

This chapter contains a process that helps you view code as a hacker would. You use tools to look for potential security holes, create a test system to use while attempting to break the code, and rely on common breaches to make your life a little easier. Hackers love the bring your own device (BYOD) phenomenon because now you have all these unsecured systems floating about using operating systems that IT may not have much experience working with. Of course, there is always the ultimate application tester: the user. Users can find more ways to break applications than any developer would even want to think about, but user testing can be valuable in finding those assumptions you made that really weren't valid.

In fact, it's the need to think along these lines that drives many organizations to hire a security expert to think about all of the devious ways in which hackers will break perfectly functional applications in an effort to gain a tangible advantage they can use to perform specific tasks. However, this chapter assumes that you really don't have anyone wearing the security expert shoes in your organization right now. You may consider it when the application nears completion, but by then it's often too late to fix major problems without incurring huge costs. Thinking like a hacker when viewing your application can save your organization money, time, effort, and most importantly, embarrassment.

Defining a Need for Web Security Scans

The basic idea behind web security scans is that they tell you whether your site is currently clean and sometimes help you consider potential security holes. If you have a large setup, then buying a web security scanner is a good idea. However, smaller businesses can often make use of one of the free web security scanners online. Of course, these products really aren't completely free. When the web security scanner does find a problem on your system, then the company that owns it will likely want you to engage it to clean your system up and protect it afterward. (There truly is no free lunch in the world of computing.)

 It isn't possible for any web security scanner to detect potential problems with your site with 100% accuracy. This is especially true of remote scanners—those that aren't actually running on a system that has the required access to the server you want to test. Scanners do a remarkable job of locating existing issues, but they can't find everything.

You must also realize that web security scanners can produce false positive results. This means that the scanner could tell you that a security issue exists when it really doesn't.

The best safeguard against either missing issues or false positives is to use more than one web security scanner. Counting on a single web security scanner really is a good start, but you'll likely end up working harder than needed to create a fully workable setup with the fewest possible security holes.

Before looking more at web security scanners, it's important to see what tasks it performs. In this case, the example will use Securi (*https://sitecheck.sucuri.net/*), which is a free scanner that can detect a number of security issues, mostly revolving around potential infections. The main page shown in Figure 9-1 lets you enter your site URL and click Scan Website! to begin the scanning process.

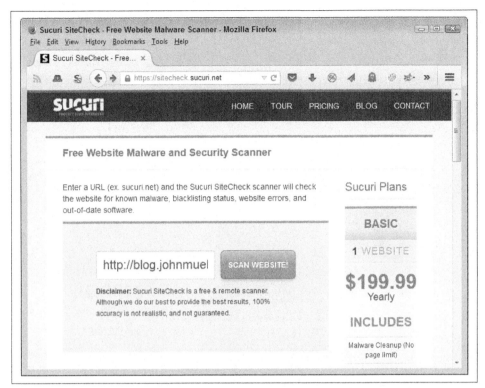

Figure 9-1. Starting the scan involves entering your site URL and clicking a button

If you do have a hosted site, make sure you check with the vendor providing the hosting services. Many of them offer low-cost web security scanners. For example, you can find the offering for GoDaddy users at *https://www.godaddy.com/security/malware-scanner.aspx*. The vendor has a vested interest in ensuring your site isn't compromised, so the low-cost offering benefits the vendor too.

After the scan is completed, you see an overview of what the scanner found and a more detailed listing of actual checks, as shown in Figure 9-2. Of course, if you want a more detailed check, you can always buy one of the Securi plans listed on the right side of the page. However, for the purposes of seeing what a scanner can do for you, the free version works just fine.

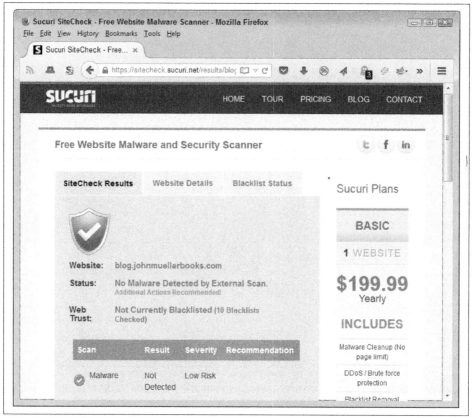

Figure 9-2. The completed scan shows any problems with your site

It can be interesting to view the site's Website Details information. Figure 9-3 shows the information for my site. Interestingly enough, a hacker could employ a scanner just like this one to start looking for potential areas of interest on your site, such as which version of a particular piece of software you use. The web security scanner helps you understand the sorts of information that hackers have available. Seeing the kinds of information everyone can find is often a bit terrifying.

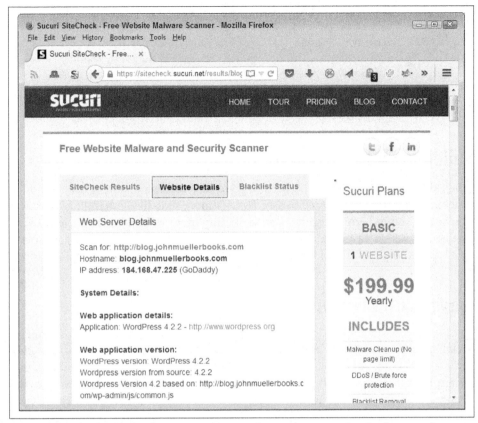

Figure 9-3. The detailed information can provide insights into what hackers can learn about your setup

The detailed information can be helpful for another reason. When you use a hosted site, as many small businesses do, it's hard to know whether the vendor providing hosting services actually keeps the software updated. The Securi (and other) web security scanners probe the site carefully and come up with lists of version information you might not even see when using the dashboard for your site. For example, it's possible for a library to still work fine, but to be outdated and have the potential for creating a security breach on your system. A call to the hosting company can usually clear matters up quickly, but you need to know about the problem before you can call anyone about it.

You can find lists of web security scanners online. One of the better lists is the Web Application Security Consortium's Application Security Scanner List (*http://projects.webappsec.org/w/page/ 13246988/Web*). The authors have categorized the list by commercial, Software-As-A-Service (SAAS), and free open source tools. Another good list of tools appears on the Open Web Application Security Project (OWASP) (*https://www.owasp.org/index.php/Phoe nix/Tools*). You can find tools for all sorts of purposes on this site.

Building a Testing System

When thinking like a hacker, it's often a good idea to have a system that you don't really have to worry about trashing. In fact, it's more than likely that the system will get trashed somewhere along the way, so it's important to build such a system with ease-of-restoration in mind. The following sections provide you with a good overview of the things you should consider when building a test setup for your organization.

Considering the Test System Uses

You need a test system so that you can feel free to explore every possible avenue of hacking. Until you fully understand just how vulnerable most applications are today, you really can't fix your own application. Developers make all sorts of mistakes that seem innocent at the time, but cause security issues later. Something as minor as the wrong sort of comment in your code can cause all kinds of problems. Using a production system to experiment is simply a bad idea because the techniques described in this chapter could potentially leave you open to a real attack. You want to use a system that you can trash and restore as needed to ensure the lessons you learn really do stick.

The idea is to test each application under adverse conditions, but in a safe manner that doesn't actually compromise any real data or any production systems. Giving a test system a virus will tell you how your application will react to that virus without actually experiencing the virus in a production environment. Of course, your test systems can't connect to your production network (or else the virus could get out and infect production systems). You can also use this environment to test out various exploits and determine just what it does take to break your application as a hacker would.

A test system need not test just your application, however. You can also use it to test the effectiveness of countermeasures or the vulnerabilities of specific configurations. Testing the system as a whole helps you ensure that your application isn't easily broken by vulnerabilities in other parts of the system setup. It's essential to test the whole environment because you can count on any hacker doing so.

Getting the Required Training

Before a developer can really test anything, it's important to know what to test and understand how to test it. You can begin the training process by using the OWASP Security Shepherd (*https://www.owasp.org/index.php/OWASP_Security_Shepherd*), which illustrates the top ten security risks for applications. The Security Shepherd can provide instruction to just one person or you can use it in a classroom environment to teach multiple students at once. The application provides a competitive environment, so in some respects it's a security game where the application keeps score of the outcome of each session. The application supports over 60 levels and you can configure it to take the user's learning curve and experience into account.

After you learn the basics, you need to spend some time actually breaking into software as a hacker would so that you can see the other side of the security environment. Of course, you want to perform this task in a safe and legal environment, which means not breaking into your own software. OWASP specifically designed the Web-Goat application (*https://www.owasp.org/index.php/Cate gory:OWASP_WebGoat_Project*) to provide vulnerabilities that an application developer can use to discover how exploits work in a real application setting. The movies at *http://webappsecmovies.sourceforge.net/webgoat/* take you step by step through the hacking process so that you better understand what hackers are doing to your application. The training includes movies on:

- General principles
- Code quality
- Concurrency
- Unvalidated parameters
- Access control flaws
- Authentication flaws
- Session management flaws
- Cross-site scripting (XSS)
- Buffer overflows
- Injection flaws
- Insecure storage
- Denial of service (DOS)
- Configuration
- Web services
- AJAX security

The final step is a WebGoat challenge where you demonstrate your newfound skills by breaking the authentication scheme, stealing all the credit cards, and then defacing the site. The point is to fully understand hacking from the hacker's viewpoint, but in a safe (and legal) environment.

It's important to understand how to perfect your security testing skills. The article at *http://blogs.atlassian.com/2012/01/13-steps-to-learn-perfect-security-testing-in-your-org/* provides you with 13 steps you can follow to improve your testing methods. This information, combined with the tools in this section, should help you test any application even if your organization lacks the resources to perform in-depth testing.

Creating the Right Environment

Any environment you build must match the actual application environment. This means having access to each of the operating systems you plan to support, browsers the users plan to use, and countermeasures that each system will employ (which may mean nothing at all in some cases). Make sure the systems are easy to access because you may find yourself reconfiguring them to mimic the kinds of systems that users have. In addition, you must plan to rebuild the test systems regularly.

Because of the kind of testing you perform using the test system, you must provide physical security for your lab. Otherwise, some well-meaning individual could let a virus or other nasty bit of code free in the production environment. You also don't want to allow access to the security setup to disgruntled employees or others who might use it to make your life interesting. The test environment should reflect your production environment as closely as possible, but you also need to keep it physically separate or face the consequences.

As part of keeping production and test environments separate, you should consider using a different color cabling for the test environment. You don't want to connect a production system to the test environment accidentally or vice versa. In addition, it's essential to label test systems so no one uses them in the production environment.

Using Virtual Machines

Most organizations won't have enough hardware to run a single machine for each configuration of operating system and browser that users expect to rely on when working with the application. The solution is to use virtual machines so that you can configure one physical computer to host multiple virtual computers. Each of the virtual computers would represent a single user configuration for testing purposes.

Using virtual machines is a good idea for another reason. When the virtual system eventually succumbs to the attacks you make on it, you can simply stop that virtual machine, delete the file holding that computer, and create a new copy from a baseline configuration stored on the hard drive. Instead of hours to set up a new test system, you can create a new setup in just a few minutes.

Virtual machines can solve many problems with your setup, but you also need to consider the need for higher-end hardware to make them work properly. An underpowered system won't produce the kind of results you need to evaluate security issues. The number of systems that you can create virtually on a physical machine is limited to the amount of memory, processing cycles, and other resources the system has to devote to the process.

It's also essential that the virtual machine operating software provide support for all of the platforms you want to test. Products, such as VMWare (*http://partner web.vmware.com/GOSIG/home.html*) offer support for most major operating systems. Of course, this support comes at an additional cost.

As an alternative to going virtual, some organizations use older systems that are still viable, but not as useful as they once were in the production environment. Because of the way in which web applications work, these older systems usually provide all the computing horsepower needed and let an organization continue to receive some benefit from an older purchase. Of course, maintaining these old systems also incurs a cost, so you need to weigh the difference in cost between a virtual machine setup and the use of older systems (or perhaps create a combination of the two).

Getting the Tools

Unless you want to write your own security tool applications (a decidedly bad idea), you need to obtain them from someone else. Fortunately, sites such as McAfee (*http://www.mcafee.com/us/downloads/free-tools/index.aspx*) provide you with all the free tools you could ever want to perform tasks such as:

- Detect malware on the host system
- Assess whether the system is vulnerable to attack
- Perform forensic analysis after an attack
- Use the Foundstone Software Application Security Services (SASS) tools to make applications more secure
- Determine when an intrusion occurs
- Scan the system for various vulnerabilities
- Stress test the system

Configuring the System

Starting with a clean setup is important to conducting forensic examination of the system after attacking it. Before you install any software or perform any configuration, make sure you zero wipe it (write all zeros to it). A number of software products let you perform this task. Writing all zeros to the hard drive ensures that any data you do see is the result of the testing you perform, rather than information left behind by a previous installation.

It's important to create a clean setup of each platform you intend to support at the outset. Make sure you make a copy of the setup image so that you can restore it later. The setup should include the operating system, browsers, and any test software needed to support the test environment. You may also want to include software that the user commonly installs on the system if the web application interacts with the software in any way.

 Products such as Norton Ghost (*http://www.symantec.com/page.jsp?id=ghost*) make it considerably easier to create images of each configuration. Make sure you have an image creation strategy in mind before you do anything to the clean configuration you create. You need clean images later to restore the configuration after you trash it by attacking it.

In addition to standard software, you may want to install remote access software so that you can access the system from a remote location outside the physically secured test area. External access must occur over a physically separate network to ensure there is no risk of contaminating the production environment. The use of remote access software lets more than one tester access the systems as needed from their usual workplace, rather than having to access the systems physically from within the secure area.

 Some organizations provide workstations that access the test systems using a KVM (keyboard, video, and mouse) switch. Using a KVM setup with a transmitter lets you easily switch between test systems from a remote location. However, the use of remote access software is probably more flexible and faster.

Restoring the System

It won't take long and your test system will require restoration. The viruses, adware, and Trojans that you use to test it are only one source of problems. Performing exploits and determining how easy it is to break your application will eventually damage the operating system, test application, test data, and the countermeasures used to

---

protect the system. In short, you need some method of restoring the system to a known state quite quickly.

Restoration also includes reconfiguring the system to mimic another environment. It pays to use images to create various test environments quickly. As previously mentioned, using virtual machines saves a lot of time because you don't have to rebuild the hard drive from scratch each time. However, make sure you also have each operating system image on a separate hard drive, DVD, or other storage media because the hard drive will eventually become corrupted.

Defining the Most Common Breach Sources

Every day sees the addition of new security breaches. It's not likely that anyone could keep up with them all. However, some security breaches require special attention and others are the sorts of things you might see in the future. Of course, it's nice to have an organized method for locating the security beaches and the checklist provided by OWASP (*https://www.owasp.org/index.php/Web_Application_Security_Test ing_Cheat_Sheet*) is a start in the right direction.

Once you know about the potential attack vectors for your application, it helps to score them so that you know which vulnerabilities to fix first. An attack that lets someone access all the pictures of the company picnic is far lower priority than one that allows access to the credit card information of all your clients. One of the best systems you can use for scoring potential attack vectors is Common Vulnerability Scoring System (CVSS) (*http://www.first.org/cvss/v2/faq*). Using this system helps you create an organized list of problems that you can deal with to make your application more secure.

Of course, it also helps you know what to test. With this in mind, the following sections describe the most common breach sources as of the writing of this book. (These sections build on the information you already obtained about basic hacks from Chapter 1.) You'll likely find even more breaches by the time the book is released because hackers are nothing if not creative in their methods of breaking software.

You can't categorize every potential breach source hackers will use. In fact, hackers often rely on misdirection (much like magicians) to keep you from figuring out what's going on. A recent news story about LOT Polish airlines (*http://www.computerworld.com/article/2938486/security/cyberattack-grounds-planes-in-poland.html*) serves to point out the results of misdirection. In this case, authorities have spent considerable time and resources ensuring that flight systems remain unaffected by potential attacks. However, they weren't as diligent about ground systems. Hackers managed to break into the ground systems and make it impossible to create flight plans for outbound passengers. Whether the attack grounded the planes by affecting their flight systems or by affecting ground control doesn't matter. What matters is that the planes couldn't take off. The hackers achieved a desired result through misdirection. The lesson is that you need to look everywhere—not just where you think hackers will attack based on the latest statistics.

Avoiding SQL Injection Attacks

There are many forms of the SQL injection attack. For example, you could mess with the form data in an application to determine whether the form is capable of sending commands to the backend server. However, it's best to start with a popular method of checking for the potential for a SQL injection attack.

Let's say that you have a URL such as *http://www.mysite.com/index.php?itemid=10*. You have probably seen URLs structured like this one on many sites. One way to check for a vulnerability is to simply add a single quote after the URL, making it *http://www.mysite.com/index.php?itemid=10'*. When you press Enter, the site sends back a SQL error message. The message varies by system, but the idea is that a backend server receives your URL as a SQL request that's formatted something like: `SELECT * WHERE itemid='10''`. The addition of another single quote makes the query invalid, which produces the error.

When you do find a problem with your application that someone could potentially exploit, it's important to make the entire development team aware of it. Demonstrating the exploit so that everyone can see how it works and what you need to do to fix it is an essential part of developer training for any organization. Products such as the Browser Exploitation Framework (BeEF) (*http://beefproject.com/*) can help you find the attack vector and then demonstrate it to others in your organization.

You can now start playing with the URL to see what's possible. For example, let's say you want to determine how many columns that query produces and what those columns are. It's possible to use the SQL `ORDER BY` clause to perform this task. Change the URL so that it includes the `ORDER BY` clause like this: *http://www.mysite.com/index.php?itemid=10'* ORDER BY 1. This is the same as typing `SELECT * WHERE itemid='10' ORDER BY 1` as a command. By increasing the ORDER BY value by 1 for each request, you eventually see an error again. Say you see the error when you try `ORDER BY 10`. The query results actually have 9 columns in this case.

A hacker will continue to add SQL commands to the basic URL to learn more about the query results from the database. For example, using the `SELECT` clause helps determine which data appears on screen. You can also request special information as part of the `SELECT` clause, such as `@@version`, to obtain the version number of the SQL server (giving you some idea of what vulnerabilities the SQL server might have). The point is that the original URL provides direct access to the SQL server, making it possible for someone to take the SQL server over without doing much work at all.

You can see another type of SQL injection attack dissected at *http://www.w3schools.com/sql/sql_injection.asp*. The underlying cause of all these attacks is that a developer used data directly from a page or request without first checking it for issues and potentially removing errant information from it.

Understanding Cross-Site Scripting

XSS is similar to SQL injection in many ways because of the way in which the exploit occurs. However, the actual technique differs. The two types of XSS are nonpersistent (where the exploit relies on the user visiting a specially crafted link) and persistent (where the attack code is stored in secondary storage, such as a database). Both attacks rely on JavaScript code put into a place where you wouldn't expect.

As an example of a nonpersistent form of XSS, consider this link: *http://www.mysite.com/index.php?name=guest*. It looks like a perfectly harmless link with a name/value entry added to it. However, if you add a script to it, such as *http://www.mysite.com/index.php?name=guest<script>alert('XSS')</script>*, the user could see a dialog box pop up with the message, XSS. This example doesn't do any damage, but the script could easily do anything you can do in a script. For example, you could craft the script in such a manner that it actually redirects the user to another site where the page would download a virus or other nasty piece of software.

 The example shows the `<script>` tag in plain text. A real exploit would encode the `<script>` tag so that the user couldn't easily recognize it. What the user would see is a long URL with an overly complex set of % values that appear regularly in valid URLs as well.

A persistent XSS attack is harder to implement, but also does a lot more damage. For example, consider what happens when a user logs in to an application. The server sends a session ID as a cookie back to the user's machine. Every request after that uses the session ID so that the application can maintain state information about the user. Let's say that the attacker sends a specially crafted script to the server as part of the login process that gets stored into the database under a name that the administrator is almost certain to want to review. When the administrator clicks the username, the script executes and sends the administrator's session ID to the attacker. The attacker now has administrator privileges for the rest of the session, making it possible to perform any administrator-level task. You can get more detailed information about persistent XSS at *https://www.acunetix.com/blog/articles/persistent-cross-site-scripting/*.

In both cases, the best defense against XSS is to sanitize any input you receive. The process of sanitizing the input removes any scripts, weird characters, or other information that isn't part of the expected response to a request. For example, if you expect a numeric input, the response shouldn't contain alphabetic characters.

 Output encoding user-supplied data can help reduce the potential for XSS. A hacker could still get around the encoding, but it would take additional time and effort to do so. Anything you can do to make things harder for the hacker will increase the hacker's desire to hack someone else, but you also need to remember that a determined hacker will always break your security.

Tackling Denial-of-Service Issues

The idea behind a DOS attack is relatively straightforward. You find an open port on a server and keep sending nonsense packets to it in an effort to overwhelm the associated service. Most servers have services that offer open ports, such as:

- DNS servers
- Email servers
- FTP servers
- Telnet servers
- Web servers

Of course, the more open ports you provide, the better the chance of overwhelming your server. A first line of defense is to close ports that you don't need by not installing services you don't require. An application server may only require a web server, so that's the only service you should have installed. As an application developer, you can recommend keeping other services uninstalled (or at least inactive). When creating a private application, using a nonstandard port can also help, as does requiring authentication.

Hackers are usually looking for services that don't have a maximum number of connections, so ensuring you keep the maximum number of connections to a value that your server can handle is another step in the right direction. It's important in a DOS attack to give the server something to do, such as perform a complex search when working with a web server. Authentication would help keep a hacker from making requests without proper authorization.

Still, it's possible to bring down any server if you have enough systems sending an endless stream of worthless requests. Some of the defenses against DOS attacks include looking for patterns in the request and then simply denying them, rather than expending system resources trying to resolve the request. You can find a host of DOS attack tools to use to test your system at *http://resources.infosecinstitute.com/dos-attacks-free-dos-attacking-tools/*. Besides looking for patterns in the attack and attempting to resolve them yourself, you can also try:

- Purchasing specialized equipment designed to help mitigate DOS attacks
- Relying on your ISP to detect and mitigate DOS attacks
- Obtaining the services of a cloud mitigation provider

Nipping Predictable Resource Location

It's possible to attack a system by knowing the location of specific resources and then using those resources to gain enough information to access the system. Some sites also refer to this type of attack as *forced browsing*. Of course, the best way to prevent this sort of an attack is to keep resources in unpredictable locations. In addition, you can ensure that the authentication scheme works and that you properly secure resources. However, let's look at how this particular attack works.

One example of this sort of attack involves identifying a URL that points out a valid resource and in turn using that URL to access another resource owned by someone else. Let's say that you have your agenda for a particular day located at *http://www.mysite.com/Sam/10/01/2015* and that you want to access Amy's agenda for the same day. Changing the URL to *http://www.mysite.com/Amy/10/01/2015* might provide the required access if the administrator hasn't configured the server's authentication correctly.

As another example, some servers place information in specific directories. For example, you might have authorized access to *http://www.mysite.com/myapp/app.html*. However, you could change the URL to see if *http://www.mysite.com/system/* exists. If you get a response of 200 back from the server, the directory does exist and you can start querying it for useful information. Of course, this assumes that the administrator hasn't properly secured the system directory and that system is a standard directory location. The administrator could always change the name of system directory and also ensure that it only allows access by those with the proper credentials.

Overcoming Unintentional Information Disclosure

Unintentional information disclosure can occur in all sorts of ways. However, the exploit always involves the hacker gaining unauthorized access to a centralized database. At one time, the source of the information would have been something like the Network Information System (NIS). However, today the information could come from any source that isn't secure or has vulnerabilities that a hacker can exploit. There are so many of these sources that it's not really possible to come up with a simple example that illustrates them all. You can overcome this type of hack by:

- Applying all required patches to the operating system, services, application environment, libraries, APIs, and microservices as required
- Configure the border routers and firewalls to block requests that could request information from a sensitive source
- Restrict access to all sensitive information sources
- Never hardcode passwords or place them where someone could easily find them
- Use two-factor authentication for any sensitive information source
- Perform audits to look for potential breaches (even if you feel the system is completely secure)
- Use assessment tools to determine whether it's possible to access the sensitive information source from anywhere other than a designated location

Testing in a BYOD Environment

The BYOD phenomenon keeps building in strength. It's important to realize that BYOD isn't going to go away. In fact, you probably already know that BYOD is going to become the preferred method of outfitting users at some point. Organizations will eventually tell users to bring whatever device is needed to get their work done and leave everything in the hands of the user. It sounds like a disaster in the making, but that's where users are taking things now.

According to Gartner, Inc., by 2017, half of organizations will no longer supply any devices to users (see *http://www.gartner.com/newsroom/id/2466615*). In addition, by 2020, 75% of users will pay less than $100 for a smartphone (see *http://www.gart ner.com/newsroom/id/2939217*), so getting a device smart enough to perform most tasks won't even be that expensive. Creating and managing applications will become harder because you must ensure that the application really does work everywhere and on any device. Of course, it has to work without compromising organizational security. The following sections will help you provide some level of testing and isolation for the BYOD environment.

It's also important to realize that users are now participating strongly in bring your own application (BYOA). The reason this new move on the part of users is so important is that it introduces yet another level of unpredictability to the application environment. You never know when another application will cause your application woe. In fact, the third-party application could provide the conduit for the next major breach your company suffers. Users will definitely continue using applications such as Dropbox, Google Docs, and CloudOn because they're convenient and run everywhere. To ensure the integrity of the application environment, you need to continue viewing these applications as contamination just waiting to ruin your day.

One of the reasons that BYOA is such a problem is that the organization loses control over its data. If the user stores organizational data in a personal account on Dropbox, the organization can't easily retrieve that data in the event of an emergency. In short, BYOA opens serious security holes that could be a problem for any application data that you want to protect.

Configuring a Remote Access Zone

When working within the BYOD environment, the best assumption you can make is that the device environment isn't secure and that you can't easily make it secure. With this in mind, a BYOD session usually has four phases:

1. The client and server create a secure tunnel to make it harder for outsiders to listen in. The intent is to prevent man-in-the-middle attacks.

2. The user supplies two forms of authentication. A two-factor authentication process makes it less likely that someone will successfully mimic the user.

3. The client makes one or more requests that the server mediates using a service mediation module. The service mediation module only honors requests for valid services. The service mediation module automatically logs every request, successful or not.

4. A service separation module provides access to public data only. It disallows access to sensitive data. The client sees just the data that the organization deems acceptable for a BYOD environment.

The remote access zone is part of phases 1 and 2. It consists of an external firewall and a VPN and authentication gateway. The remote access zone provides a first level of defense against intrusion.

The information gleaned from the user must appear as part of your application strategy. A BYOD access is different from local access from a desktop system the organization owns in that you have no idea of where this access occurs or whether the device itself is secure. When a user accesses your application in such a manner, you need to provide a role that matches the device used. This means that you don't allow any sensitive information to appear on the device and could potentially limit access to other sorts of data. For example, your organization might decide that it's acceptable to obtain a listing of sales for a particular client, but the list is read-only, which means that the user can't make any changes to the sales list in the field. In order to make these changes, the user would need to log in to the account from a local system.

The use of a remote access zone also implies that your organization configures mobile device management (MDM). This is a set of products and services that help ensure the mobile device remains as secure as is possible. For example, the MDM could check mobile devices for patch requirements and ensure the user patches the device before you allow application access (you could simply patch the device automatically). Even with an MDM in place, you can't assume the device is secure when:

- The device reports values that imply a secure configuration, but your organization doesn't actually implement the specified values. A malware developer won't know which values to report and will simply report them all.

- Other authorities can override the device settings. For example, if a smartphone vendor can automatically patch the device outside your control, you must assume that some of those patches could contain viruses or other malware.

- It isn't possible to enforce settings on the mobile device. The device may not provide the required support, your application may not be configured to support the device, or malware interferes with the updates.

Checking for Cross-Application Hacks

A cross-application hack is one in which one application gains access to data or other resources used by another application. In many cases, the hack occurs when two applications have access to the same data source (cross-application resource access or XARA). One such recent hack is for the OS X and iOS operating systems (read about it at *http://oversitesentry.com/xara-an-old-way-to-hack-cross-application-resource-access/*).

Another type of cross-application problem is cross-application scripting (CAS). In this case, the bug causes a problem where JavaScript code executes within certain types of applications. You can read about one such exploit for Android at *http://news.softpedia.com/news/Apache-Cordova-for-Android-Patched-Against-Cross-Application-Scripting-453942.shtml*.

The best way to verify that your application isn't potentially exposing data through this kind of exploit is to stay on top of any news for the platforms you support. It takes a security expert to find potential problems of this sort. Unfortunately, barring a patch from an operating system or browser vendor, you can't really do too much about this particular hack except to remain vigilant in checking your data stores for potential damage. Of course, this particular kind of problem just lends more credence to creating a remote access zone (see the previous section of this chapter).

Dealing with Really Ancient Equipment and Software

Research firms love to paint pretty pictures of precisely how the future will look. Of course, some of those dreams really do come true, but they don't take into account the realities of the range of user equipment in use. For example, it might trouble some people to discover that (as of this writing) 95% of all ATMs still rely on Windows XP as an operating system (see *http://info.rippleshot.com/blog/windows-xp-still-running-95-percent-atms-world*). The US Navy is still using Windows XP on 100,000 desktops (see *http://arstechnica.com/information-technology/2015/06/navy-re-ups-with-microsoft-for-more-windows-xp-support/*). Yes, old, archaic, creaky software still exists out there and you might find it used to run your application.

According to NetMarketShare (*http://www.netmarketshare.com/operating-system-market-share.aspx?qprid=10&qpcustomd=0*), Windows XP still powers upwards of 14.6% of the systems out there. It's important to realize that your main concern when creating an application may not be the shiny new smartphone with the updated, fully patched operating system and the latest in browser technology. The real point of concern may be that creaky old Windows XP system loaded with Internet Explorer 8 that your users insist on using. It's interesting to note that Internet Explorer 8 still commands about 25% of the desktop market share (see *https://www.netmarketshare.com/browser-market-share.aspx?qprid=2&qpcustomd=0*).

Of course, you can always attempt to force users to upgrade. However, if you've dealt with the whole BYOD phenomenon for long enough, you know that users will simply ignore you. Yes, they might be able to show you a shiny new system, but they'll continue to use the system they like—the older clunker that's causing your application major woe.

About the only effective means you have of dealing with outdated equipment is to check the browser data during requests. Doing so lets you choose whether to allow the request to succeed. When the browser is too old, you can simply display a message telling the user to upgrade their equipment. The article at *http://sixrevisions.com/javascript/browser-detection-javascript/* describes how to perform browser version checking. You can see your actual browser information at *https://www.cyscape.com/showbrow.asp*. The only problem with this approach is that it's possible to thwart the check in some cases and some browsers also report incorrect version information.

Relying on User Testing

Nothing can test software in a more violent and unpredictable manner than a user. Most developers have seen users try to make software do things that it quite obviously shouldn't because the user doesn't realize the software shouldn't do that. It's this disconnect between what the software appears to do and what the user makes it do that provides the serious testing that only a user can provide.

The important part of the process is the part that will cause the most pain to developers. Any attempt to create an organized approach to user testing will only result in testing failures. Users need to have the freedom to play with the software. Actually, play time is good for everyone, but it's an essential element of user testing. The following sections describe how you can get the user to play with your software and come up with those serious security deficiencies that only users (and apparently some hackers) seem to find.

Interestingly enough, you don't actually have to perform your own user testing any longer. If you really want a broad base of test users, but don't have the resources to do it yourself, you can always rely on sites such as User Testing (*http://www.usertesting.com/*). Theoretically, the site will provide you with honest evaluations of your application in as little as an hour (although one quote provided on the main page said the results were delivered in 20 minutes). Most of these third-party testing sites offer web application, mobile application, and prototype testing.

A few third-party testers, such as Applause (*http://www.applause.com/web-app-testing*), specifically offer "in the wild" testing where your application actually sees use on the Internet from unknown users, just as it would in the production environment. Of course, the difference is that that testing occurs without any risk to your equipment and Applause provides the tools required to obtain measurable results. In general, you would want to save this level of testing for a time when your application is almost ready for release and you want to perform a sanity check.

Letting the User Run Amok

Sometimes the best way to test your application is to give your user a set of printed steps and a goal. Watching how the user interacts with the application can tell you a lot about how the user perceives the application and where you need to make changes. Actually videotaping the user at work can be helpful, but you need to be aware that the act of videotaping will change the user's behavior. Keylogging and other techniques are also helpful in keeping track of what the user does with the application without actually standing over the top of the user to observe (which would definitely change user behavior and your testing would fail).

Fortunately, you don't have to rely on just the resources you have at hand. Sites such as Mashable (*http://mashable.com/2011/09/30/website-usability-tools/*) provide you with a wealth of testing tools you can use to check your web application for problems. The site documents the tools well and tells you why each tool is important. Most importantly, the site helps you understand the importance of specific kinds of testing that you might not have considered. For example, Check My Colours (*http://www.checkmycolours.com/*) verifies that people with various visual needs can actually see your site. Yes, using the wrong colors really can be a problem and testing for that issue can help you avoid potential security problems caused by user error.

Another good place to find testing tools is The Daily Egg (*http://blog.crazyegg.com/2013/08/08/web-usability-tools/*). Some of the tools on this site are the same as those on the Mashable site, but you obtain additional insights about them. A few of the tools are unique. For example, the list of page speed testing tools is better on The Daily Egg and the list includes GTMetrix (*http://gtmetrix.com/*), which can help you locate the actual source of slowdowns on your page.

Developing Reproducible Steps

Part of user testing is to obtain a set of reproducible steps. Unless you gain this kind of information, you can't really fix application issues that cause problems. This is the reason that you need specific testing software that records what the user does in detail. Asking the user to reproduce the steps that led to an error will never work. In many cases, the user has no idea of how the error occurred and simply feels that the computer doesn't like them. Trying to get the user to reproduce the steps later will likely lead to frustration and cause the user to dislike the application (which usually leads to more errors and more security problems). Therefore, you need to get the steps required to reproduce an error on the first try.

In order to create an environment where you can obtain the best level of testing and also ensure that the user has a good chance of finding potential errors, you need to perform specific kinds of testing. Letting the user run amok to see what they can do without any sort of input is useful, but the chaos hardly produces predictable results. When working through user testing, you need to consider these kinds of tests:

Functionality
> It's important to test all of the application features. This means asking the users to try out forms, perform file manipulation and calculation tasks, search for information using application features, and try out any media features your application provides. As the user tests these various features, make sure that the tests also check out the libraries, APIs, and microservices that your application relies upon to perform most tasks.

User interface and usability

The user interface must keep the user engaged and provide support for anyone with special needs. As part of this level of testing, you need to check navigation, accessibility, usefulness from multiple browser types, error messages and warnings, help and any other documentation you provide, and layouts.

Security

Although you have tested the application to determine whether it suffers from any of the common security breaches listed in "Defining the Most Common Breach Sources" on page 189 you need to have the user test for them as well. See if the user can get the application to break in the same ways that you did. Look for ways in which the user's method of interacting with the application creates new breach conditions.

Load and scalability

It's impossible for you to test an application fully to determine how it acts under load. You need to ensure that the application scales well and that its performance degrades gracefully as load increases. However, most importantly, you need to verify that load doesn't cause issues where a security breach can occur. It's important to know that the application will continue to work properly no matter how much load you apply to it. Of course, the application will run more slowly when the load exceeds expectations, but that's not the same as actually breaking it (i.e., causing a failure that could let someone in).

Giving the User a Voice

Interviewing a user or allowing users to discuss the application in a gripe session after working with it is a good way to discover more potential problems with the application. In many cases, a user will be afraid to perform certain steps due to the perception that the application will break. This problem occurs even in a test environment where the user is supposed to break the application. You may not want to hear what the users have to say, but it's better to hear it during the development stage than to put the application into production and find out that it has major issues later.

As an alternative to confrontational approaches to obtaining user input, you can also rely on surveys. An anonymous survey could help you obtain information that the user might otherwise shy away from providing. It's important to consider the effects of stress and perceived risk on the quality of user input you receive.

Using Outside Security Testers

Penetration testing relies on the services of a third party to determine whether an application, site, or even an entire organization is susceptible to various kinds of intrusion. The attacker probes defenses using the same techniques that a hacker uses.

Because the attacker is a security professional, the level of testing is likely better than what an organization can provide on its own. Most organizations use outside security testing services for these reasons:

- Locating the vulnerabilities missed by in-house audits
- Providing customers and other third parties with an independent audit of the security included with an application
- Ensuring the security testing is complete because the organization doesn't have any security professionals on staff
- Validating the effectiveness of incident management procedures
- Training the incident handling team
- Reducing security costs for the organization as a whole

 It's a bad idea to allow someone to penetration test your application, site, or organization without having legal paperwork in place, such as a nondisclosure agreement (NDA). Don't assume that you can trust anyone, especially not someone who is purposely testing the security of your setup. Make sure you have everything in writing and that there is no chance of misunderstanding from the outset.

Considering the Penetration Testing Company

Of course, like anything, penetration testing comes with some risks. For example, it's likely that you expect the third-party tester to be completely honest with you about the vulnerabilities found in your application, but this often isn't the case. In some cases, the third party fails to document the vulnerabilities completely, but in other cases, the penetration tester might actually be sizing your company up to determine whether a real intrusion would be a good idea. It's important to ensure you deal with a reputable security tester and verify the types of services rendered in advance. You should spend more time checking your security services if you experience:

- Disclosure, abuse, or loss of sensitive information obtained during a penetration test
- Missed vulnerabilities or weaknesses
- Availability of the target application or site is impacted
- Testing doesn't occur in a timely manner
- Reporting is overly technical and hard to comprehend

- Project management looks disorganized, rushed, or ill-considered

When it comes to penetration testing, you tend to get what you pay for. Your organization must consider the trade-offs between cost, timeliness, and quality of testing when hiring a third party to perform penetration testing. The less you pay, the more you tend to wait, the less you get for your money, and the more likely it is that something negative will happen as a result of the testing.

In some cases, a trade-off in amount of testing works better than other trade-offs do. Testing just one application, rather than the entire site, will cost less and you'll be able to hire a higher-quality security firm to perform the task. Of course, if you test just one application, you can't check for issues such as trust relationships between the target and another system.

Managing the Project

Before you allow anyone to perform penetration testing, you need a proposal that outlines the scope, objectives, and methods of testing. Any penetration testing must include social engineering attacks because most hackers employ them. In fact, the people in your organization are the weakest link in your security. An application can provide nearly perfect security, but a single disclosure by the wrong person can thwart all your attempts at maintaining a secure environment.

Ensure that the testing methodology is well-documented and adheres to industry best practices. For example, many security firms adhere to the Open Source Security Testing Methodology (OSSTMM); check out the Institute for Security and Open Methodologies (ISECOM) website (*http://www.isecom.org/*) for details. If the tester uses some other methodology, make sure you understand precisely what that methodology is and what sorts of benefits it provides.

The proposal should state what type of feedback you receive as part of the testing. For example, it's important to decide whether the penetration testing includes full disclosure with a demonstration of precisely how the system is penetrated, or does the report simply indicate that a particular area is vulnerable to attack.

Defining the time of the attack is also important. You might not want to allow testing during the busiest time of the day to avoid risking sales. On the other hand, you may need to allow testing at less convenient times if you truly want to see the effects of load on the system.

Covering the Essentials

Any organization you engage for penetration testing should have a single point of contact. It's important that you be able to reach this contact at any time. The leader of your development team and the penetration team contact should be able to contact each other at any time to stop testing should the need arise. The contact should also have full details on precisely how the testing is proceeding and specifics about any potential issues that might occur during the current testing phase.

You should also know whether the tester has liability insurance to cover any losses incurred during testing. The liability insurance should include repayment of time invested in recovering data, downtime for the system, and any potential loss of revenue that your organization might incur.

The testing team must also demonstrate competency. You don't want just anyone penetration testing your system. The team that appears in the proposal should also be the team that does the actual testing. Look for certifications such as:

- GIAC Certified Incident Handler (GCIH)
- Certified Ethical Hacker (CEH)
- OSSTMM Professional Security Tester (OPST)

Getting the Report

The results of any penetration testing appear as a report. To ensure you get a report that you can actually use, make sure you request an example report before testing begins. The report should include a summary of the testing, details of any vulnerabilities, a risk assessment, and details of all the actions the penetration testing involves. The report must contain enough technical information that you can actually fix the problems found during testing, but still be readable by management staff so you can procure the time and resources required to perform the fixes.

Along with the report, you should also receive log files of every action taken during the testing phase. The log files should show every packet sent and received during testing so that you can go back later to follow the testing process step by step.

The security company you hire should also keep an archive of the testing process. You need to know how they plan to maintain this archive. Part of the reason for checking into the archive process is to ensure your confidential data remains confidential. It's important that the archive appear as part of offline storage, rather than a network drive on the vendor's system.

CHAPTER 10

Creating an API Safety Zone

Any API you create or use as part of your application has the potential for creating a large array of problems. However, unlike libraries, you can actually make using an API much safer because an API executes in its own address space and in its own process. Placing the API in a sandbox or virtual environment (essentially a protected environment) makes it possible to:

- Control precisely what actions the API can take, the resources it can access, and the ways in which it interacts with your application. Of course, you can also starve the API for resources or make it impossible for the API to complete a task by making the sandbox or virtual environment too inclusive. There is a balance you must maintain between risk (security) and being able to perform useful work.

- Control how the application interacts with the API. For example, you make it less likely that errant or malicious input will cause any sort of disastrous effect. The application inputs are strictly controlled and unexpected inputs tend to have a reduced effect or no effect at all. Of course, this kind of protection can also make it hard to experiment with the API or perform certain types of testing.

This chapter helps you understand the concept of an API sandbox/virtual environment and determine precisely how you can use one with your next programming project to keep things safe. As part of working with API sandboxes, this chapter also discusses some sandboxing and virtual environment solutions. Not every solution works in every situation, so it's a good idea to know about a number of potential solutions.

Like any other security solution, using an API sandbox isn't a silver bullet. It won't keep every hacker at bay and it won't keep every API from damaging your application or its associated data. Using an API sandbox reduces risk. You need to determine whether the API sandbox reduces the risk enough or whether you need additional measures to keep your application safe. Security isn't about just one technique or one measure. A secure system relies on a number of security layers to get the job done.

The final section of the chapter discusses a sandboxing alternative, virtualization. Even though it might seem that a virtual environment and a sandbox are essentially the same thing because they achieve largely the same goals, they really are different technologies; therefore, this last section helps you understand the differences in detail. A virtualized environment tends to make it appear to the API that it executes in a completely open environment. However, a virtualized environment is completely cut off from everything else and the API works through a strict access scheme.

The point of this chapter is to help you create an environment where an API can execute without truly connecting with other parts of the application. The environment is strictly controlled. It shows two methods to achieve this goal and helps you understand when to choose one technology over the other. Choosing the right kind of safety zone is essential if you want to obtain usable results from your application testing and ultimately application usage.

This book uses the term *safety zone* to refer to the goals achieved by both sandboxes and virtual environments. It's essential to remember that the goals of the two technologies are basically the same, but how the technologies achieve these goals is significantly different. Because of the differences, you may find that choosing one technology over the other gives you advantages with certain application development needs.

Understanding the Concept of an API Safety Zone

An API safety zone provides a secure and flexible method of testing or using any API you create. It's always a good idea to use an API safety zone during testing to ensure you can recover from mistakes quickly. You may decide to continue using an API safety zone after moving the API to the production environment for the security features that it provides.

Using a sandbox does provide additional security. However, many organizations aren't concerned about security when they implement a sandbox environment. In addition to security, a sandbox can provide you with these benefits:

- Reduced costs by controlling resource usage
- Controlled access of third-party APIs
- Improved testing and development environment in the form of better control
- Decreased time to market
- Simulated error scenarios for testing
- Monitored API performance

Organizations also use virtual environments for purposes other than simply securing the API. As with a sandbox, a virtual environment reduces costs by controlling resource usage, controls access to third-party APIs, and improves the testing and development environment. A virtual environment has many advantages from the organizational perspective including:

- Reduced recovery time after an API crash
- Enhanced speed and network bandwidth control
- Improved energy usage
- Diminished hardware footprint
- Faster provisioning
- Reduced vendor lock-in
- Increased uptime (even when security and reliability events are rare)
- Extended application life

The choice between using a sandbox or virtual environment may come down to the additional features that each provides if the API will work equally well with either option. It's essential to consider the security aspects of each option first, however, if you want to maintain the kind of security required by today's applications.

Defining the Need for an API Safety Zone

Security is about risk management. Making requests of any API incurs risk because you don't know that the API hasn't been compromised, assuming that the API was free of potential problems in the first place. The need for policing any API that you use becomes apparent when you read about the damage done by APIs online. Any API you use could send data that turns out to be a virus, script, or other malware in disguise. Because of the way in which APIs are used, you'd only find out about the issue when everyone started to complain that the application was down or you found confidential information in a place you didn't expect to find it (assuming someone else doesn't find it first).

The reverse issues occur when you own the code for an API. Your API may provide a valuable service for your customers. It may offer access to all sorts of confidential data, some of which the customer should access, and some that should remain hidden. The wrong sort of input could cause your API to react in unexpected ways—causing damage to the API, its data, and the server in general. Consequently, you need to find ways to sanitize the input data, but also to provide protection when it turns out that the sanitation process didn't work as well as anticipated.

Whether your API sends or receives data as the result of a request, using the API in a sandbox or virtual environment only makes sense because doing so will reduce your risk. Keeping the bad guys out completely may not work, but you can minimize your risk and the effects of any breach you experience. The following sections build a case for working with APIs in a sandbox or virtual environment.

Ensuring Your API Works

Security is about risk management. Ensuring your API works as anticipated reduces risk by reducing the potential for someone making the API work in a manner you hadn't considered. Hackers often do their dirty work by looking for ways to make code misbehave—to do something the owner doesn't want it to do. Using an API safety zone lets you test your code in ways that you normally couldn't test it without creating problems on the test server. You can perform these sorts of tests to ensure your API works as intended:

- Verify that the correct inputs provide the correct responses
- Use range checks to ensure that the API responds correctly to out-of-bounds data
- Input data of the wrong type to ensure the API sanitizes data by type
- Check data length by using data inputs that are both too long and too short
- Purposely input invalid data that hackers might use, such as scripts, tags, or binary data
- Leave required data out
- Add extra inputs
- Create null data inputs
- Overload the API
- Starve the API of resources

Enabling Rapid Development

Placing your API directly on the server means that you have one copy of the API for everyone to use. Naturally, the second that any of the developers decides to try something radical that causes the API or the server to crash, everyone else has to stop work as well. You want your developers to feel free to experiment because you can be sure the hacker will certainly feel free to do so. Creating a constrained environment where everyone has to play by the rules is almost certain to hide security holes that a hacker will use to breach your server.

Sandboxing helps enable rapid development by making it less likely that the server will crash. If the API experiences problems, you can usually recover quite quickly. The sandboxed environment will also make it quite easy to simulate all sorts of conditions that could occur in the real world, such as a lack of resources or resources that are completely missing. However, you still typically have one copy of the API running, so it's not quite as free as you can make the development environment.

Using a virtual environment makes it possible for each developer (or group of developers) to have an individual copy of the API. Of course, you use more server resources to make this scenario happen, but the point is that you end up with an environment where no one developer can intrude on any other developer's programming efforts. Everyone is isolated from everyone else. If one developer thinks it might be a good idea to attack the API in a certain way and the attack is successful (bringing the API or the virtual environment down), those efforts won't affect anyone else. The point is to have an environment in which developers feel free to do anything that comes to mind in search of the perfect application solutions.

The trade-off to consider in this case is one of resources versus flexibility. The sandboxing approach is more resource friendly and probably a better choice for small organizations that might not have many hardware resources to spare. The virtual environment is a better approach for organizations that are working on larger APIs that require the attention of a number of developers. Keeping the developers from getting in each other's way becomes a prime consideration in this case and the use of additional hardware probably isn't much of a problem.

 Think outside the box when it comes to acquiring hardware for development and testing purposes. The system that no longer functions well for general use might still have enough life in it for development use, especially if your goal is to test in constrained environments. In short, don't always think about new hardware when it comes to setting up a test environment—sometimes older hardware works just as well and you may have plenty of it on hand as a result of equipment upgrades.

Certifying the Best Possible Integration

A problem with integration testing in many cases is that the testing looks for positive, rather than negative results. Developers want to verify that the:

- API works according to specification
- Functionality of the API matches the expectations for any business logic the API must enforce

It turns out that there are a number of solutions that you can use for integration testing that will also help you find potential security issues. The following sections describe the most popular techniques: sandboxing, creating a virtual environment, using mocking, and relying on API virtualization.

Sandboxing integration testing

Using a sandboxed environment makes it possible to perform true-to-life testing. In some cases, you can get false positives when the sandboxed environment doesn't match the real-world environment in some way. In addition, using the sandboxed environment typically doesn't show the true speed characteristics of the API because there is another layer of software between the API and the application. Speed issues become exaggerated when multiple developers begin hitting the API with requests in an environment that doesn't match the production environment.

 If you find that the tests you create produce unreliable or inconsistent results, then you need to create a better test environment. When it's not possible to input specific values and obtain specific outputs, then the testing process produces false positives that could take you days to resolve. False positives are especially problematic when working with security issues. You can't have a particular set of conditions produce a security issue one time and not the next.

Virtualizing integration testing

The alternative of a virtual environment provides the same true-to-life testing. Because of the way in which a virtual environment works, it's possible to mimic the production environment with greater ease, so you don't get as many false positives. Actual testing speed usually isn't an issue because each developer has a private virtual environment to use. However, unless you have the right kind of setup, you can't reliably perform either application speed or load testing because the virtual environment tends to skew the results. Recovery after a failed integration test is definitely faster when using a virtual environment.

Mocking for integration testing

Some developers use mocking for API integration testing. A mocked API accepts inputs and provides outputs in a scripted way. In other words, the API isn't real. The purpose of the mocked API is to test the application portion separately from the API. Using a mocked API makes it possible to start building and testing the application before the team codes the API.

The advantage of mocking is that any tests run quite quickly. In addition, the response the application receives is precise and unchangeable, unlike a real API where responses could potentially vary. (A mock doesn't perform any real-world processing, so there is no basis for varied responses.) However, mistakes in the mock can create false positives when testing the application.

Examples of mocked APIs exist online. For example, if you want to test your REST-based application, you can use Mocky (*http://www.mocky.io/*) to perform the task. You use Mocky to create a canned anticipated response that an application can query, as shown in Figure 10-1. Mocky makes it possible to create various response types as well. Not only do you control the HTTP response, but you also control the content response type and value.

A number of mocks provide both SOAP and REST support. For example, mockable.io/ supports both SOAP and REST, as shown in Figure 10-2. In order to use this service, you must sign up for an account. A trial account lets you perform testing, but any data you generate isn't private. In order to create a private setup, you must obtain a paid account.

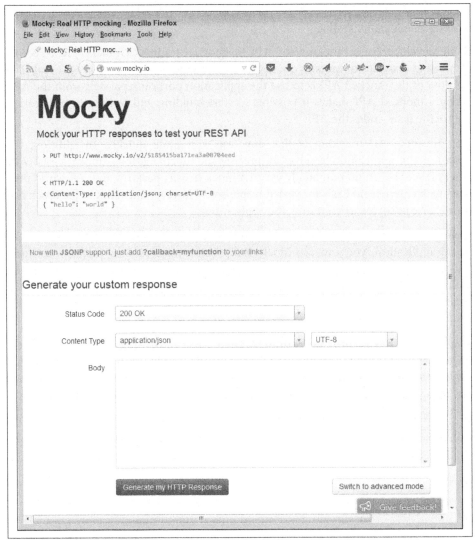

Figure 10-1. Mocky provides a simple form you fill in to configure testing

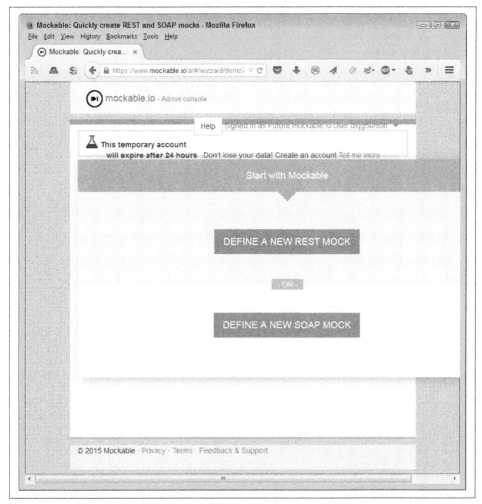

Figure 10-2. Use mocks such as mockable.io when you need SOAP support

In this case, once you select the kind of mock you want to create, you fill out a form to perform the actual testing process. As shown in Figure 10-3, the list of settings you can change for the mock is extensive. In this case, you also select items such as the verb used to create the call. The point is that a mock provides an environment where you provide a specific input in a specific way and get a specific result back.

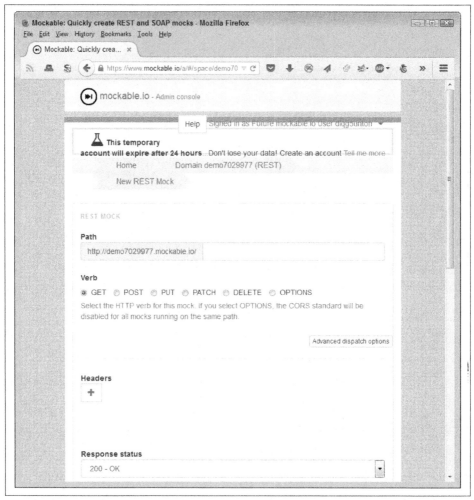

Figure 10-3. Some mocks provide a significant amount of control over the testing interface

The more advanced mocks, such as Apiary (*https://apiary.io/*), offer a range of services to make the mocking process easier. You can use this service to generate documentation, integrate coding samples, perform debugging tasks, and automate testing. Naturally, as the complexity of the mock increases, so does the price.

Integrating using API virtualization

A sandbox environment makes it possible to do something that you normally couldn't do easily—virtualize a missing API. It's entirely possible that your development schedule won't match the schedules of some of the third parties you depend upon for services. When this problem occurs, companies are often left twiddling their thumbs while waiting for the dependent API. Of course, you could always reinvent the wheel and create your own version of the API, but most organizations don't have that option and it really isn't a good option even when you do have the resources.

 Never confuse API virtualization with server virtualization or the use of virtual machines. In the latter two cases, you create an entire system that mimics every part of a standard platform as a virtual entity. API virtualization only mimics the API. You couldn't use it to perform tasks such as running an application directly.

Virtualization is the process of creating a representation of an API that you can use for testing and other purposes. The representation acts as a sort of black box that you can use in lieu of having the actual API to rely on. This black box ultimately provides access to the actual APIs, but it could also provide access to a mock instead. The point is that the API virtualization layer provides a consistent means of interacting with the API and integrating an application with it, even if the API isn't completely finished. Figure 10-4 shows how the API virtualization layer looks.

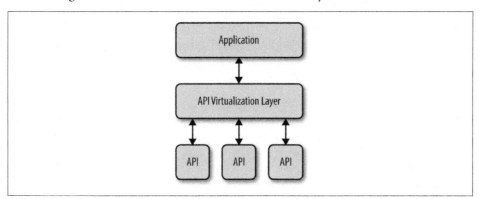

Figure 10-4. The API virtualization layer separates the application from the APIs

Using API virtualization hardens your application against the sorts of failures that hackers love. The virtualization layer makes it possible for the application to continue running even when the API itself isn't functioning correctly. For example, you could create a mock to stand in for the API when a failure occurs and the application will simply continue running. The user might not even notice any difference. Later, when the API is back online, you can perform any required recovery in the background. The point is that a hacker won't be able to get the application to fail simply by over-loading the API.

In some cases, you can create an even better environment by combining a sandbox product with API virtualization. For example, SmartBear provides two products:

VirtServer and Ready API! (*http://smartbear.com/product/ready-api/overview/*), that make it possible to create a two-layer approach to working with APIs (read more at *http://smartbear.com/product/ready-api/servicev/features/share-virtual-services/*). The idea is to gain additional flexibility in working through complex API interactions.

Verifying the API Behaves Under Load

Load testing is important for security reasons because hackers often overload an API or an application in order to cause it to fail in a specific way. After the API or application fails, the hacker uses various tricks to use the disabled software as an entry point to the network. Consequently, knowing how your API will degrade when loaded is essential because you want it to fail gracefully and in a manner that doesn't open huge holes for the hacker to enter. It's essential to keep in mind that every API is going to fail at some point if you put enough of a load on it. Despite promises you might have read in the past, there isn't any way to make software scale to the point it can accept an infinite load (assuming that it's even possible to test for such a thing).

In order to perform load testing, you must be able to simulate a load, which usually means adding software to the system that will make the required calls, reduce resources as needed, and perform any required logging. Most developers use a sandboxed environment for load testing because it provides the most realistic testing environment. Look for tools that work with all the platforms you need to support. Some products, such as LoadUI (*http://www.loadui.org/*), provide versions for Windows, Mac, and Linux testing. Before you get any tool, try to download a trial version to see if it works as promised.

A starting point for any API load testing is determining how to test it. You need to obtain statistics that tell you how to load the API to simulate a real-world environment. To ensure the API works as advertised, you need to determine:

- Average number of requests the API receives per second
- Peak number of requests the API receives per second
- Throughput distribution by endpoint (the locations that make calls to the API)
- Throughput distribution by user or workgroup

It's also important to decide how to generate traffic to test the API. You may decide to start simply. However, it's important to test the API using various kinds of traffic to ensure it behaves well in all circumstances:

- Repetitive load generation (where the testing software uses the same request sequence)
- Simulated traffic patterns (a randomized version of the repetitive load generation or a replay of API access log data)

- Real traffic (where you have a test group hit the API with real requests)

After you establish that the API works under standard conditions, you need to vary those conditions to simulate a hacker attack. For example, a hacker could decide to flood the API with a specific request, hoping to get it to fail in a specific manner. The hacker could also decide to keep adding more and more zombies in a distributed denial-of-service (DDoS) attack that simply loads the API down to the breaking point. Get creative. It's important to determine what will break your API and cause it to fail, and then see how the API fails. Knowing how the API will fail will help you determine the level of risk that each kind of hack poses so that you can better prepare for the consequences.

Keeping the API Safe from Hackers

After you have performed all of the other testing described in this chapter, you might think that your API is safe. The problem is that you haven't thought about all the ways in which the hacker will attack it. If someone is truly determined to break your API, they'll find a way to do it. Chapter 9 discusses the need to think like a hacker. Of course, that's a good start, but once you have ideas on how someone could break your API, you need to test them. The only way you can do that safely is to try creating an API safety zone.

In this one case, testing with both a sandboxed and a virtualized environment will help you get the best results. Each environment provides specific advantages to the tester that will help ensure the API will behave itself in the production environment.

 It's never a good idea to test your application and its associated APIs in a production environment unless absolutely necessary. Many developers have tried it and found that the testing procedures actually damage the data the application was supposed to protect. In addition, you generally won't be able to schedule time for testing that's convenient to users. Because users add variations to the testing environment, you need to test at a time when users aren't actively engaged in performing tasks. Otherwise, you can't be sure that a failed test is the result of testing or of user input.

Developing with an API Sandbox

Visualizing an API sandbox is relatively simple. It's the same idea as a sandbox for children. The API has access to everything contained within the sandbox, but nothing outside of it. Keeping an API in a sandbox has important security implications because it becomes less likely that an API, even one that is under attack by a hacker, could potentially do anything to harm the application or its data. By keeping the API sequestered, it can only damage resources that are already set aside for it. This means that the API is effectively unable to do damage in an unmanaged way unless the designer implements the sandbox incorrectly or ineffectively.

Nothing comes free. By placing an API in a sandbox, it's also quite possible that the API will no longer function as expected or will work slowly in the resource-starved environment. It's essential to create the API sandbox such that the API functionality remains robust. Creating a balanced API sandbox can be difficult and it requires an in-depth knowledge of precisely how the API works with the application to perform specific tasks. (It's not necessary to understand every detail of the API because it's unlikely that the application uses the entire API.)

Many articles make a big deal out of sandboxes, but really, it isn't anything all that much different than working with any modern operating system. At one time, the application had full access to the entire machine. Today, an application has controlled access to system resources that include memory and processing time. The application must share with other applications running on the system, so the operating system controls access to resources. What you have with a sandbox is an additional layer of control, but the control is similar in functionality and effect to any other sort of application control.

Once you establish good reasons for developing an API sandbox, it's time to develop one for use with your application. Actually, you need an individual sandbox for each API you use in your application. Some applications use quite a few of them and it doesn't help to contaminate one API's environment with problems generated by another API. Keeping everything separated and unable to destroy anything else is always a good idea. In some cases, you might have to become creative in the way that you build an application so the APIs continue to work as they should, but the idea of keeping APIs in completely separate and controlled environments is a great idea.

Beginnings of the Sandbox

You might think that the sandbox is a relatively new construct. However, the concept of a sandbox has been around for quite a long time, since the 1970s, in the form of the Hydra operating system. The Carnegie Mellon multiprocessor operating system for minicomputers featured a sandbox where developers could experiment with artificial intelligence (AI) applications in relative safety (*http://research.microsoft.com/en-us/um/people/gbell/Computer_Structures_Principles_and_Examples/csp0366.htm*). Each application ran as a user application, which meant it didn't have access to lower-level operating system functionality that could cause a system failure.

Other developers noticed the functionality provided by Hydra and reproduced it in other environments. For example, Sun provided the concept of Dynamic System Domains (*http://www.filibeto.org/~aduritz/truetrue/e10000/dynamic-sysdomains.html*) to provide error protection and application isolation (among other goals). FreeBSD actually locked applications up by putting them in jails (*https://www.freebsd.org/doc/handbook/jails.html*). Therefore, the idea of the sandbox has been around for a long time—however, using them for APIs is relatively new.

Today, many applications run in a sandbox. For example, in 2012, Apple started requiring developers to include sandbox features as part of the applications found in Apple's Mac App Store (*https://developer.apple.com/app-sandboxing/*). Google's Chrome browser (*https://tools.google.com/dlpage/res/chrome/en-GB/more/security.html*), Microsoft's Internet Explorer (*http://securityintelligence.com/internet-explorer-ie-10-enhanced-protected-mode-epm-sandbox-research/*), and Apple's Safari (*http://www.cnet.com/news/safari-matches-rivals-with-sandboxed-flash-for-better-security/*) all have sandboxes. The only browser without a sandbox is Mozilla's Firefox (*http://www.extremetech.com/computing/178587-firefox-is-still-the-least-secure-web-browser-falls-to-four-zero-day-exploits-at-pwn2own*).

Using an Off-the-Shelf Solution

Building your own sandbox could be a lot of fun, but it's more likely a waste of time. You want to focus on your application, rather than build an environment in which to use it safely. That's why you need a good off-the-shelf solution that you can trust. The following list describes a few of the available sandbox solutions:

AirGap (https://spikes.com/isolation-is-the-new-prevention.html)
This is an interesting idea. Instead of allowing the browser to run on the client system, it runs on a server in the cloud. The user relies on a viewer application that provides isolation from the browser. You see the browser window and interact with it as you normally would, but the only thing that is running on the client system is the viewer. The vendor promises physical, connection, session, and

malware isolation using this approach. You'd need to try it with your application to see if the viewer approach would actually do the job.

 A solution such as AirGap works fine for many users. However, you must consider where the browser is running. If you are in a regulated industry or your application deals with sensitive information, then AirGap won't work for you. The browser really does need to run on the host system to work correctly and to maintain the confidentiality that the legal system (or common sense) requires.

Sandboxie (http://www.sandboxie.com/)
You can use Sandboxie to run any application on the host system, not just browsers. This means that you can use Sandboxie to perform all sorts of tasks that other solutions might not support. Because it runs on the client system, all your sensitive data remains fully protected from view. The vendor provides a trial version you can test. When you choose to buy a license, you have a choice between a home and small business version or an enterprise version. Only the enterprise version comes with a support package. Sandboxie only works with the Windows operating system.

Spoon.net (https://spoon.net/browsers)
Sometimes you need to test a lot of different browsers, but downloading and installing them all on your system is difficult. Configuring all these browsers as you need them configured adds additional steps. You can avoid all this pain by accessing the browser through the environment provided by Spoon.net. To use this product, you install a plug-in for your browser and then choose the browser you want to use, as shown in Figure 10-5. The browser selections aren't limited to those that your platform would normally support. For example, even if you're using a Windows system, you can load Safari or Firefox Mobile to perform required testing.

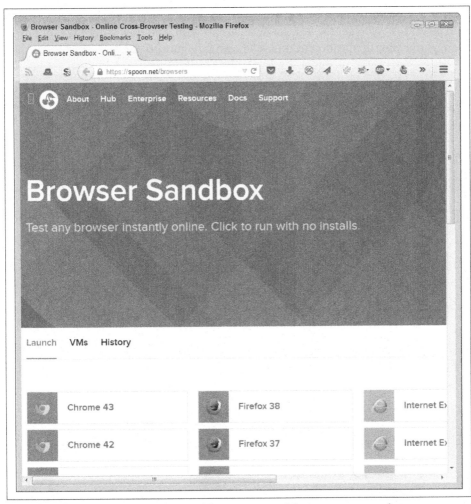

Figure 10-5. Spoon.net makes it possible to use any of the most common browsers

Using Other Vendors' Sandboxes

There are situations where you use a sandbox whether you want to or not. For example, when writing an application that uses the eBay API, you must first use the sandbox (*https://go.developer.ebay.com/developer-sandbox*) to write your application code and then test it. Only after eBay certifies the application can you run it in the production environment. Because of the high risks involved in the API environment, you will likely find that you spend considerably more time using third-party sandboxes to test your code.

Access to most of these sandboxes relies on specialized keys. Vendors, such as eBay, want to know who is using their sandbox and for what purpose. The key uniquely identifies you and you must have it in order to make a sandbox call. When working with eBay, it's easy to get the key, create a user account, and then enter the sandbox to begin performing application testing, as shown in Figure 10-6.

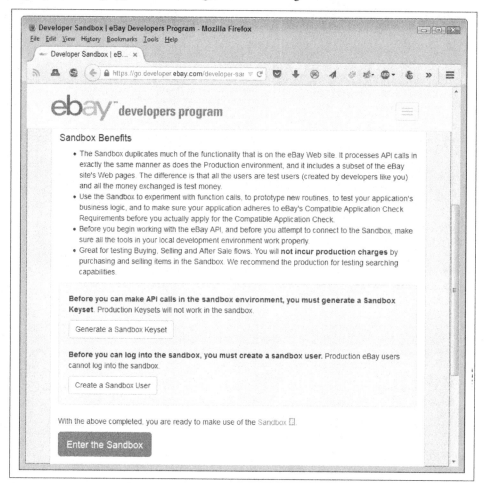

Figure 10-6. Most vendors will require some sort of access control to use their sandbox

A problem can occur when you need to use multiple APIs in your application and each of these APIs has its own sandbox environment. Trying to get the application certified means getting each of the vendors to sign off on it. Make sure you create a plan for getting your application signed off by each of the vendors before you begin coding. In some cases, you may have to break your application into separately testable pieces in order to gain the approval you need.

The use of multiple APIs in a single application has become so common and so complex that many developers now turn to API aggregation for help. Using API aggregation makes it possible to reduce complexity by creating an API mashup. Working with API aggregation is well outside the scope of this book, but you can find some excellent information about it in "Api Aggregation: Why It Matters and Eight Different Models" (*http://www.programmable web.com/news/api-aggregation-why-it-matters-and-eight-different-models/2013/12/13*) and "Extending REST APIs with API Aggregator" (*http://tech.3scale.net/2013/04/18/accelerate-your-mobile-api-with-nginx-and-lua/*). Of course, there are many other resources you can consult for information about aggregation, but these articles are good places to start.

Considering Virtual Environments

Sometimes your API requires a virtual environment in which to work. A virtual environment gives the feeling of being the real thing without letting the API do things that would cause problems. Throughout the chapter, you've seen comparisons between sandboxing and virtual environments. From a security perspective, both provide protection against hacker activity, but do it in a significantly different manner. However, the bottom line is always to separate the API, application, application components, or any other software item that you might want to isolate from the operating system. The isolation allows you to intercept and cleanse data, as well as keep the software under control so hackers do less damage. The following sections discuss virtual environments in more detail.

Defining the Virtual Environment

A virtual environment can refer to any software that provides the means to isolate other software. Think about it as you do a container, because that's what it is. Previous sections of the chapter have described various kinds of virtual environments. However, this part of the chapter describes the kind of virtual environment you use for development purposes, rather than running an application as a user.

The basic reason to use virtualization is to isolate all or part of the development environment so that you can play with the application. Finding security issues truly does mean experimenting with the software in ways that you would never use in a standard operating system (especially not one connected to the network where your mistake could take down everyone).

Some languages come with their own virtual environment tools. For example, Python users have a number of tools for creating virtual environments at their disposal. These tools make it easier to set up and configure specific environments for specific languages. You can read about the Python offerings at *http://docs.python-guide.org/en/latest/dev/virtualenvs/*. The point is to look for language-specific tools whenever possible to create virtual environments designed to work with that language.

Virtual environments can also include so much more than a sandbox does. It's possible to create virtual environments with specific operating systems, development tools, application setups, and browsers. The virtual environment emulates every part of the development experience so that you can create an Apache server setup using one virtual environment and an IIS server setup using another. Both virtual environments can exist on the same machine without any problems with conflicts.

Differentiating Virtual Environments and Sandboxing

Virtual environments and sandboxes have many similarities. The rest of the chapter has described the most common similarities, such as keeping your API safe. The basic differences between most virtual environments and sandboxing are that virtual environments are:

Repeatable
> When you move the virtual environment file to another system, that system runs the virtual environment precisely as it would run on the original system. What this means is that every developer sees the application in the same way, using a prescribed development environment, so the results seen on one system are repeatable on another system. Differences between setups make it hard (sometimes impossible) to verify the presence of security issues.

Movable
> Depending on the virtualization software you use, you could move the virtual environment just about anywhere. As long as the developer receiving the virtual environment file has the correct software, it's possible to re-create the precise virtual environment needed to work with the project.

Recoverable
> Virtual development environments rely on a special kind of file that defines how to create the required emulation. If your experiments cause the virtual environment to crash, all you need to do is close that copy of the virtual environment and start another. Recovery takes only as long as needed for the software to load, which may be just a few seconds.

Re-creatable

There are times when you need multiple copies of the same project running on your system. You can create as many copies of a virtual environment as needed for your purposes. The special nature of virtual environments means that every copy you create will begin with precisely the same resources, software loaded, environment, and so on. Consequently, every copy is a clone of every other copy on your system.

Implementing Virtualization

One of the more interesting virtual development environments is Vagrant (*https://www.vagrantup.com/*). This particular product runs on any Windows, OS X, or common Linux system (there are versions of Linux that don't work with Vagrant, so be sure to check the list to be sure Vagrant supports your Linux distribution). To use this product, you install it on your system, configure the kind of environment you want to use for development purposes, and place the resulting file with your project code. Any time you want to start up the development environment you need for a particular project, you simply issue the `vagrant up` command and it configures the correct environment for you. The product will create the same environment no matter where you move the project files, so you can create a single environment for everyone on your development team to use. Vagrant is a better choice for the individual developer or a small company—it's inexpensive and easy to use.

Another useful virtual environment product is Puppet (*https://puppetlabs.com/*). This product relies on VMware (*http://www.vmware.com/*), with Puppet performing the management tasks. The combination of Puppet and VMware is better suited toward the enterprise environment because VMware comes with such a huge list of tools you can use with it and it also provides support for larger setups.

Relying on Application Virtualization

All sorts of virtual environments exist to meet just about any need you can think of. For example, Cameo (*http://www.cameyo.com/*) makes it possible to shrink any application down into a single executable (*.exe* file) that you can copy to any Windows machine and simply run without any installation. If you need to support other platforms, you can copy the application to the Cameo cloud servers and execute it from there.

Application virtualization is a packaging solution. You create a virtual environment that specifically meets the need of just that application. Figure 10-7 shows how the virtual application environment might appear. As far as the application is concerned, it's operating in its native environment, even though it's using a completely different operating system to perform tasks.

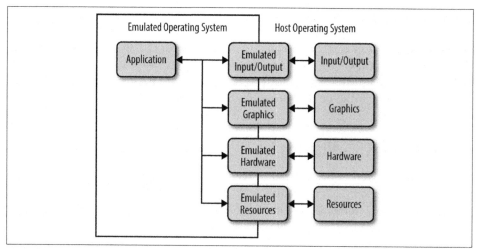

Figure 10-7. Application virtualization is a kind of packaging technology

Another product that provides an application virtual environment is Evalaze (*http://www.evalaze.de/en/evalaze-oxid/*). This product emphasizes the sandbox environment it provides along with the application virtualization. You can use it to run an application from all sorts of places, including memory sticks. This is a great solution to use if your application requires a specific browser and you want to be sure that the user's environment is configured correctly.

Researching an appropriate kind of virtualization will take time and you need to pursue your research with an open mind. Some of those odd-looking solutions out there may be precisely what you need to create a secure environment for your application.

CHAPTER 11

Checking Libraries and APIs for Holes

Before you can know that a particular piece of software will behave in a particular way, you need to test it. Yes, you do have a specification and you created the code in accordance with that specification. You even debugged the code to ensure that there aren't any obvious errors in it. However, you still don't know that the code will function as originally intended until you perform some level of testing on it. Testing ensures that software behaves as you expect it should.

This chapter does discuss testing in the traditional sense, but it also views nontraditional sorts of testing. A standard testing suite will provide specific inputs and then validate the expected outputs. However, the real world doesn't always provide the kind of input that libraries and APIs expect, so it's important to test that sort of input as well. Of course, when you test in this manner, you don't know what to expect as output. The library or API design must contain functionality that helps with recovery from errant input so that the system doesn't crash, but you don't know whether this functionality is even present until you perform the required level of testing.

Testing can and should happen at multiple levels. Unit testing, the testing of individual pieces of code, comes first. A developer begins performing this sort of testing shortly after writing the first bits of code. Next comes integration testing as the application components are put together. Finally, the application is tested as a whole with all of the completed software in place. All these levels of testing (and more) require security testing as well—checking for unexpected inputs and determining whether the code acts in an acceptable manner. During this time, the developers also create a testing harness—test routines that automate the process of testing so that it becomes more reliable and consistent.

Each programming language can also have particular issues that developers must check. The final part of this chapter discusses how to check for specific programming language issues as you perform your security testing. Unlike other areas of testing, language-specific issues tend to revolve around security because hackers often look for these differences as the means for causing the application to crash in a specific manner or for logic errors that the hacker can employ to gain access. Tracking potential language flaws is just as important as tracking flaws in third-party libraries and APIs. You need to test every part of an application from every possible angle to ensure your application will behave in a predictable manner.

Testing Outside the Box

Code depends on procedures. Yes, the code may be event driven or it might not include the concept of state, but deep down, code relies on a set of steps to accomplish tasks. That set of steps is a procedure. Whether the procedure is complete or not is beside the point for the sake of this discussion.

I got my first view of testing outside the box in grade school. It's hard to remember most events from that time in my life, but one event has stood out all these years as a life skill to remember. The teacher had asked us all to write a procedure for making toast. It seems like a simple enough request. However, we all failed. It turns out that everyone thought to get the loaf of bread out and to stick individual pieces into the toaster. Waiting for the toast to pop up was no problem, nor was buttering the toast afterward.

The sticking point was taking the pieces of bread out of the wrapper. When the teacher followed our procedure to the letter, she, of course, tried to stick the individual pieces of bread, wrapper and all, into the toaster. We had all made an assumption that meant the procedure was flawed. Computers are literal like my teacher. We make assumptions about what the computer will do based on common sense and experience—neither of which are present in the computer. Testing outside the box means looking for that bread in the wrapper assumption that everyone made while developing the code. Security holes are often the result of assumptions that the developer shouldn't have made.

Creating a Testing Plan

Every testing scenario requires a testing plan. Although you want to test outside the box, you do need to have some sort of structured method to perform the testing. Otherwise, testing becomes inconsistent and incomplete. In order to perform a useful purpose, testing needs to be methodical, yet flexible enough to provide a capacity for additional tests as it becomes obvious you need them. With this in mind, the following sections help you define a testing plan from a development perspective.

It's important to note that testing plans often have a number of phases and orientations. Every stakeholder in an application development effort will want to perform some level of testing to ensure the application meets specific goals and objectives. These points of view could conflict, but in most cases, they merely augment each other. For example, a DBA may want to verify that the application interacts with the database in a manner that's consistent with company guidelines.

Considering Goals and Objectives

Application testing can't succeed unless the development team defines both goals and objectives for the testing. A goal is as simple as determining whether the application meets the technical and business requirements that an organization requires of it. An objective is to determine that the application can successfully perform a set of tasks within the business environment provided for it. For example, an objective might be to add new users to a database without causing errors, duplicating users, or leaving out essential information. The following sections discuss goals and objectives that testing must meet in order to provide a useful result.

Defining the Testing Alternatives

Testing isn't the only way to check an application. The main point of testing is to verify that the application performs in a certain way. Other techniques can achieve the same goals. The most common alternatives to testing are code review, static analysis, model checking, and proofs. Each of these alternatives has its place as part of your strategy for improving overall application security and ensuring the application behaves in a reliable manner.

Code review is a check performed by human specialists. A team walks through the code and verifies that the design and implementation fulfills the requirements of the specification. Using code review can help locate potential coding problems that automated methods might miss. In fact, it's entirely possible that an application will compile and execute with significant flaws that code review will reveal. You can read more about code review at *https://www.owasp.org/index.php/Code_Review_Introduction*.

Static analysis is the same process as code review, but uses automated tools in place of human reviewers. The advantages of static analysis are consistency and speed. Automated tools check every facet of the application in precisely the same way and tend not to make mistakes brought on by tiredness. In addition, automated tools can work faster than humans. However, automated tools can also miss errors that humans would see almost immediately. You can read more about static analysis at *https://www.owasp.org/index.php/Static_Code_Analysis*.

Model checking verifies that application properties satisfy the requirements of the specification. In most cases, this means verifying that the application provides solutions for elements such as algorithms. This kind of testing is automated, but requires substantial human input to perform. You can read more about model checking at *https://www7.in.tum.de/um/25/target.html*.

Proofs often appear as some form of stress testing on the application. A proof verifies that the application will perform as needed, even when substantial loads are placed on the application.

Defining the goals

Goals define a condition that a person or entity intends to meet. You can set all sorts of goals for application testing, such as computing the precise value of pi within 42 picoseconds. Of course, the goal isn't achievable because it isn't possible to calculate a precise value for pi. Some organizations set the same sorts of goals for applications and are disenchanted when it becomes obvious that the testing process hasn't achieved the goal. Real goals are accomplishable using the resources available within the time allotted.

In addition, a goal must define a measurement for success. It isn't just a matter of knowing whether testing succeeded—it's a matter of knowing how well testing succeeded. In order to obtain an answer to how well the testing proceeded, the goals you set must provide a measure that defines a range of expected outcomes, such as the application calculated the correct result within the given timeframe 99% of the time.

The precise goals you set for your application depends on what you expect from it and the time you have in which to implement the goals. However, it's possible to generalize the goals under the following categories:

Verification and validation
> The verification and validation process does bring faults to light. However, it also ensures the application provides the designed output given specific inputs. The software must work as defined by the specification. From a security perspective, you must test the software for both expected and unexpected inputs and verify that it responds correctly in each case.

Priority coverage
> The most secure application in the world would have every function tested in every possible way. However, in the real world, time and budgetary constraints make it impossible to test an application fully. In order to test the software as fully as possible, you must perform profiling to determine where the software spends most of its time and focus your efforts there. However, other factors do come into play. Even if a feature isn't used regularly, you may still have to give it higher coverage when it can't fail (a failure would cause a catastrophic result). The prioritization of coverage must include factors that only your application possesses.

Balanced

The testing process must balance the written requirements, real-world limitations, and user expectations. When performing a test, you must verify that the results are repeatable and independent of the tester. Avoiding bias in the testing process is essential. It's also possible that what the specification contains and what the users expect won't match completely. Miscommunication (or sometimes no communication at all) prevents the specification from fully embracing the user's view of what the application should do. As a result, you may also need to consider unwritten expectations as part of the testing process.

Traceable

Documenting the testing process fully is critical in repeating the testing process later. The documentation must describe both successes and failures. In addition, it must specify what was tested and how the testing team tested it. The documentation also includes testing harnesses and other tools that the team used to perform software testing. Without a complete set of everything the testing team used, it's impossible to re-create the testing environment later.

Deterministic

The testing you perform shouldn't be random. Any testing should test specific features of the software and you should know what those features are. In addition, the testing should show specific outcomes given specific inputs. The testing team should always know in advance precisely how the tests should work and define the outcomes they should provide so that errors are obvious.

Testing performance

Many people equate performance with speed, but performance encompasses more than simply speed. An application that is fast, but performs the task incorrectly, is useless. Likewise, an application that performs a task well, but makes the information it processes available to the wrong parties, is also useless. In order to perform well, an application must perform tasks reliably, securely, and quickly.

Each of these performance elements weighs against the others. Increasing security will necessarily make the application slower because the developer adds more code to perform security checks. Adding code makes the application run more slowly. Likewise, reliability will cause an application to slow because more checks are added in this case as well. Security checks can decrease application reliability by reducing risk at the expense of functionality—a reliable application is one that provides all the expected functionality in every given circumstance (it doesn't fail). In short, all elements of performance work against each other, as shown in Figure 11-1.

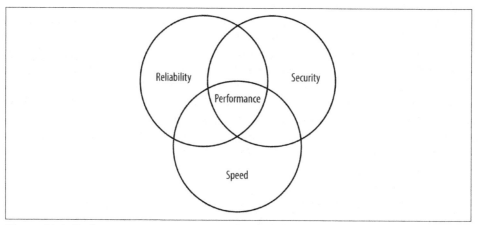

Figure 11-1. Performance encompasses speed, reliability, and security

In order to test the performance of an application, you must verify the balance between speed, reliability, and security. Balanced applications perform well and don't place a burden on the user, but still handle data reliably and efficiently.

Testing usability

Many testing scenarios fail to test usability. Determining how well the user can interact with the software is essential because the goal of software is to help users become more productive (whether those users are human or machine is immaterial). A confusing or otherwise unhelpful interface causes security issues by keeping the user from interacting with the software correctly. The testing process needs to consider the physical and emotional needs of the user in addition to the steps required to accomplish a task. For example, asking a colorblind user to click the red button may not obtain the desired result. Failing to differentiate the button in a manner other than color is almost certainly going to cause input problems that will eventually lead to security issues.

 It's easy to become complacent when performing testing steps. A user can typically rely on keyboard and mouse input as a minimum, so you need to test both. However, users may have a broader range of access options. For example, pressing a Control key combination may perform tasks in a manner different from just using standard keyboard keys, so you need to test this type of input as well. It's not essential to test every kind of input in every possible situation, but you should know that the application is able to handle the various input types correctly.

Testing platform type

Software behaves differently depending on the platform used. Throughout the book, you've seen that users can and will use various kinds of devices to interact with any application you create. It isn't possible to test your application on every conceivable platform because some platforms aren't even available at the time of testing. Consequently, you must create platform types—devices that fall into specific categories depending on capabilities and features. For example, you may be able to group smartphones into two or three categories depending on the functionality that your application provides.

 An organization is unlikely to know every type of device that users rely upon to perform work-related tasks. It's important to perform a survey during the application design process to obtain a list of potential user devices. You can use this list when creating testing scenarios for specific device types.

When working through platform-type issues, it's especially important to look at how devices differ both physically and in the way in which the interface works. Differences in the level of standardization for the browser can make a big difference as well. Any issue that would tend to cause your application to work differently on the alternative platform is a test topic. You need to ensure that these differences don't cause the application to behave in a manner that you hadn't expected.

Implementing testing principles

A testing principle is a guideline that you can apply to all forms of testing. Principles affect every aspect of application testing and are found at every level. When you perform API unit testing, you apply the same principles as when you test the application as a whole during integration testing. The following principles are common to testing of all sorts:

Making the software fail
> The objective of testing is to cause the application to fail. If you test the application to see it succeed, then you'll never find the errors within the application. The testing process should expose as many errors as possible, because hackers will most definitely look for errors to exploit. The errors you don't find are the errors that the hacker will use against you.

Testing early
> The sooner you find an error, the lower the cost of fixing it. The cost of fixing a bug increases with time, as shown in Figure 11-2. The more each bug costs to fix and the later you find each bug, the fewer bugs you can fix due to cost and time considerations and the less secure the application becomes.

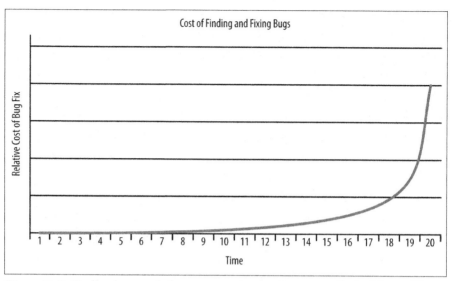

Figure 11-2. Finding bugs early leaves more time and money to find additional bugs

Making testing context dependent

The context of an application helps determine how you test it. For example, an application used for a safety-critical need requires different testing than an application used for an ecommerce site. The development approach also affects the testing context. An application developed using the waterfall approach requires different testing than an application that relies on the agile approach. Using the correct testing context helps improve application security by making it more likely that you'll find the bugs most likely to cause problems.

Creating effective test cases

The more complete and precise you can make the test cases, the more effective the testing becomes and the better the potential security becomes. The test cases must include both user and application architecture requirements. Each test case consists of the precise input to the application code and a description of the exact output expected because of the input. It's essential that inputs and outputs use measurable quantities to avoid ambiguity.

Reviewing test cases regularly

Using the same test cases repeatedly creates a test harness that eventually fails to find errors. It's essential to review test cases as potential application issues become known so that the tests continue to push the application harder and find more bugs. As part of the review process, you should also perform exploratory testing to locate potential bugs that no one has thought about yet, no user has stumbled upon, and no hacker has exploited.

Using a variety of testers

Some organizations rely on different testers during test phases, such as release, acceptance, integration, and unit testing. Using level testing does work, but employing a variety of testers throughout the development process will yield better results. For example, relying on users to help test during the early application stages could help locate security issues in interface design at a time when they're easy and inexpensive to fix.

Performing both static and dynamic testing

Using static testing probes application depth and demonstrates the developer's understanding of the problem domain and data structure. Using dynamic testing probes application breadth and reveals the application's ability to handle extremes of input. Using both static and dynamic testing helps ensure that the testing process yields as many bugs as possible within the allotted timeframe.

Looking for defect clusters

Errors tend to occur in clusters. The probability of finding errors in a particular code segment is directly proportional to the number of errors already found in that code segment.

Performing test evaluation

Each test case requires evaluation on completion to determine its success or failure. When the number of test cases are low or of a critical nature, you rely on human inspectors. When the number of test cases is high, you must include automated inspection in addition to the human inspector.

Avoiding the error absence myth

Just because an application runs with no detectible errors doesn't mean that it's error free. Applications can have all sorts of nontestable errors, such as an inability to meet user needs. In addition, tests can only check what the developer created them to check. A test may not find an error simply because it doesn't test for it. Applications generally have errors, many of which are undetectable.

Ending the testing process

Theoretically you can continuously test an application looking for errors (and continue to find them). However, testing normally comes to an end at some point that is based on the combination of money, time, and software quality. When the risk of using an application becomes low enough and users agree that the application is usable enough, the testing process normally stops even though there are still issues to consider. As a consequence, any piece of software you employ for any purpose likely contains errors that will pose security risks.

Understanding testing limitations

Testing can't provide you with an absolute picture of software performance. It can help you ascertain specific facts about the software, but not guarantee that the software won't break. It's essential to set realistic expectations about the testing process and to perform that process understanding that the result is incomplete. Here are some limitations you need to consider:

Testers aren't clairvoyant

Testing can only demonstrate the presence of errors, but never their absence. The testing process determines the presence of known issues. A tester can't test for unknown or undiscovered issues.

Testing isn't a decision-making tool

Testing can only help you determine the state of the software. It can't help you determine whether the software is safe to use or whether you should release it with some bugs in place.

Users will find an environment that doesn't work

Testing only makes it possible to determine that the software will work reasonably well in a specific environment. If a user installs the software in an environment with different conditions, the software could fail. In fact, any change to the environment you create for the software could cause failures that you couldn't find during testing.

Root causes are invisible to testing

Testing is about determining the effect of a failure given a specific input—it doesn't tell you the original source that caused the failure in the first place. All you know after the testing process is that a failure exists; you must determine where it came from.

Relying on Testing Tools to Fill the Gaps

Manual testing techniques, augmented with testing harnesses and scripts, can provide you with a significant advantage in locating potential security holes in your application. However, most developers also rely on tools to help fill in the gaps left by these longtime standbys. Testing tools make it possible to look for specific kinds of security issues that standard testing may not locate, such as SQL injection, Cross-Site Scripting (XSS), buffer overflow, and flash/flex application and Web 2.0 exposure. Here are some of the tools you should consider adding to your developer toolbox to fill in the gaps:

WebInspect (http://www8.hp.com/us/en/software-solutions/webinspect-dynamic-analysis-dast/)

Provides you with a Dynamic Application Security Testing (DAST) tool that automatically looks for commonly used hacks. The tool simulates how your

---

application behaves when under attack from these hacks so that you can easily identify potential security holes. The tool works on both web applications and services.

AppScan (http://www.ibm.com/developerworks/downloads/r/appscan/)
Performs a broad range of testing, including DAST, runtime analysis, and static taint analysis on both applications and services. The emphasis of this tool is on vulnerability management over the lifecycle of the software.

Burp Proxy (https://portswigger.net/burp/proxy.html)
Installs a proxy server on your system that intercepts all traffic between the application and other endpoints, making it possible for you to analyze application request and response traffic. Using this tool makes it possible to look for suspicious activity that might not normally attract attention, but could serve as a precursor to an attack by a hacker.

Paros (http://sourceforge.net/projects/paros/)
Creates a proxy server environment that makes it possible to review and edit all incoming and outgoing traffic for your application. This tool also provides some scanning capabilities that makes automated testing easier.

Testing Internal Libraries

When testing internal libraries—those that you control and own—you have access to the source code and can perform unit testing on each of the elements before you even put the library together. This approach gives you additional control over the testing process, lets you test and fix bugs when the costs are lower, and ensures you can perform both static and dynamic testing in order to locate potential problems with greater efficiency.

Of course, the fact that you own the code also means that you're writing the library at the same time as the rest of the application. Other developers will want to perform testing as well. What this means is that you must employ mocking, as described in Chapter 10, to ensure that development can progress as anticipated. As you perform individual unit testing and are certain that the library elements work as anticipated, you can replace the mocked elements with real elements.

As part of the testing process, you can also create a testing harness for the library as described in "Creating a Test Harness for Libraries" on page 240. However, instead of creating the whole test harness at once, you create it a piece at a time as the real library elements become available. Creating the test harness in this manner will help you keep track of how library elements are interacting with the application and make changes as needed (when the cost of doing so is low).

Testing Internal APIs

As with internal libraries, you own the code for an internal API. Because an API isn't part of the application—it runs in a different process—you need to create a server setup for interacting with the API. However, you won't want to use a production server for the task because the code you create will have all sorts of issues. It pays to configure the application such that you can change just one configuration item to point the application to the production API once you release the API.

Any API you create will also need to rely on mocking so that application developers can begin writing the application code while you continue to work on the API. As the real code becomes available, you need to replace the mocked elements with real elements. It pays to develop the whole set of test scripts for an API at the outset using the techniques found in "Creating Testing Scripts for APIs" on page 241, realizing that the mocked elements will provide canned responses. In fact, the canned responses will clue you in as to which elements are still mocked.

It's essential to test your internal APIs using the same criteria as the external APIs and to configure the testing and development environments to match your production environment. Otherwise, you could end up with a situation where an internal API actually becomes a pathway for a hacker to gain access to your network. Even disconnected software is subject to various kinds of hacks (as described in previous chapters).

Testing External Libraries

An external library (including frameworks and all sorts of other library-like coding structures) is one that someone else owns. The library is complete before you even begin writing your application and theoretically, the third party tests and maintains the library code. However, the library is simply a black box in most respects. Your ability to perform a full static test is limited to the public-facing modules that the third party makes available. Due to the complexities of working with most third-party libraries, a full static test is out of the question, which leaves dynamic testing.

Before you begin writing your application, during the proposal and design stages, you need to ensure any third-party library you choose is safe and fully meets the criteria for your application. The most popular libraries provide you with a test harness or you can find a third-party test harness for them. However, when working with a smaller, less known library, you need to set up testing yourself.

It would be easy to assume that just because a library, framework, API, or microservice is popular that it's automatically safe to use. Even with such well-known products as jQuery, you can find security issues on sites such as *http://www.cvedetails.com/vulnerability-list/vendor_id-6538/Jquery.html*. In addition, even if the product is supposedly safe, using it incorrectly can cause all sorts of security issues. You need to review articles such as "How to Safely and Wisely use jQuery: Several Key Issues" (*http://resources.infosecinstitute.com/safely-and-wisely-use-jquery/*) to discover the issues that could cause you problems later. Every piece of code has vulnerabilities, every piece of code has usage issues, every piece of code is unsafe—just keep repeating these three phrases to yourself and you'll be all right.

Testing External APIs

External APIs are popular precisely because someone else owns the code and it doesn't even run on the local system. You won't download the code or do anything with it except to make calls. The siren call of external APIs lulls even the careful developer into a false sense of security. Previous chapters have told you all about the terrifying potential for APIs to cause you woe. If anything, you need to script tests for external APIs with even greater care than any other code you use because unlike external libraries (and by extension, frameworks) you won't ever see the code. There is no possibility whatsoever of performing a static test so your dynamic tests had better run the API through its courses before you make a decision about using it.

Unlike libraries, it's unlikely that you'll find a ready-made scripting suite for an API. In order to verify that the API works as anticipated, you really do need to create a scripting setup and send inputs of all sorts to the API. It's essential to track the responses you receive, especially to errant inputs. You don't know how an API will respond to errant inputs. Consequently, you don't know how to code your application to react to errant input feedback. In other words, you need to know how the API will react when it receives data that is out of range or potentially of the wrong type.

The assumption of most developers is that the errant input will come from application users. However, errant input to the API can come from a botched man-in-the-middle attack or from other sorts of hacks. The errant input could also come from other sources on your system that reflects some type of infection or other problem. By being aware of how an API reacts to errant input, you can create a sort of security indicator that tells you something is wrong. Consider it a canary in the mine strategy. Errant inputs don't just happen in most cases—there is a cause and knowing the kind of errant input that provides an unexpected response can provide clues as to the source of an issue.

Extending Testing to Microservices

You test microservices using the same techniques as you do APIs. As with APIs, you only have the ability to perform dynamic testing unless you happen to own the microservice code. In addition, it's essential to track responses to unexpected data inputs, especially when you plan to use multiple microservices to perform the same task (with the alternatives providing backup to a main microservice that you select). The responses you receive may vary between microservices, which will mean your error handling code becomes trickier.

The biggest issue to consider with microservices, however, is that the developer purposely keeps microservices small. You can't test the most commonly used features because every feature is commonly used. In short, your testing scripts must now test every microservice fully, which could add a burden to the testing group.

Testing Libraries and APIs Individually

The first level of testing generally works with libraries and APIs individually. The testing process for microservices is similar to APIs, except you don't need a complex test harness because microservices are decidedly simpler than APIs. The following sections describe strategies you can use when unit testing both libraries and APIs (and, by extension, microservices). It's important to note that you can test APIs and microservices either directly or as part of an API virtualization layer.

Creating a Test Harness for Libraries

A test harness is a set of instructions within the application code or as part of a special addition to the code that performs various tests. Because libraries exist as part of the application, the instructions for testing the library also appear as part of the application.

Test instructions normally appear in debug code as some sort of `assert()` function, or by making use of logging or screen outputs. JavaScript lacks an `assert()` function (there is talk of adding one). However, you can use the `error` object to create an assert-like function that provides the same sort of information. In using an `assert()` setup, you create assertions in the code that look something like this:

```
assert(typeof myArg === "string");
```

The `assert()` function would look something like this:

```
function assert(condition, message)
{
    if (!condition)
    {
        message = message || "Assertion failed";
        if (typeof Error !== "undefined")
```

```
        {
            throw new Error(message);
        }
        else
        {
            throw message;
        }
    }
}
```

In this case, when the value of an argument or some other code condition fails, the test ends with an error. You can choose to log the error or work with it in other ways, but you know the test failed. Testing the condition isn't a problem with any browser. However, you may find different browsers support the `error` object in different ways, so simply throwing the message (rather than re-throwing the `error` object) is a good fallback position.

The in-code element does perform tests, but you still need input for those tests. To obtain this part of the puzzle, you normally need to employ scripted manual testing, which is always error prone, or a third-party product to script the required inputs. The tests you run against the library will tell you precisely how well the library meets the requirements of your application.

Creating Testing Scripts for APIs

API support consists of making calls. It's possible to test an API without even using the application. All you need is a script that makes calls and checks responses. A number of third-party products perform this task or you can create a simple application to perform the testing manually. Using a script ensures you get the same testing results each time, so using a scripting product is usually the best choice. Any test you create should check for these conditions as a minimum:

Range
> Responds correctly within its range and provides a correct error response when values are either too high or low.

Type
> Verifies that the user supplies the right data type as input and provides a correct error response when the input is of the wrong type.

Size
> Validates the length of the data so that it's not possible for someone to send a script instead of the expected string.

Characters
> Tests for invalid characters within the input to ensure the user can't send control or other incorrect characters as part of the input.

After you start using the API from the application, you need to perform integration testing, which consists of providing inputs to the application and then requiring the application to make the required calls. Again, you can use a scripting product to make this task easier.

Extending Testing Strategies to Microservices

As with APIs, you want to use some type of scripting product to make calls and check responses when working with a microservice. However, you need to ensure that the microservice is checked thoroughly because each one represents a separate piece of code. It's not possible to make assumptions about a microservice in the same way that you can with an API.

When you do perform integration testing, you need to determine the performance profile of the application. Every microservice should receive at least one test. However, microservices you plan to use more often should receive more testing. The purpose of this strategy is to verify code that has a higher probability of causing problems and to keep testing costs lower.

Developing Response Strategies

The focus of all testing is on the response provided by the library, API, or microservice to a given input. Unless the code reacts in the proper manner, the application won't work as originally envisioned. More importantly, hackers look for discrepancies in behavior to exploit. When defining responses, you must consider two response types: direct and mocked. The following sections discuss each response type.

Relying on direct results

A direct response comes from the active library, API, or microservice. In this case, you obtain an actual response to the input provided. If the code under test is working correctly, the response you receive should precisely match the specifications defining the test cases. The direct results actually test the code you plan to use with your application.

Relying on mocked results

Mocked results come from mocking software that simulates the library, API, or microservice. Using mocked results lets you start working on the application and testing it before the library, API, or microservice code is ready to use. Using this approach saves time and allows development to progress much faster.

However, there is another consideration. You can use mocking to test the viability of your testing harness for a library or testing scripts for an API. Because you already know that the mocking software will provide a precise response for a given input, you can validate that the testing software is working as anticipated. It doesn't pay to perform a test unless you can count on the testing software to perform the task correctly.

Performing Integration Testing

Once you have tested the individual elements of an application for issues, you begin integrating the actual libraries, APIs, and microservices into the application. The easiest, most complete, and least complex method of integration testing is to use a phased approach where libraries, APIs, and microservices are added to the application in small groups in an orderly manner. The use of phased integration testing helps you locate and fix problems quickly. Transitioning an application from mocked data to real data one piece at a time may seem time consuming at first, but the process does make it possible to locate errors quickly, ultimately saving a lot of time. The goal of integration testing is to create a completed application that works as anticipated and doesn't contain any security holes.

 It's never possible to create a bulletproof application. Every application will contain flaws and potential security holes. Testing does eliminate the most obvious issues and you need to test (and retest) every change made to any part of the application because security holes appear in the oddest places. However, never become complacent in thinking that you've found every possible problem in the application—a hacker will almost certainly come along and show you differently.

Developers have come to rely on a number of integration testing models. Some of these models are designed to get the application up and running as quickly as possible, but really only accomplish their task when nothing goes wrong. Anyone who writes software knows that something always goes wrong, so the big bang model of integration testing will only cause problems and not allow you to check for security concerns completely. With this in mind, here are three testing models that use a phased approach and allow a better chance of locating security issues:

Bottom up
> In this case, the development team adds and tests the lower-level features first. The advantage of this approach is that you can verify that you have a firm basis for applications that perform tasks such as monitoring. The raw source data becomes available earlier in the testing process, which makes the entire testing process more realistic.

Top down
> Using top down means testing all of the high-level features first, checking first-level branches next, and working your way down to the lowest-level features. The

advantage of this approach is that you can verify user interface features work as intended and that the application will meet user needs from the outset. This sort of testing works best with presentation applications, where user interactivity has a high precedence.

Sandwich

This is a combination of both bottom up and top down. It works best with applications that require some use of data sources to perform most tasks, but user interactivity is also of prime consideration. For example, you might use this approach with a CRM application to ensure the user interface presents data from a database correctly before moving on to other features.

Testing for Language-Specific Issues

A huge hole in some testing suites is the lack of tests for language-specific issues. These tests actually look for flaws in the way in which a language handles specific requests. The language may work precisely as designed, but a combination of factors works together to produce an incorrect or unexpected result. In some cases, the attack that occurs based on language deficiencies actually uses the language in a manner not originally anticipated by the language designers.

Every language has deficiencies. For example, with many languages, the issue of thread safety comes into place. When used without multithreading, the language works without error. However, when used with multithreading and only in some circumstances, the language suddenly falls short. It may produce an incorrect result or simply act in an unexpected manner. Far more insidious are deficiencies where the language apparently works correctly, but manages to provide hackers with information needed to infiltrate the system (such as transferring data between threads).

The following sections describe the most common language-specific issues that you need to consider testing for your application. In this case, you find deficiencies for HTML5, CSS3, and JavaScript—languages commonly used for web applications. However, if you use other languages for your application, then you need to check for deficiencies in those languages as well.

 Many testing suites check for correct outputs given a specific input. In addition, they might perform range checks to ensure the application behaves correctly within the range of values it should accept and provides proper error feedback when values are out of range. The reason that most test suites don't check for language deficiencies is that this issue is more security-related than just about anything else you test. When testing for language-specific issues, what you really look for is the effect of deficiencies on the security of your application.

Devising Tests for HTML Issues

When working with HTML, you need to consider that the language provides the basic user interface and that it also provides the avenue where many user-specific security issues will take place. With this in mind, you need to ensure that the HTML used to present information your application manages is tested to ensure it will work with a wide variety of browsers. With this in mind, here are some language-specific issues to consider:

- The HTML is well formed and doesn't rely on tags or attributes that aren't supported by most browsers.
- The document is encoded correctly.
- Any code within the document performs required error handling and checks for correct input.
- The document output looks as expected when provided with specific inputs.
- Selection of user interface elements reduces the potential for confusion and errant input.

 There are many tools available for HTML testing. Two of the better products are Rational Functional Tester (*http://www-03.ibm.com/ software/products/functional*) and Selenium (*http://www.sele niumhq.org/*). Both products automate HTML testing and both provide the record/playback method of script creation for performing tests. Rational Functional Tester, a product from IBM, also features specialized testing strategies, such as storyboarding. If you need to perform a manual check of a new technique, try the W3C Markup Validation Service at *https://validator.w3.org/dev/tests/*. The site provides HTML-version-specific tests you can use.

Part of HTML testing is to ensure all your links work as intended and that your HTML is well formed. Products such as WebLight (*http://www.illumit.com/weblight/*) automate the task of checking your links. A similar product is LinkTiger (*http://linktiger.com/*). The two products both check for broken links, but each provides additional capabilities that you may need in your testing, so it's a good idea to view the specifications for both.

Devising Tests for CSS Issues

The original intent for CSS was to create a means for formatting content that didn't involve the use of tables and other tricks. The problem with these tricks is that no one used a standard approach, and the tricks tended to make the page unusable for people with special needs. However, CSS has moved on from simple formatting. People have found ways to create special effects with CSS. In addition, CSS now almost provides a certain level of coding functionality. As a result, it has become important to test CSS just as fully as you do any other part of the application. CSS has the potential for hiding security issues from view. With this in mind, you need to perform CSS-specific tests as part of the security testing for your application—it should meet the following criteria:

- The CSS is well formed.

- There aren't any nonstandard elements in the code.

- Special effects don't cause accessibility problems.

- The choice of colors, fonts, and other visual elements reflect best practice for people with special needs.

- It's possible to use an alternative CSS format when the user has special needs to address.

- Given an event or particular user input, the CSS provides a consistent and repeatable output effect.

 As the uses for CSS increase, so does the need for good testing tools. If you're a Node.js user, one of the better testing tools you can get is CSS Lint (*http://csslint.net/*). You use CSS Lint for checking code. When you want to check appearance, you need another product that does screenshot comparisons, such as PhantomCSS (*https://github.com/Huddle/PhantomCSS*). When the screenshot of your site changes in an unpredictable manner, PhantomCSS can help you identify the change and ferret out the cause. If you need a manual validator for checking a technique you want to use, rely on the W3C CSS Validation Service at *https://jigsaw.w3.org/css-validator/*.

Devising Tests for JavaScript Issues

JavaScript will provide most of the functional code for your application. With this in mind, you test JavaScript code using the same approach as you would other programming languages. You need to verify that for a given input, you get a specific output. Here are some issues you need to consider as part of your testing suite:

- Ensure the code follows the standards.

- Test the code using a full range of input types to ensure it can handle errant input without crashing.

- Perform asynchronous testing to ensure that your application can handle responses that arrive after a nondeterministic interval.

- Create test groups so that you can validate a number of assertions using the sample assertion code found in "Creating a Test Harness for Libraries" on page 240 (or an `assert()` provided as part of a test library). Test groups magnify the effect of using assertions for testing.

- Verify that the code is responsive.

- Check application behavior to ensure that a sequence of steps produces a desired result.

- Simulate failure conditions (such as the loss of a resource) to ensure the application degrades gracefully.

- Perform any testing required to ensure the code isn't susceptible to recent hacks that may not be fixed on the client system. Using a security-specific analyzer, such as VeraCode (*http://www.veracode.com/*), can help you locate and fix bugs that might provide entry to hackers based on recently found security issues.

The tool you use for testing JavaScript depends, in part, on the tools used for other sorts of testing the organization and the organization's experience with other tools. In addition, you need to choose a tool that works well with other products you use with your application. Some organizations rely on QUnit (*https://qunitjs.com/*) for testing JavaScript because of the other suites (such as JQuery and JQuery UI) that the vendor produces. In some cases, an organization will use RhinoUnit (*https://code.google.com/p/rhinounit/*) to obtain Ant-based JavaScript Framework testing. Many professional developers like Jasmine (*http://jasmine.github.io/*) coupled with Jasmine-species (*http://rudylat tae.github.io/jasmine-species/*) because the test suite works with behaviors quite well. If you're working a lot with Node.js, you might also like to investigate the pairing of Vows.js (*http://vowsjs.org/*) and kyuri (*https://github.com/nodejitsu/kyuri*). Another Node.js developer favorite is Cucumis (*https://github.com/noblesa murai/cucumis*), which provides asynchronous testing functionality.

One of the issues you need to research as part of your specification and design stages is the availability of existing test suites. For example, the ECMAScript Language test262 site (*http://test262.ecmascript.org/*) can provide you with some great insights into your application.

Considering the Essence of an Attack

It's important to understand that many attacks don't actually look like they accomplish anything because you don't know what the attacker is trying to do. For example, an attack on the Transport Layer Security (TLS) protocol, which relies on Rivest Cipher 4 (RC4) encryption, may look more like someone is trying to turn the system into a zombie. If you're a developer who is trying to figure out what is going on with the application, you almost have to know the kind of attack taking place, which is why you want to ensure you have a security professional on your team.

In this case, one attack depends on generating a request with a repeated piece of information, such as a cookie. The sender will include this cookie with every request, but every request is encrypted such that the information looks different. Only after obtaining enough samples is it possible to break the encryption and start obtaining data from the compromised browser.

At least two groups have broken RC4 enough to obtain data from a browser using TLS. The first technique requires somewhere in the neighborhood of 2,000 hours, while the second requires a mere 75 hours. Obviously, unless the information obtained has significant value, the technique probably isn't worth the average hacker's time to employ. Even so, the fact that the techniques exist at all means you need to think about what an attack is attempting to accomplish.

The most interesting part of this attack is that the attackers rely on JavaScript to implement it (impressive for a language that developers once regarded as useful only for scripting). The attackers upload the code to the target browser using script injection or a man-in-the-middle attack. You can read more about this particular attack at *http://www.computerworld.com/article/2948937/security/encrypted-web-and-wi-fi-at-risk-as-rc4-attacks-become-more-practical.html*.

The fix for this sort of attack is to use a more modern cipher as part of the TLS protocol. TLS supports a number of ciphers including Advanced Encryption Standard (AES). To keep your application reasonably safe, you need to ensure that the server is configured not to accept RC4 as a cipher, but to request a more modern cipher instead.

CHAPTER 12

Using Third-Party Testing

Third-party testing involves hiring an external entity to perform tests of various sorts on your application, including security tests. The third party can offer a range of services—some are quite comprehensive. Of course, you need to know that you can trust the third party before you even begin any sort of testing. Once testing has started, you need to ensure the third party receives proper input from your organization, has the correct level of monitoring, and provides a desirable level of output. The third party might perform tests similar to those that you'd employ, but you need to know that the skill level of the third party is higher than that provided by your own organization or there is less of a reason to hire the third party in the first place.

There are many reasons you might want to rely, at least partially, on third-party testing. The most common reason for hiring a third party is time. However, many organizations lack the skills and other resources to perform a complete testing job properly. Organizations sometimes hire a third party to keep in-house testers honest and to ensure the in-house testers haven't missed anything. Working with third-party vendors commonly follows the four steps described in this chapter:

1. Locate the third-party testing service you want to use.

2. Create a test plan (using the third party as a resource) that defines precisely how the third party is to test the software.

3. Implement the test plan after the third party has had a chance to sign off on it.

4. Validate the application based on the reports and other outputs you receive from the third party.

Although this book has spent considerable time working with desktop, browser, and mobile applications, it's important to remember that the principles described apply to other sorts of applications too—some of which almost always require third-party testing. For example, automobile manufacturers could have probably avoided the recent recall of many connected automobiles by employing third parties to ensure the testing process completely tested all aspects of connectivity (see *http://www.computer world.com/article/2953832/mobile-security/senators-call-for-investigation-of-potential-safety-security-threats-from-connected-cars.html*). The fact is that hackers know how to break into these vehicles and so do many third-party testers (see *http://www.comput erworld.com/article/2954668/telematics/hacker-shows-he-can-locate-unlock-and-remote-start-gm-vehicles.html*).

Third-party testers can also check for exotic sounding types of hacks that may become all too common in the future (see *http:// www.computerworld.com/article/2954582/security/researchers-develop-astonishing-webbased-attack-on-a-computers-dram.html*). Although techniques such as rowhammering sound quite far-fetched today, you can bet that hackers will employ them tomorrow and that it will take a skilled third-party tester to ensure your setup isn't vulnerable to this sort of attack.

Locating Third-Party Testing Services

You can't go to "T" in the phone book and find a listing for testers. It would be nice if you could simply look up an interested third party in the yellow pages and know that they'd do a great job of testing your application. Unfortunately, finding a third-party tester requires a bit more research on your part and you want to make sure you verify that the third party can do the job you're asking them to do. The following sections help you understand some of the issues surrounding the search for a third-party tester and describe how to ensure the third-party tester really has your best interests in mind.

Defining the Reasons for Hiring the Third Party

There are many reasons you might have for hiring a third party to perform application testing for you. The reasons vary by organization, application type, and the problem domain the application solves. Before you hire a third party to perform testing, it's important to know why you're hiring the third party. If you don't have this piece of essential information, the testing effort is doomed from the start because you have unstated and potentially unrealistic expectations of the testing process. In short, you can't know that the testing is a success because you have no idea of what you expected in the first place. With this in mind, the most common reasons for hiring a third party are:

Quality

Using someone who specializes in testing can improve the quality of your software because an organization devoted to testing will know all the latest techniques for performing tests in your particular problem domain. These testers also perform testing tasks every day, so they know about potential bugs and issues that commonly occur with software that uses a particular programming language, operating system, platform, and addresses specific user needs. It's also quite possible that the quality of the reports you receive from the testing process will be better than anything produced by your own organization because testers fill out this type of report every day.

Cost

A professional tester can perform the testing tasks faster and with greater accuracy than someone who performs the task on a part-time basis. The tester can also avoid tests that won't provide anything with your particular application—a problem that occurs regularly within organizations (wasting both time and money). In addition, it's possible to outsource the testing to a location in the world where the actual costs of hiring someone to perform this task is much lower than in your location.

Training

A hidden cost that many organizations don't consider is the time and expense of training a team to perform the testing tasks. Even if team members perform the task part time, they won't have the experience that professional testers do and may need additional training for each new kind of application tested. The only time that it pays to have an actual testing team is if your organization writes enough software to keep the team engaged in testing full time.

Time

Setting up a testing lab, training the testers, and waiting for the testers to become proficient in performing the required work takes time that many organizations simply don't have. In order to get a product to market on time, it becomes necessary to test during the writing process, using techniques that are as efficient as possible, on systems that match the production system as closely as possible, and with reports back to developers that help locate and fix problems as quickly as possible.

Expertise

Your organization may have recently made an update in platform, equipment, or other resources that require another cycle of testing. The application or related services haven't changed, but the environment in which they operate has. If you find that the newness of the setup causes problems for your existing testing team, it may be time to get third-party help in discovering what these changes mean to the software and to get new checks established. The third party can also provide much needed training.

Considering the Range of Possible Testing Services

The essential benefit of using a third-party tester is ensuring that you get full value out of the services provided. However, the best testing service in the world can't possibly know everything about every possible sort of testing. You need to define precisely what sort of testing you want done and then use these specifics when choosing a testing company. As a first step, you need to define the environment:

- Platform
- Operating system
- Programming language
- Problem domain
- Organization type
- User type

Not every testing company performs every sort of testing available. Once you get past the environmental factors, you need to consider the sorts of testing you need done. To get the best results, it's important that the third-party tester provide facilities for performing all the tests you need. Here are the most common types:

- Security
- Functional
- Automation
- Performance
- Integration

 There are many kinds of testing on all sorts of levels. You can find longer lists of test types at *http://www.softwaretestinghelp.com/ types-of-software-testing/*, *http://www.aptest.com/testtypes.html*, and *http://www.testingexcellence.com/types-of-software-testing- complete-list/*. However, even these lists are incomplete. Remember that you also need to consider both static and dynamic testing techniques when you own the software and the third-party tester could be involved at both levels.

Some testing companies offer just one thing—testing. However, you may decide that you need other services in order to succeed in your application development task. A full service company typically charges a lot more than one that offers just testing. The number of services doesn't always affect the bottom line, but it can and you need to choose just those services you actually need. Here are some common add-on services:

Developer coaching

In some cases, the testing problem may turn up issues that your developers simply haven't encountered. The use of developer coaching helps your team locate and fix problems faster. In addition, it provides a level of training that is specific to your application, which means that the information learned is organization-specific and focused (increasing its value).

Program management

You may need some help managing the testing effort. Just as your development team may lack testing experience, the management team may lack experience in managing certain aspects of the product lifecycle. Some testing companies can help your organization overcome this problem.

eLearning

An organization as a whole may require some additional training to make the application work better. For example, many users are unaware of the issues surrounding security, so they make mistakes that could cause a security breach. The use of eLearning modules helps people discover the skills needed to use the application successfully during times when the user actually has the motivation and availability to complete the training.

It's also important to consider the specifics of the security testing for your application. The third-party tester may offer some types of security testing, but not others. In addition, you need to know what the third party should provide as part of the service. Here are some things to consider:

Environment

You need to define whether the testing is against staging or production environments. Staging environment testing works best during the early development stage of the application. Production environment testing works best during the final development stages and when the application is first released to the production environment.

Testing level

Some testers perform a basic suite of tests to ensure that the security risks for your application remain low. However, this basic testing might not tell you enough to fix the problems your application contains. You may want the test to provide full proof of concept exploits, with sample code, so you can see precisely how the hacks work in order to provide a better fix. (The third party can some-times help perform triage on your application as well.)

Resource usage

Testing uses resources on your system. In order to prevent loss of application functionality or availability during testing, you need to specify resource usage rules. The third-party tester can configure testing tools to remain within what-ever guidelines you set. In addition, make sure you specify resource usage as a function of day and time. For example, you may want the third-party tester to focus testing on evenings or weekends when the system under test receives less use and you can relax some of the resource usage rules.

Testing stop conditions

You don't want security testing to result in a data breach or other security issue. In some cases, security testing could actually result in a security issue. Defining stop conditions helps prevent the testing scenario from turning into a situation where you actually need to perform data recovery or make a public statement about a data breach.

Ensuring the Third Party Is Legitimate

Anyone can come to you saying that their company provides superior testing services in a timely manner and at the lowest possible cost. It doesn't mean that they actually deliver on their promises. What it could mean is that they have a great marketing staff that can write above-average material, but that none of the write-up will ever come to fruition. A bad third-party tester could cost you everything by allowing a competitor to deliver product first, causing a data breach that drives customers away, or makes it impossible for people in your organization to perform their jobs. Conse-quently, ensuring the vendor can actually deliver on promises made is an essential part of finding a vendor.

Security testing is one of those areas where you really don't want to take any chances, so ensure the third party you hire has all of the required certifications. The American Software Testing Qualifications Board (ASTQB) (*http://www.astqb.org/*) is a good place to start looking for the certifications the third party requires. Another place to look is the International Software Certifications Board (*http://www.softwarecertifica tions.org*). No matter which group you choose to support, make sure the company you hire has testers with the appropriate certifications. In addition, get guarantees in writing that only the certified testers will work on your project (or else the company might substitute substandard help that is marginally supervised by those who possess the certifications).

It also pays to look at vendor stability. An annual report can tell you a lot about the health of an organization, which in turn tells you whether the organization is success-ful in completing tasks. Successful organizations tend to do a better job of testing and you want the best for your application. You should also dig into organization statistics such as the amount of turnover (which indicates employee happiness) and determine whether the organization has ever had bad press attached to its name.

Reviews from previous customers can help. However, it's essential to remember that reviews are simply opinions and customers are extremely biased at times. In addition, an organization can seed positive reviews to make it appear that it provides better service than it really does. Check out the reviews and ensure that the customer actually had work done by the company when possible. Contact the customer to see what sort of testing it had done (again, if possible).

Interviewing the Third Party

At this point, you know precisely why you want third-party help, that you have found a company that provides the services you need, and that the company is legitimate. It's time to have a discussion with the people in the company and determine whether you can create a working relationship with them. This isn't like an interview for hiring someone for your organization—you're hiring an entire company to perform testing on your application in order to ensure that the application is secure. This means getting all the stakeholders in your company involved with the interview and determining the best candidate for the job. The stakeholders include management, of course, but they also include developers, trainers, users, and anyone else who is affected by the application. The question you need to answer is whether the company you're hiring really can do the required levels of testing to obtain a usable application. If you need other services, then you also need to interview the company about the support you can expect (which is where the users could excel if the company is providing training support).

Performing Tests on a Test Setup

Before you sign on the dotted line, make sure you know that the company you're hiring can do the work. Have the company provide some sort of limited demonstration that walks through a generalized testing process if at all possible. You should be able to see a walkthrough or some other evidence that the company can actually do the work. Otherwise, it's really hard to know what you're getting until it's too late to back out of the deal. Some demonstration of proficiency is always a good idea, even if it's a dry run-through of the process the company plans to employ.

Creating a Testing Plan

It isn't possible to test any piece of software without some sort of testing plan. You discovered this requirement in previous chapters. However, creating just a general plan won't quite do it when working with a third party. You need to create a plan that spells out what you expect of the third-party tester. The document needs to split up the work between your organization and the tester. In addition, the plan must consider what constitutes a successful test under these conditions. You don't have to worry about the pass/fail state of the application alone, but whether the collaboration between your organization and the third-party tester met specific goals needed to ensure the application is reasonably secure. The following sections describe how to create a testing plan.

Specifying the Third-Party Goals in Testing

Chapter 9 discusses the need for goals in application testing. Chapter 11 further emphasizes the need for goals and describes them in some detail. However, these are goals for your application as a whole and your organization as a whole. A third-party tester is a partner in the testing process, which means that it only works through a part of the process. The goals of a third-party tester are similar to your goals in that the testing must still reflect specific principles; however, the goals now also include the need to communicate all testing criteria and methodologies clearly. In addition, you must provide goals that include the concepts of your organization's management strategy. Consequently, the goals described in Chapter 9 and Chapter 11 are a good starting point, but you must now augment them to ensure the third party knows precisely what is required and how to respond to requests for reporting information.

Generating a Written Test Plan

You always need to create a written test plan. However, when working with a third-party tester, you must go over the written test plan to ensure the third-party testing roles are clear and that the third party completely understands all the testing requirements. Where questions exist, the third-party tester should be able to provide input that helps clarify the testing requirements. In fact, this input is invaluable as training for future test plans. A third-party tester should be able to help you create a test plan that fully adheres to industry best practices and helps you obtain the precise results you want from the testing process.

As part of the testing plan, you need to list the tests to conduct using the third-party tester's list of services as input. In other words, the test plan should clearly state which of the third-party tester services are part of the testing process so that no ambiguity exists once testing starts. Make sure you understand precisely which tests are run and why these tests are necessary to ensure the application works as anticipated. A third-party tester must articulate the need for the tests and other services clearly. Otherwise, the testing process could fail due to a lack of communication.

It's important to build a trust relationship with the third-party tester during this initial process. Of course, trust begins with the knowledge that the third-party tester really does know how to perform application testing in your problem domain. Verifying that the third-party tester is legitimate is a good starting point, but make sure your experts are already on hand to oversee tasks that specify how the testing process should proceed. Getting third-party tester input is only useful when you know the third-party tester is really on your side (and not trying to scam you in some way).

Enumerating the Test Output and Reporting Requirements

The test plan must contain a section that describes the expected outputs precisely. In addition, the test plan must detail what to do when tests fail so that the response is organized and well considered before the testing process begins. The third-party tester can usually help provide additional information about expected outputs and potentially additional individual test types so that you can verify that your application truly is secure against the latest threats. It's unlikely that your own staff will know about every potential threat, so part of the third-party tester's job is to ensure you test for security issues that you don't know about in addition to those you do know about. The test plan should include detailed outputs for every test.

When a test cycle is complete or some other event occurs, the test plan should specify some type of written report. The report need not appear on paper, but simply in a permanent form that everyone can review and study as needed. The reports are usually tied to tests or other significant events and the test plan should detail precisely which tests generate specific reports.

Make sure you obtain copies of sample reports from the third-party tester. Ensure you understand the content of these reports. In many cases, the third-party tester can make changes to the report so that it works better with your organization's style of testing. In addition, you may need reports in a specific format to meet regulatory or legal requirements, so make sure the third-party tester is aware of these requirements and can provide the reports in the form needed.

Considering Test Requirements

Tests are more than simple inputs and outputs conducted in a specific environment. As part of your test plan, you must consider how the testing company performs the tests. It can become a sticking point in some situations. For example, you may have only the United States in mind for a market. If your testing company is in Hong Kong, they're used to speaking UK English. The differences are small, but enough to make testing less useful in some situations. Consider parsing words that vary slightly between the two English forms, such as *color* and *colour*. Your code may not parse *colour* correctly. The reverse also holds true. A testing company needs to support all the languages you intend to support.

Considering how you test an application is important from all sorts of angles. For example, if your application is designed to meet specific healthcare requirements and the testing company doesn't place enough emphasis on accessibility testing, the application may provide everything but the essential of making access easy. It doesn't matter if the application is secure when the user can't interact with it in the first place.

Creating this portion of the testing plan is especially difficult because you have already trained any testing staff in your organization to look for the special requirements of your application. It's easy to make assumptions about how the testing company will view testing based on what you already do. The key issue is to assume nothing when it comes to testing—write everything down.

Implementing a Testing Plan

Once you have a testing plan in place, you need to consider just how to implement it. Having goals is a good start, but providing a process to achieve those goals is necessary for successful completion of the testing. When implementing a test plan, you must consider the need to perform monitoring. This isn't a matter of snooping, but one of directing—to help the third party achieve the testing in the way you expect, you must provide the required direction. The act of implementing the plan could also cause unexpected issues to surface. You need some procedure in place for handling these issues or the testing could slow to a standstill. The following sections describe the techniques needed to implement a testing plan.

Determining Organizational Participation in Testing

It's important to involve your organization in the testing process. Otherwise, you can't be sure the testing company is performing the task correctly. However, monitoring the testing process differs substantially from hands-on participation. You may even choose to divide the testing process into functional areas—those that your organization already has the expertise to perform and those that the testing company specializes in. The testing plan should spell out precisely what level of participation each entity provides.

Implementing the test plan often shows that the best plans on paper still lack real-world usefulness. You may find that the test plan doesn't include every area of participation (leaving areas to split after the fact) or that it fails to consider the logistics of performing the tests in the manner specified. The test plan may not define the required level of communication adequately or you might find that the communication process is chatty, which wastes time. Performing a dry run of the testing process usually tells you about these issues before they become a problem.

Beginning the Testing Process

After all the planning and dry runs, it's time to start the testing process. You may try to psyche yourself into believing the first day will go well, but you'll be disappointed. It's smarter to assume that some problems will occur during the testing process and that you need to deal with them up front. What this means to the developer is communicating issues such as missing source code files to the testing organization as quickly as possible. You may also find that the testing company can't access online resources, such as libraries, APIs, and microservices, required to run the application. The best idea is to set the first few days of testing aside to work out kinks in the system so that a general rush to get going doesn't compound the issues you confront during startup.

Depending on your application configuration, purpose, and resources, you should also plan to address a number of security issues. The testing company may not have access to paid online resources or you might have to provide additional rights to resources that your organization owns. Make sure you have all the people necessary to make the application work available during the first few days of testing as a minimum. For example, if your application requires database access, ensure that a DBA is available to help create the required access levels. Coordinating the effort is a good job for DevOps, assuming your organization has someone assigned to this task. Don't forget to include management staff as needed.

 Never give the testing company carte blanche to your organization's resources. The testing company should have access to the minimum number of resources required to make the application run. In addition, you should provide the minimum number of rights to those resources. If the testers don't require administrator access, then you should limit that access to some appropriate user level instead. The main reason to limit access is to protect your resources. However, even assuming that the testing company is completely trustworthy, it's important that the testers check the application using the same rights that everyone else will have (an especially important factor during security testing).

Performing Required Test Monitoring

Monitoring the testing company is an essential part of ensuring the tests go as planned. You need to ensure that the testing company performs all required tests (and doesn't simply sign off on them), yet doesn't perform any unauthorized (and potentially chargeable) testing. It also pays to monitor resources during testing. For example, the DBA should ensure that the testing process doesn't damage any database data, even if that data is used specifically for testing purposes. Some application failures aren't immediately apparent unless you perform the required monitoring.

Handling Unexpected Testing Issues

Testing is an antagonistic process. After all, you're trying to force an application to fail. Any antagonistic process is going to produce unexpected results at times. You can spend as much time as you like stating that a given input should provide a given output, but the emphasis of that statement is on the word *should*. The reason you perform testing is to find those times when the results are different than you expected.

Of course, the testers handle most of these unexpected results using whatever system you have in place for reporting bugs. However, some unexpected results come from external sources, such as miscommunication between test team elements. In this case, reporting the issue as a bug won't help because the problem isn't within the application—it's the result of some external source acting on the application or its testing process. To handle this sort of testing issue, you need a process in place that works outside the bug reporting system.

A common way of addressing these sorts of issues is to hold an impromptu meeting. The problem is that meetings can become unfocused, are hard to schedule, and may not produce any usable results because stakeholders need time to research issues. Some organizations rely on private forums or wikis to address these sorts of issues. In fact, products exist for handling this issue in all sorts of ways. You can see a list of 25 common developer collaboration tools at *https://blog.profitbricks.com/top-25-collaboration-tools-for-developers/*.

Using the Resulting Reports

The third-party tester could simply tell you that your software is absolutely amazing and works with flawless integrity rarely seen in the development community. However, a verbal report doesn't provide you with any means of performing analysis later or of creating a plan to fix the problems found by the third-party tester. You need reports of various kinds to present the facts to various members of the organization. Many of these members won't have any programming skills whatsoever, so you need reports that break things down simply and other reports to provide detailed analysis you can use to create fixes. The following sections describe the use of reports as a means of using the third-party testing results in an efficient manner.

Discussing the Report Output with the Third Party

The reports that describe application performance during testing can vary and the parties involved vary as well. For example, most applications today rely on third-party libraries, APIs, and microservices. You may choose to report issues with these third-party elements to the vendor that created them as a means of making your application work better. Of course, you don't want to share the entire report, including the reports on your personal code, with these third-party vendors. A third-party tester can address the need to contact other third parties about their code, but you need to have some policy in place for managing this issue. If you have the third-party tester perform the work, the third-party stakeholder can simply upload new versions of their code to the tester—greatly simplifying your role in the task. (You still need to know about any changes to third-party code because these changes could affect other applications.)

Reports that the tester generates need to address the various audiences in your organization. A management team may only want to see an overview that provides status information and the big numbers. Users may only want to know about issues that affect usability and the sort of interface the application presents. Developers want detailed reports that specify precise error locations and potential fixes for them. A DBA may only want to know the specifics of issues that affect the database. In short, reports come in various forms to address the needs of specific audiences.

Presenting the Report to the Organization

The application testing process generates the vast majority of the reports you need automatically, as part of running the test. A routing mechanism can ensure everyone who needs a report gets one through some method, such as email. However, getting a report to a stakeholder isn't quite the same as getting the stakeholder to read it. Of course, the question is why anyone should care about this issue given that the stakeholder should take responsibility for reading the material. The problem is that stakeholders tend to ignore information until they really do need it, which is usually too late when it comes to application development. Stakeholders need to remain engaged in order to ensure that the application performs as expected when testing completes.

Depending on the development model you use, you may need to present reports to the organization as often as weekly. Some models actually call for a Monday meeting. Each Monday you present a report of the project process, any issues, and then follow it with a demonstration. Stakeholders who can see progress each week tend to become more involved in the project and provide better input, which means you get fewer questions about adding features at the end of the process when it isn't possible to add them any longer.

Using Monday as the presentation day also gives the development, testing, and other teams time to react to suggestions or needs for application development. Instead of trying to rush a fix on Sunday, the various teams have the whole week in order to produce an updated application version that will amaze the stakeholders on Monday. As a result, the various teams actually get some rest and are able to do a better job.

A worst-case day for presenting reports to the organization is Friday. To begin with, no one is paying attention anyway because they're already thinking about weekend plans. Even if they do pay attention, they're tired after a week of work and less likely to provide the creative input you really need to design an appealing application that performs useful work. The various teams will also feel obliged to work the weekend in order to start on fixes while the need for the fixes is fresh in their minds. If you want to get practical input on your application, avoid making your reports on a Friday.

Acting on Testing Recommendations

The result of testing, reports, discussion, and so on is that the various teams need to fix problems found by the various testers. Some problems are more important than others are and are most likely to cause problems after application deployment, so you work on these issues first. Part of the testing team and stakeholder interaction is to assign values to each problem that defines the importance of that problem. For example, you wouldn't want to fix a low-priority fit and finish issue before you fix that showstopper issue that causes the application to crash on nearly everyone's machine.

However, just fixing the problem doesn't get the job done. In some cases, a problem has more than one answer and you might choose to create versions of the application that implement each answer to determine which one is best. The various stakeholders need to review the potential fixes and decide which one works best for them (which may not be the same fix in all cases). Creating and exercising all the potential useful fixes for a problem is part of acting on testing recommendations.

It's also important to have the fix tested by the testers. However, you might decide not to have the fix tested immediately. Perhaps an interaction makes it hard or impossible to test the fix without repairing other problems in the application first. It's essential to look at the dependencies of a particular issue and be sure to address the dependencies as well as the original problem.

PART IV

Implementing a Maintenance Cycle

Software can and does break. If nothing else, it gets old or stops interacting with newer hardware. In some cases, users outgrow the software or find that it no longer meets their needs. The new, exciting, and brightly polished piece of code you deliver today will soon turn rusty and decay into a has-been of yesterday's code—a museum piece that people will gawk at if it becomes famous enough. It's hard to hear that your code will eventually end up on the trash heap after spending so much time and sweat putting it together. Of course, you can avoid this destiny entirely by simply maintaining your code, which is the point of this part of the book. If you truly want your application to provide service for as long as possible, you must have a plan in place for keeping it viable from the outset.

This part of the book breaks the task of maintaining software into three distinct parts: determining when to update the software (Chapter 13), deciding how to perform the update (Chapter 14), and using reports to monitor the update requirement (Chapter 15). By following this three-part process, you can keep your application bright and shiny so that people will continue to admire and use it successfully.

Clearly Defining Upgrade Cycles

Your application is constantly exposed to threats online, and so is every other piece of code that your application relies on. In order to reduce the risk incurred by known threats, you need to perform upgrades to your application regularly. These upgrades help improve your application in several ways, all of which affect security:

- Usability to reduce user mistakes
- Outright coding errors
- Speed enhancements that keep users from doing the unexpected
- Fixes to functional code that reduce the potential for breaches
- Fixes required to upgrade third-party libraries, APIs, and microservices

This chapter views the upgrade process from several levels. You can't just make fixes willy-nilly and not expect to incur problems from various sources, most especially angry users. Upgrades require a certain amount of planning, testing, and then implementation. The following sections discuss all three levels of upgrades and help you create a plan that makes sense for your own applications.

Developing a Detailed Upgrade Cycle Plan

Part of the process for introducing upgrades to your application is creating a plan for implementing the changes. The problem is that you often don't know about the upgrades needed for third-party software, don't understand the requirements for creating the upgrade, can't put the upgrades in any particular order, and then encounter problems with upgrade implementation plans. It's essential to create an orderly way to evaluate updates, which is why you want to create an upgrade cycle plan. Figure 13-1 shows a process you can follow in performing this task.

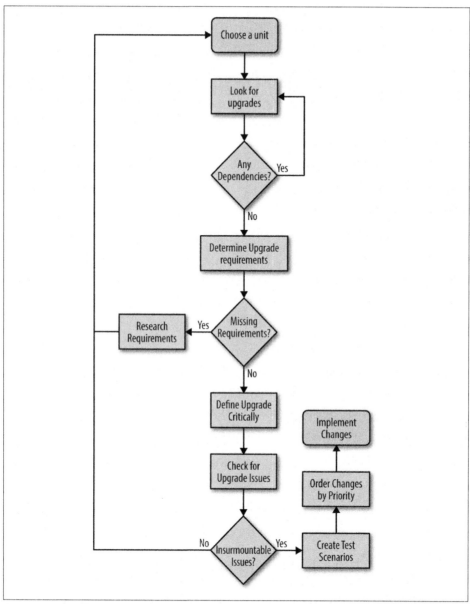

Figure 13-1. Following an orderly process when creating an upgrade cycle plan saves time and money

The idea is to work through one unit at a time and ensure that you test everything associated with that unit. Even if you test a particular dependency as part of another unit test, you must also test it with the unit under observation because the observed unit might use the dependency in a different way or affect it in a different manner.

Now that you have an idea of what sort of process you can follow, you need details on how to perform the task. The following sections discuss the issues surrounding an upgrade cycle plan. After reading this section, you should have a better idea of how to create a plan that specifically meets the needs of your application.

Looking for Upgrades

The trouble tickets collected by support as the result of user complaints and system outages usually tell you what you need to know about upgrades for your own application code. If the trouble tickets don't tell you everything needed, they at least provide enough information for you to perform the research required to discover precisely what upgrades you need to create. However, third-party application software is a different matter. Unless a developer or other interested party locates a fix for a problem as the result of debugging in-house code, an upgrade can remain invisible. It's important to look for upgrades to third-party software and ensure you have a complete listing of them. Otherwise, you can't maintain your application's security state and the unknown risk potential for a security breach increases. Many organizations end up blindsided by the upgrade it didn't realize it needed to make.

 Some third parties offer automatic update notifications. The use of automatic notifications is one way to ensure you know about them, but you can't depend on them. A notification tells you that an update is definitely available, but you must also be proactive in checking for the updates you didn't hear about. Even if a vendor is studious about providing notifications, the notifications can still get lost or end up in a junk folder.

Checking the vendor site can tell you about upgrades you need to incorporate into your application when working with public libraries, APIs, and microservices. In many cases, vendors offer beta versions of upgrades so that you can begin working with them early. It pays to spend time reviewing precisely what the upgrade affects so that you know how much importance to attach to it with regard to your application. An upgrade that doesn't affect any of the features your application uses is less important than an upgrade that affects all of the features your application uses. However, you should still incorporate the upgrade at some point, even if you're sure your application is unaffected because upgrades often have dependency interactions that even the vendor doesn't know about (or hasn't fully tested).

Trade press articles and vendor press releases can also tell you about upcoming upgrades. In addition, you can keep your eyes peeled for articles that talk about any deficiencies in the product you're using and the vendor plans for fixing them. All this information feeds into your upgrade plans. You get advance notice of what will likely happen so you can start thinking about it long before you have to do the work.

Don't downplay the effects of personal communication when it comes time to upgrade. A vendor insider can often let you know about an upgrade before anyone else knows about it. Knowing about an upgrade in advance gives you a competitive advantage because you can prepare for the upgrade sooner than anyone else does. Time is a critical resource in the computer industry, and the company that frequently releases upgrades as soon as they're needed is the company that keeps customers and attracts new ones. The ability to plan also reduces the stress on staff and makes it possible for everyone to create better upgrades (rushed upgrades can sometimes create more work than the problems they fix).

As you hear about needed upgrades (either for your own code or for code provided by a third party), you need to place the information about it on a list. Everyone in your development group should have access to the list and remain apprised of future upgrade requirements. Encourage your team to communicate about potential upgrades and the effect the upgrades will have on your application. Anything you can do to keep people thinking about upgrades and how to perform them will reduce the work you need to do later when time is critical.

Determining Upgrade Requirements

Knowing the specifics about an upgrade is a good first step. However, it isn't good enough to start doing anything concrete about the upgrade. You must determine the requirements for making the upgrade. In some cases, an upgrade can pose the same problems in logistics that creating a new application can. Predicting how long a complex upgrade will take and how many resources it requires can become nearly impossible. The following list provides you with some idea of what to consider as part of an upgrade requirement specification:

Determine the resource requirements
> Not all upgrades require additional resources—the surprising fact is that most do. Resources can include all sorts of things: memory, processing cycles, hard drive space, data sources, screen real estate, input types (such as sensors), network bandwidth, and so on. The list can become quite large and you need to consider it carefully because resource changes can have nasty side effects, such as the inability to run the application on a device that the user has relied upon in the past.

Obtain any required platform changes
> Keeping an eye out for deprecated features is always a good idea. Deprecated features cause all sorts of problems because sometimes they exclude older platforms from consideration. You need to consider precisely how a platform change will affect users. Perhaps an upgrade excludes an older, but popular, operating system that the user loves. Rather than hearing endless complaints about the platform

change, you need to learn about it and consider its effect on your organization, the application, and the users before starting the process of implementing it.

Consider the time required to create, test, and deploy the upgrade

The hardest upgrade requirement to consider is the time required to create, test, and deploy the upgrade. No matter how carefully you try to compute this requirement, it often falls short. Most people predict that they can accomplish the task in far less time than it will actually require. When determining this upgrade requirement, make sure you use realistic numbers and add time and resources for those unplanned emergencies that always occur in a software project.

There are many causes of issues when trying to calculate a time requirement. One of the issues that you don't see covered in books very often is the need to consider the human element. The humans on your team will have many tasks tugging at them as they work on the project. If they feel they can put your project off for a while to complete a more critical task, they'll definitely do so. This is the procrastination factor and you need to deal with it in some positive way as part of your planning process. Unless the members of your team feel there is a criticality about your project, the procrastination factor will step in every time to cause you problems. The project you could complete on time suddenly becomes the project that is late, due entirely to the human factor you didn't account for in your planning.

Create a list of personnel and skills required to create the upgrade

A common problem with upgrade projects is that the original planning didn't include a list of personnel and skills required to accomplish it. The tendency is to think that a small subset of people or perhaps just one person can accomplish the upgrade without any problem. Unfortunately, this isn't the case. An upgrade requires every bit of careful planning that a new project does. You need access to the same experts that the original project had in order to ensure the upgrade meets the same high standards.

Upgrades often forget to include users as part of the team. As a result, the upgrade breaks user interfaces and causes other problems that a user would see quite quickly, but a developer will miss completely. Make sure you include all the required personnel as part of your upgrade process to ensure you end up with an upgrade that actually works and remains secure.

Define the potential effect of the upgrade on data sources

Upgrades can affect data sources in all sorts of ways. For example, you may find that you need to add additional fields to databases or you need access to an entirely new data source. The data source might be an input from a sensor or some other nontraditional information that your application now requires in order to function properly. Think about all of the inputs that the application could require as you consider the ramifications of an upgrade.

Unlike applications of old, you can no longer simply consider your application as part of the requirements list or the needs of your organization as the operating environment. Your upgrade requirements list will need to consider the use of third-party libraries, APIs, and microservices as part of the picture. In addition, you now need to consider the environments in which those pieces of your application run as part of the overall requirements list.

It's also important not to forget your user in all this. When users relied on desktop systems, it was easy to create a controlled environment in which the user's needs were easy to consider. Today, a user might try to use your application on a smartphone in the local restaurant. The application could see use while the user is the passenger (and hopefully not the driver) in a car or when the user is taking alternative transportation, such as a local train or bus. The upgrade requirements need to consider all sorts of devices used in all sorts of environments.

Defining Upgrade Criticality

Upgrades affect applications in many ways and the risk of not providing an upgrade varies by application, platform, and need. The criticality of an upgrade is directly proportional to the risk not applying the upgrade presents. As an upgrade becomes more critical, its priority on your upgrade list increases. Part of the planning cycle involves the assignment of priorities to upgrades so that your organization applies the highest priority upgrades first. Otherwise, you can't be sure that the upgrade process will truly represent a reduction in risk to your organization. When working through priorities, consider these criteria:

Security risk

Security upgrades always have a high priority because someone has already proven they provide some method of damaging your system. However, not all security upgrades represent an immediate risk because no known hacker uses the vulnerability for an attack or the attack requires a special condition, such as physical machine access. When prioritizing by security upgrade need, consider the amount of risk that the security issue imposes on your application.

Damage potential

Upgrades that fix a problem that could result in some sort of application or data damage usually rank high on the list of upgrades. Depending on the risk that a problem poses, upgrades that fix problems can supersede security upgrades in many cases. In this case, you must ascertain the probability that such damage will occur and the result of that damage.

Error potential

Errors created by user input or other problems can pose a significant risk, but you can also overcome many of these errors with additional user training or by implementing new company policies. Even so, you must assign a priority based on the probability of the error occurring, the damage that the error could cause, and the ability of the organization to overcome, catch, and correct the error.

Natural events

Some upgrades address the potential for natural events to cause application errors. The presence of line noise can cause single bit errors in a data stream, so one solution is to include error-correcting code (ECC) routines to root out and fix the single bit errors. In most cases, with the emergence of technology that automatically fixes the most egregious of these errors, you can give these issues a lower priority. You must still create upgrades to fix them, but the security issues that will definitely cause problems have to come first.

It's essential to assign values to your priority list. These values make it easier to determine whether a change is critical (because it fixes a security hole) or is simply convenient (because it makes an interface change that a user requested that is more fit and finish than usability). Figure 13-2 shows the potential interplay between the various priority criteria when using a five-level priority system (your system may contain a different number of levels).

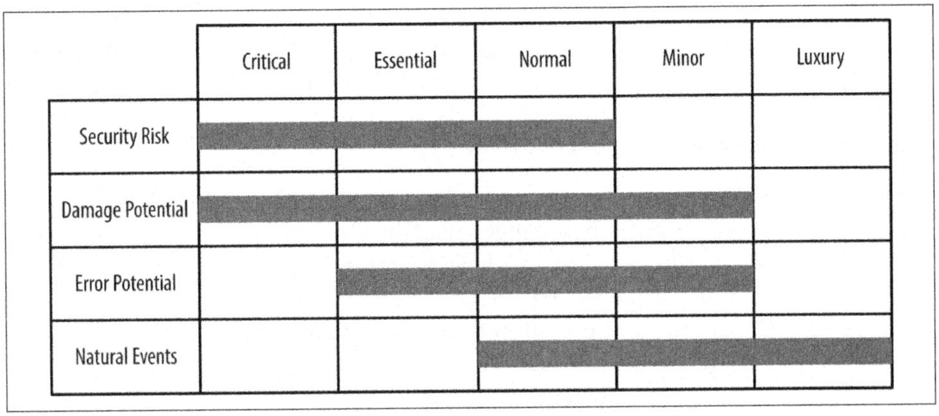

	Critical	Essential	Normal	Minor	Luxury
Security Risk	▓	▓	▓		
Damage Potential	▓	▓	▓	▓	
Error Potential		▓	▓	▓	
Natural Events			▓	▓	▓

Figure 13-2. Balancing priorities is an essential part of the testing process

It's important to update the priorities of upgrades that you need to create for your application constantly. As you create new change requirements, it's important to increase the priorities of existing upgrades accordingly. Likewise, the addition of new change requirements may reduce the priority of some existing upgrades. In order for a listing of required upgrades to perform its designed purpose, you must keep it updated.

Checking Upgrades for Issues

Any time you make an upgrade of an existing product, there is a potential for compatibility or other issues to creep in unnoticed until the upgrade moves to the production environment. By that time, it's really too late to do much about the issues except react to them and hope for the best. A better solution is to look for potential upgrade issues during testing, which means having a substantial testing group or relying on a third-party tester (see Chapter 12 for details). However, even before you get to the testing stage—even before the upgrade is implemented in any way—you can use various techniques to discover whether the upgrade will create issues. The following list describes a few of the more common techniques:

Check the vendor site
> Vendors will often provide detailed write-ups of known issues with their products, including compatibility issues. In fact, in order to move a product forward sometimes, a vendor may purposely introduce a breaking change that will definitely cause problems for your application. Once you become aware of such issues, you need to consider whether the security and reliability implications of the upgrade are worth the new features obtained.

Look through forums dedicated to the product or vendor
> In some cases, a vendor is either unaware of a breaking change or unwilling to admit it. Other users will tell you about potential breaking changes. Those odd error messages that keep popping up are telling you about a potential problem with the software. When you start seeing patterns in forum messages, you need to investigate the upgrade further before using it in your own application and suffering the same fate as others have.

Read the trade press
> The worst possible breaking changes usually appear in the trade press somewhere. Expert developers who also have a writing career to support are always looking for product changes that make it nearly impossible to use the product correctly. In some cases, you even find workarounds for issues. When a breaking change appears in the trade press, you can be sure that most vendors are already working on a fix for the problem and it may be better to wait for the fix to appear, rather than implement the upgrade immediately.

Perform testing directly on the new third-party code
> The use of testing harnesses and testing scripts (see Chapter 11) is an essential part of looking for potential issues. The tests may not turn up every problem, but

when an issue is big enough, you can bet that testing will give you an indicator of the problem.

Develop a test scenario for a subset of the functionality

If you suspect a breaking change is in the code, but can't find a definitive source of information about it, try creating a small test application that focuses on that particular feature. Creating a test application that runs just a part of the library, API, or microservice through its paces won't take much time and will help considerably if you do find a problem. The test application can serve as a means for developing a workaround or detecting when the vendor fixes the issue.

Obtain third-party expert input

Some testing companies and many consultants can offer expert input on libraries, APIs, and microservices because they work with the code all day in a manner designed to break it. Spending all your work time hammering away at code definitely provides advantages that merely working with the code to build an application doesn't provide.

Many organizations make the decision to introduce many changes as part of a single, consolidated upgrade package in the belief that a single upgrade is far better than multiple upgrades. It's true that a single upgrade can be less disruptive when absolutely everything goes as planned. The fact of the matter is that things seldom go as planned and the use of multiple upgrades in a single package complicates the process of finding what has gone wrong. Using a phased approach to introducing change is always better. The production environment is usually going to present some issues that you didn't see in the test environment, so phasing in changes helps you locate these new problems quickly so that you can squash them before they become a major problem.

It's unlikely that you'll find any third-party code update that is completely without issues. Any change to the code is likely to introduce bugs, breaking code changes, interface changes, design strategy changes, and all sorts of other issues that are simply unavoidable because change really does represent a two-sided coin containing the good changes on one side and the bad on the other. Flipping the coin often determines whether you end on the good side or the bad side of the changes. (Of course, coins also have an edge and some changes truly are neutral.)

At some point, you need to decide whether the issues you find are going to cause so many problems that the upgrade isn't worth your time. When you decide that the upgrade isn't worth the implementation time, you must also consider dependency issues. The code you rejected may affect some other upgraded code or your application in some manner that you can't foresee without analysis. It pays to take your time and determine whether breaking issues really will cause enough pain to make the upgrade untenable. Calling off an application upgrade and waiting for fixes is preferable to releasing flawed software that will upset users and potentially cause security issues.

Creating Test Scenarios

Testing an upgrade does follow many of the same processes found in Chapter 11 and Chapter 12. However, the upgrade process demands that you perform some mandatory tests to ensure the upgrade works as expected. The use of test cases can help ensure that you test an upgrade fully before releasing it. The following list provides you with ideas on the sorts of test scenarios that you must include as part of the testing process for an upgrade:

Trouble ticket content

Every trouble ticket that your upgrade addresses should include enough information to create a test case. When this isn't the case, you need to work with the developer responsible for researching a fix for the problem. Every bug you fix in an application (whether a coding error or some other noncoded problem) requires a test case to ensure you test the changed code completely.

Action items

Sometimes a problem doesn't generate a trouble ticket because you can't replicate the problem or you can't fix the issue for other reasons (such as lack of code access). Even when you only suspect an issue, it's important to try to create a test case to look for it. A coding change often makes an intermittent error become more visible, creating the potential for fixing it. However, you only find these opportunities through testing.

Third-party code changes

Every third-party code change should generate a specific test case for your application. You need to know that the third-party code change hasn't affected your application in a negative way. Unfortunately, you often find these sorts of problems during integration testing unless you have a great test harness or set of test scripts for checking the third-party code.

Environment and configuration changes

All sorts of environment and configuration changes can cause problems. For example, a company policy may change how IT grants user access to resources. The change is a positive one because it keeps the resource more secure and reduces the access to the resource so the application runs faster. However, a lack of access can also spell trouble with users, so you need to ensure users can still access the resources they need. Other types of environment and configuration changes can have similar effects on the application, and you won't know about it until after you perform the required testing.

Implementing the Changes

At this point, you've considered every element of an upgrade. The point of all this work is to ensure the upgrade:

- Works as intended
- Remains stable
- Provides proper security
- Improves reliability
- Creates a great user interface
- Seals any security breaches

The implementation process should begin with the highest-priority items on your list first, rather than trying to implement everything at once. A problem that many organizations face is that an upgrade becomes overwhelming. The changes often do take place, but at the expense of testing and ensuring the changes meet the specifications set for them. As a result, the upgrade ends up needing an upgrade. At some point, the code becomes so much spaghetti that no one understands fully and certainly that no one can secure. What you get is the kind of software that hackers love because it's easy to overcome any defenses built into the software and easier still to hide the hack.

Creating an Upgrade Testing Schedule

At some point, you'll have the coding for your upgrade started. You don't want to wait until the process is too far along to start testing. It's important to begin testing as soon as possible, especially when working with a third-party tester. The sooner you can find potential issues, the less costly and time consuming they are to fix. Consider using mocking so that you can perform upgrade testing as the features become available, rather than waiting for the upgrade as a whole due to dependencies. With this in mind, the following sections get you started with creating and implementing a testing schedule for your upgrade.

Performing the Required Pre-Testing

Once the upgrade process begins, you need to begin the testing process immediately. A lot of people wonder what the rush is, but most organizations run out of money before they run out of things to fix. In order to ensure testing takes its proper place, you need to start testing immediately. You must perform the following levels of testing during the upgrade coding process:

Unit

Make sure you test each change as you complete the coding. Otherwise, you can't be sure that the code will even work. Using mocking helps make the testing process possible at this level.

Dependency

The changes you make will affect other code. Within reason, test dependencies in related code so that you can ease the way into integration testing with a reasonable chance of success.

Configuration

It's important to ensure that configuration settings still provide the effect and level of flexibility that the various IT specialists expect. Otherwise, the application will fail during integration testing when you begin to configure it in various ways.

Security

You can't simply assume that the repairs you made to your code will actually work as expected. Sometimes a security fix doesn't actually fix the problem. You need to perform testing on the code that failed to determine whether the fix sealed the breach. In addition, you must make sure that the fix doesn't actually open new holes.

Some developers take security testing to mean looking for holes in the code. Yes, that's one sort of security testing. However, you must test all aspects of security. For example, a commonly missed level of security testing is to ensure that users end up in the proper roles and that they have the required levels of access. A manager performing a user-level task should be in a user role, rather than in a managerial role. A hacker can use role issues to gain access to the system at a higher privilege level than should be possible.

Data connectivity

Applications manage data. Otherwise, there isn't much of a reason to create the application. Part of your testing must ensure that the unit under test can still connect to the required data sources and manage them successfully. It's sometimes surprising to find that a fix to repair a security or other issue actually ends up making data inaccessible or damages the application's ability to manage the data safely.

Performing the Required Integration Testing

As you put the upgrade together, you need to look for integration issues. Because you aren't creating the code from scratch, integration issues can be trickier to find. You're mixing new code that everyone has worked with recently with old code that no one has seen for a long time. The ability of the development staff to understand integration issues is less than when working exclusively with new code. As a result, you need to perform the kind of integration testing described in Chapter 11, but with an eye toward those interfaces between new and old code.

 It helps to have someone available who has actually worked with the old code and understands it fully. Given that people change jobs regularly, you might actually have to find a good candidate and hire them on as a consultant to help with issues that turn up in the older code. Hiring someone who is familiar with the old code will save a lot of time and effort trying to figure the old code out. In addition, someone who worked on the previous development team can fill in gaps as to why some code works as it does and why the team did things in a certain way. Documentation is supposed to provide this kind of information, but documentation is usually inadequate and poorly composed, so that sometimes it presents more questions than answers.

Be sure you test using your existing testing harness and scripts to ensure that the application still meets baseline requirements. You may have to perform updates on the testing harness and scripts to ensure they provide testing functionality for new features and remove testing for deprecated features. Maintain a change log for the changes you make to the testing harness and scripts. Otherwise, you might find it difficult to reverse changes later should one of your upgrades prove incorrect.

Moving an Upgrade to Production

Once the testing is finished and you're certain that the upgrade will work as advertised, you need to move it to a production environment. If your organization is large, try moving the upgrade to just one group of users first so that if the users find an error, you can fix it without taking the entire organization offline. The important thing to remember is that the application must remain reliable and secure with the upgrade in place, yet provide the speed and interface experience the user requires. Otherwise, the upgrade will fail because users will refuse to use it. They'll attempt to use the version that feels more comfortable to them, even if that version is likely to cause data breaches and other security issues.

Part of the reason you want to employ users as testers is to ensure that they tell others about the new upgrade. When users get excited about an upgrade, you get a better response and it takes less time to get everyone started with the new product. Of course, you want to make sure that the tester experience is a good one.

From a security perspective, it's often helpful to intrusion test an upgrade using a third-party tester. Yes, most people would say that you're supposed to complete all of the required testing on the test server, and they're right for the most part. However, intrusion testing doesn't just check the application for errors. It also provides a sanity check on these items:

- Network connectivity
- Intrusion detection software
- Intrusion prevention software
- DMZ reliability
- Required firmware updates for all hardware
- Server setup
- Required updates for all software
- Application environment
- Third-party libraries, APIs, and microservices
- Application
- User processes
- Database connectivity

It simply isn't possible to check all of these items using the test setup. For example, you can check the production server's vulnerability to attack by using the test setup. Although it might seem as if some of these test issues are well outside the purview of moving an upgrade to production, any change to the server setup, including the application software, really does require such a test. The interactions between the various components make it impossible for you to know whether the server is still reliable and secure after the change. Unfortunately, many organizations fall down on the job in this area because no one seems to understand what has happened to the server setup. The bottom line is that the server could now be vulnerable and you wouldn't even know it.

Testing the software isn't the only thing you need to consider. It's also important to get user feedback on interface changes. The user works with the application at a detailed level for many hours each day. It's likely that the user will encounter potential security issues brought on by interface changes before the development staff does. In fact, experience shows that the development staff is often clueless that a particular change causes an issue that is completely obvious to application users. It isn't that the development staff is insensitive or doesn't do the job correctly—simply that the user has a completely different viewpoint on how the application should work.

Checking with administrators, DevOps, DBAs, and other skilled individuals is also a priority for an upgrade. You need to discover whether changes affect these specialized users in any negative way. For example, configuration changes that take too long to propagate through the system represent a potential security issue. If it takes 24 hours for a user deletion to take effect, a disgruntled user can cause all sorts of problems that would be hard to track. All it takes is one issue of this kind to cause an organization all sorts of woe, so ensuring the IT professionals in your organization can perform their job is an essential part of the upgrade.

CHAPTER 14

Considering Update Options

Updating means bringing new information, features, or interface elements into the application. Improving application accuracy also falls into the realm of an update. An update may not even affect application code in a significant manner, but can still affect security in a number of ways. For example, you can update a database to include a field that shows who last edited a record, which can improve security by making it possible to track the source of an error or infection that has occurred on the system. Changing prompts so the information you want from a user becomes clearer is a security fix that doesn't necessarily require any recoding, especially when the prompts exist in an external file. The idea behind an update is to make the application better in some way so that a coding fix may become unnecessary. It's important to know when to differentiate between an upgrade and an update, so the first part of this chapter spends time comparing the two processes and how they affect your application.

An update won't always fix a security issue, just as an upgrade is sometimes overkill. In order to use organization resources effectively, you need to know when to use an update and when you really do need to perform an upgrade. The upgrade process appears in Chapter 13 and provides you with details on how this process works. This chapter compares updates with upgrades and helps you understand how the update process works.

Updates can fall into a number of categories. For example, you could choose to update your programming language suite. The new suite could provide better debugging, optimized code output, and faster executables. None of these features directly affect your application code, but they do affect how your application works. The simple act of recompiling your application modules produces effects that everyone can see.

In some cases, you need to perform emergency updates. Selling management on an update can be hard because updates often don't affect the application code at all. It's hard to tell a manager that you need time, resources, and personnel to make an update that won't change a single line of code in the application. Trying to demonstrate the benefits of the change can also be hard until you actually make the changes and can quantify their effect to management in a way that demonstrates a return on investment.

As with upgrades, you need to test your updates. However, some update testing is significantly different from upgrade testing because, again, you don't necessarily deal with code when working through an update. In summary, this chapter provides you with a complete primer on performing updates of various sorts so that you can better gauge when to use an upgrade versus an update.

Differentiating Between Upgrades and Updates

Both upgrades and updates affect the security of your application. However, an upgrade differs significantly in scope and purpose from an update, so it's important to know the difference between the two. Most upgrades create significant new functionality and affect the code base at a deeper level than an update will. In fact, many updates don't touch the code base at all. An update performs tasks such as:

- Changing the database managed by the application. For example, a database that supplies catalog information may have an update to descriptions that help a user make better decisions.

- Modifying existing features to make them friendlier or less prone to producing errors. For example, menu entries may now include speed keys so that users don't have to guess about which key combinations to use.

- Reconfiguring user interface features to make them better suited to user needs. An update may include support for more languages so that a user can see the user interface in a preferred language, rather than as a secondary or tertiary language that's less clear.

- Including more specific user interface options, such as changing a textbox entry to a radio button selection so that the user can make specific choices. Every element of chance removed from an application inherently improves application accuracy and enhances security.

In most cases, updates are more subtle from the developer's perspective. It's quite likely the developer may not even make the changes in some situations. For example, you need the services of a DBA to update the database, rather than rely on the developer to do it. A DBA can perform the task faster and more accurately in most cases. Designers can make many user interface changes using the coding techniques available today, making it unnecessary for the developer to change the code base at all. However, developers do become involved in the process when it comes time to test the update to ensure it performs as expected. Sometimes an update also requires a few code tweaks to make it work as expected.

Even if a developer isn't involved in an update in a significant way, the team should always include developers in the discussion. In fact, updates, like upgrades, should have the full support of all stakeholders in the development team. This process includes user testers who verify that an update actually performs as requested and determine the update won't cause significant new user errors or other potential problems (such as slowing users down or causing a huge spike in training costs).

One thing that upgrades and updates do have in common is a need for testing. Some organizations make the mistake of assuming that updates require lighter testing, or possibly no testing at all. The problem with this viewpoint is that putting an update on the production server will likely reveal issues that testing would show earlier and would make easier to fix. It's important to remember that testing doesn't just check the code base; it also checks for issues such as a user's inability to interact with the application properly at some level. An update could actually open a security hole by making it possible for a hacker to interact with the application in a new way (especially when the update involves new user interface functionality). However, the emphasis of update testing is on the areas that are changed. For example, you still test every aspect of the application, but if the user interface has changed, then the focus of the testing is on the user interface and you make more checks in that area.

Some update decisions fall outside the purview of the direct oversight of the development team. For example, a third-party update to a library, API, or microservice might occur automatically. In this case, you still have to test the update, but the testing actually occurs after the production system receives the update in many cases. Reversing the update may also prove impossible, so that breaking changes could cause an organization to look for a new third-party product or create an upgrade that fixes the problem. As a result, it's essential to keep track of updates of all sorts and to be ready to test them at any time.

Determining When to Update

Third-party software could present a problem when it comes to updates. More than a few third-party vendors have tried to slip unannounced updates past development teams when the nature of a fix could prove embarrassing to the vendor. Security updates sometimes fall into this category—they just magically appear one day and no one is really sure when the third-party vendor released them. These updates can snowball and cause your application to stop working, or worse still, start acting in an unpredictable manner. One day you simply find that support starts receiving lots of irate calls from users who can't quite seem to get the application to work.

Updates you make to your software or the updates made for you by third-party vendors, do require some level of planning, even when the third-party vendor forgets to mention the update or why it was made. You need to know that the change actually falls within the realm of an update and isn't actually an upgrade in disguise. With this in mind, the following sections discuss some of the issues you should consider when determining an application requires an update.

Working Through Library Updates

- Library updates can be the hardest to make because a library becomes part of the application code. Because you import it directly into the application, some changes are hard to hide from view. In addition, some changes can cause odd problems to surface—bugs that have always been in the library, but never showed up because the application allocated memory or other resources in a different manner. The update may not even appear in the application after including the new library because the calls may have a slightly different name. These issues are all common to any sort of library update you wish to make. The following sections divide libraries into those that you incorporate from a third-party source and those that you develop on your own.

Dealing with third-party library updates

When working through a third-party update, the first step is to obtain a list of the changes—assuming the vendor provides one. Work through this list to determine which changes actually affect your application. Use a unit test to help determine whether the documented change reflects the actual change in the function before you begin making plans for the update.

Unfortunately, the list won't tell you about some issues, such as name changes, in a way that appears as a change. In many cases, the vendor lists a name change as a new feature. Consequently, you must also review the list of new features looking for features implemented as a change to a function that you already use. For example, the new feature might have the name MySpecialFunction2() when it replaces MySpecial Function(). The change could reflect new features, which means you have to review the update carefully to ensure you understand the ramifications to your code.

If you can obtain a copy of the code, use static testing techniques to better understand the changes the vendor made to the library. Running the code through a debugger to see the code in action can be helpful as well. You may not have these options available in most cases, but it doesn't hurt to consider them.

Developing in-house library updates

Performing in-house library updates provides you with more control over the update process. You can perform all levels of required testing because you own the code. The most important issue is to document every change the update creates fully so that you don't find reliability and security issues later. Many security issues occur when an update changes how a function works and the code continues to use the old approach to working with the function. The mismatch can cause security holes.

A worse situation occurs when an update appears as a renamed function, but the lack of documentation causes people who work with the library to continue using an older, buggy function. The result is that the team working with the library knows that the library contains a security fix, but the team working on the application has no idea that the security fix exists. Hackers actually review such library changes when possible and use the mismatch to discover security issues. Exploiting the mismatch is easier than looking for actual coding errors because the renamed function acts as a beacon advertising the fix for the hacker.

Employ static testing to ensure that the documented change actually matches the coded change in the library. After performing a static test, use unit testing to verify that the fix works as advertised. "Creating an Update Testing Schedule" on page 295 provides you with additional information about the testing process.

The worst-case security hole is one where everyone thinks that a fix is in place, but the fix is missing, doesn't work as advertised, or developers don't implement the fix in the application. Always verify that developers actually implement updates in a consistent manner. Even if a fix fails to work as advertised, consistent implementation makes a follow-on update much easier to implement because everyone is using the function in the same manner.

Working Through API and Microservice Updates

APIs and microservices both suffer from the same problem—they work as black boxes for the most part. It's possible to sneak an update in without anyone knowing. Some vendors have actually done this in the past, and it isn't unheard of when working with in-house code either. The black box issue can cause all sorts of problems when the API or microservice fails to work as expected. Tracking down the culprit can be difficult. With this in mind, it's essential to ensure that the development team fully documents every change to the internal workings of an API or microservice call and that the outputs remain the same for a given input. The following sections discuss the differences between third-party and in-house updates.

Application developers base their ability to trust an API or microservice on the assurance that for a given input, the output remains the same. An update can make the calls more secure, faster, or reliable, but it can't change the outcome. If any element of an interface is changed by an update, then you need to create new calls to access that element. This approach ensures that developers will need to use the new calls in order to obtain the benefits provided by the update.

Dealing with third-party API and microservice updates

When working with third-party API and microservice code, you won't have any access to the update code and won't be able to perform any type of static testing. What you can do is perform intensive unit testing to ensure that the following considerations are true:

- Each of the calls still produces the advertised outputs for given inputs with the range originally specified for the call.
- The call doesn't accept inputs outside the range originally specified.
- Any tests involving exploit code (to ensure security enhancements actually work) fail.
- Speed testing shows that the call successfully completes tasks within the time tolerance of the original call or faster.
- Reliability testing shows that the call doesn't fail under load.
- Any documented changes to the code actually work as anticipated.

Developing in-house API and microservice updates

Always perform static testing as a first measure of in-house updates. During the process, you want to verify that the documentation and the code changes match completely. A significant problem with updates is that the API or microservice development team thinks that an update works one way when it actually works another. It's also a good idea to match documented updates against trouble tickets to ensure that the fixes address the issues described in the trouble tickets. This visual checking process might seem time consuming, but performing it usually makes subsequent testing far easier and reduces the probability of a security issue sneaking into the code accidentally significantly less. The black box nature of API and microservice code makes the static check even more important than it is for libraries.

Your in-house code will also benefit from the same sorts of checks you perform on third-party code (see "Dealing with third-party API and microservice updates" on page 286 for details). However, you can now perform these checks with the code in hand to better understand why certain checks fail.

A particularly tricky issue when working with microservice updates is that many organizations now rely on a microservices API to make the various microservices look like a custom API. The use of a microservices API reduces the programming burden on developers and ensures that every platform has the required resources using protocols available to that platform. Figure 14-1 shows a typical microservices API setup.

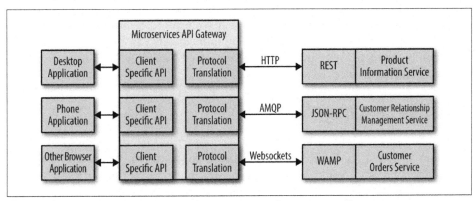

Figure 14-1. When using a microservices API, test the API as well

It's essential to test the various microservices directly to ensure the update hasn't changed the way in which the microservice works natively. However, you must also test the microservice API to ensure that the API still responds correctly to all the platform types that the application supports. Otherwise, you can't be certain that the microservice API will continue to provide correct results in a secure and reliable manner.

Accepting Automatic Updates

Some vendors now make it as hard as possible to ignore automatic updates. An automatic update is one that a vendor pushes to a client in some way. In some cases, the vendor simply changes the software at the server so you end up using the update automatically. These are the main reasons vendors like automatic updates:

- Fewer security or reliability issues due to using an outdated version
- Reduced support costs
- Smaller staffing requirements
- Improved ROI

Of course, the question isn't one of whether automatic updates are good for the vendor, but whether they're good for your organization. In many cases, using automatic updates proves problematic because the organization isn't prepared for the update and breaking changes usually create support issues. The most severe cases result in data loss or security breaches, which run counter to making an update in the first place.

Most organizations try to avoid automatic updates when possible in order to reduce the potential for unexpected side effects. When a third-party vendor insists on automatic updates and you have no alternative for third-party software, then you really do need to have someone tracking the third-party software to determine when an automatic update will appear. Testing the update immediately can help you avoid problems with breaking updates and potentially improve the ability of your organization to react to sudden changes as well.

Updating Language Suites

Web applications fall into a somewhat special category in that users who speak any of a number of languages could simply find them while searching for something else. Any public application you create, even if you only mean for one group to use it, does sit on the world stage of the Internet where anyone from anywhere can access it. Theoretically, you can try to block access, but that's a counterproductive strategy. If you suddenly find that your application is receiving accolades from places you never imagined, you may need an application update that addresses language-specific issues. The following sections discuss some of the issues you need to consider, especially when it comes to maintaining a secure application environment.

Creating a Supported Language List

Not every application supports every world language. Trying to make this happen would be a logistics nightmare and it isn't necessary because not everyone will actually want to use your application. However, you may find that you need to support more than just one language as the application becomes more popular. Modern server software generally makes it possible to track the locations that access your application. The location itself may not provide everything needed. For example, it may surprise you to know that Romania has a number of official languages:

- Romanian
- Croatian
- German
- Hungarian
- Romani

- Russian
- Serbian
- Slovak
- Ukrainian

However, these are just the official languages. Your application user might actually speak a different language, such as Italian. It isn't possible to know precisely which language to support based solely on location. The point is that if you suddenly find that your application is receiving lots of requests from Romania, you already know that the user is not likely to speak English natively (or perhaps at all). If your application only supports English, then you might find the user is confused, makes mistakes, and potentially causes both security and reliability problems.

 In some cases, you can make assumptions about language support based on the application environment. An application running in a private environment in the United States, for example, might only need to support English and Spanish as options. When the application runs in Romania, you might want to support all of the official languages to ensure that everyone can access your application. Considering application environment is an important part of working through the language support list.

Using location does provide you with a good starting point, but you need to obtain language statistics in some other way. About the only effective means to ensure you get good data is to provide feedback forms or conduct user surveys. As you accumulate statistics about application use, you see patterns emerge and can start deciding which languages to support. Creating a list of supported languages is important because you need to know which languages you can actually afford as part of an update and you want to be sure you target the most popular languages first.

When creating an update to support multiple languages, you typically want to provide different URLs for each language. Otherwise, it becomes nearly impossible for someone to find the language they need. In addition, using different URLs makes it possible to detect information the browser provides and make a reasonable language selection for the user. The two common methods for creating unique URLs for each language are:

Language-specific URL

>The same domain hosts multiple languages. An URL such as *http://www.mysite.com/en/stuff.html* would support the English language, while *http://www.mysite.com/de/stuff.html* would support the German language. The benefit to this approach is that you save money by not having to buy multiple top-level domains (TLDs). This approach focuses on language.

Multiple TLDs

>Each language has its own domain. An URL such as *http://www.mysite.us/stuff.html* supports users in the United States, while *http://www.mysite.ro/stuff.html* would support users in Romania. The benefit of this approach is that search engines, such as Google, will offer a separate link for each language you support, rather than treat all of the languages as duplicated content and display only one link. This approach focuses on country. You can find a list of the TLDs on Wikipedia (*https://en.wikipedia.org/wiki/List_of_Internet_top-level_domains*).

Obtaining Reliable Language Specialists

If you choose to perform a language-specific update of your application, you can only ensure that it works reliably and securely when the update looks as if you originally wrote it in the target language. Everyone has worked with instructions or other written communication that someone originally wrote in another language and then translated to whatever language you speak. When the translator exercises less than the usual skill, the results are often hilarious. The actual meaning behind the various bits of information becomes lost and no one can take the information seriously. However, the security issues that this kind of miscommunication causes are no laughing matter.

However, even a great translator will do a less than perfect job if you don't provide the right environment in which to perform the translation. The following steps provide insights into the techniques you can use to create a better application translation and ensure users can actually follow your prompts as a result:

1. Place all hardcoded strings in the application in a database of some type. Identify each string by its location within the application.

2. Replace each hardcoded string with a placeholder control that you fill with the correct language string when the page loads.

3. Create a separate database file for each language and ensure the database name reflects the language content.

4. Fill each language database with the translated strings provided by the translator. Use precisely the same identifiers for each of the strings so that the identifier always matches the screen prompt.

5. Add code to the application to perform the task of filling the controls with the correct prompts from the database.

6. Test the application initially with the original language to ensure that the prompts work as intended.

 It's always a good idea to obtain a second check on language updates, especially when no one in the organization speaks the language natively. There is always a potential for errors when making a translation. In addition, you need to consider social mores of the people who speak the language. The most problematic issue is that some languages won't have a direct translation for some words. As a result, you must choose the correct approximation and then ensure there is little room for misinterpretation of the approximate translation. Having an independent check of the translation will save embarrassment later, in addition to making the application more secure by reducing the potential for input errors.

Verifying the Language-Specific Prompts Work with the Application

Simply translating the prompts isn't enough in many cases. You need to rely on your language specialist to ensure that every prompt on every screen reflects how people who speak the language natively expect to see the prompts. For example, some languages read from left to right, while others read right to left. The orientation of the prompts is important, as is the formatting. You may need to provide application hints and formatting to ensure that people using the application can actually interpret the prompts correctly.

Ensuring Data Appears in the Correct Format

Different areas of the world format data in different ways. Some countries use a comma, instead of a period, for the decimal place. These same countries might use a period, in place of a comma, for the thousands place indicator. Imagine what would happen if a user changed values based on the wrong formatting in this situation. A user could enter values that could cause the application to misbehave, crash, or simply do something odd. The result could be a security breach or an opening that a hacker needs to create a security breach. Many security issues come out of seemingly silly errors that a hacker exploits to gain the small advantage that leads to a big payoff.

The presentation of data in the right form ensures there are no misunderstandings. Creating a potential security issue simply because of a mix-up between commas and periods seems like a problem that you can easily solve, but sometimes proves absurdly difficult. You can find examples of thousands indicators and decimals points by language at *http://docs.oracle.com/cd/E19455-01/806-0169/overview-9/index.html*. The graphic guide at *http://www.statisticalconsultants.co.nz/blog/how-the-world-separates-its-decimals.html* is also interesting.

Defining the Special Requirements for Language Support Testing

Testing your application becomes a lot harder when you start adding multiple languages. Unless you plan to keep those language specialists around for the life of the application, you need some other means to verify that updates aren't causing language support problems. Proper planning, change documentation, and verification in the original language are your best starting points. Whenever you create a change to the application that affects a prompt in the original language, you must consider changing the prompts in all of the other supported languages as well. To make this process as easy as possible, use these suggestions:

Plan

Make sure you check each change carefully. Sometimes a designer will try to tweak prompts when they don't really require any change. Keeping the number of changes small will reduce costs, ensure the application remains reliable, and help improve security by reducing the potential for miscues.

Document

Every change to every prompt in the original language must also appear in every other language your application supports. A security and reliability issue starts when the language editions get out of sync. It's essential that this part of the update process runs smoothly and without error or you'll find yourself hiring that language specialist again to clean up the mess.

Verify

Ensuring that every change occurs in every location is hard because you probably don't have staff that speaks the language you support. A good way to verify the language update is to use screenshots. Compare the original screen to the updated screen to verify that the prompt changes really did take place. The only problem with this approach is that you can't be sure that prompt change is completely correct.

 Because of the manner in which the application uses prompts, you don't need to test the underlying code for each language. What you change for each language is the interface and that's where the focus of your testing takes place for language-specific issues. Ensuring you get good prompts and that those prompts appear in the correct places is the basis of language support testing.

Performing Emergency Updates

Upgrades are always well planned and timed carefully. Most upgrades receive the proper planning and timing too. However, when a hacker has just exposed some terrifying hole in your application that you need to act on immediately, sometimes an update can't wait—you must create an interim fix and deploy it immediately or suffer the consequences. No one likes emergencies. The more critical the application and the more sensitive the data affected, the less anyone likes emergencies. The following sections help with the emergencies that come in the middle of the night, lurking, waiting for your guard to go down.

Avoiding Emergencies When Possible

Everyone experiences an emergency at some point in the application support process. It just goes with the territory. However, you can avoid most emergencies by planning for them before they happen. Here are some issues you need to consider as part of avoiding emergencies:

- Perform full testing of each update and upgrade before deployment.
- Deploy updates and upgrades only when system load and availability supports it.
- Avoid deploying updates and upgrades when staffing levels are low or key personnel are absent.
- Ensure the application has access to all required resources from multiple sources if possible.
- Plan for overcapacity situations and ensure you have adequate additional capacity available to meet surge requirements.

- Assume a hacker is going to attack at the worst possible time and plan for the attack (as much as possible) in advance.
- Test system security and reliability regularly.

Creating a Fast Response Team

Your organization needs a fast response team—a group of individuals that are on call to handle emergencies. It doesn't have to be the same group of individuals all the time —everyone needs a break—but you should have an emergency response team available at all times, especially those times when hackers love to attack (such as weekends). An emergency response team must contain all of the individuals that an application requires for any sort of update. If you require a DBA to make an update normally, then you need a DBA on your emergency response team. The team should train together specifically on handling emergencies to ensure they're ready to go when the emergency occurs.

 Never perform an upgrade as an emergency measure. Upgrades deeply affect the code and you can't properly test the code with the short response time that an emergency requires. When you release an upgrade without proper testing, you likely include some interesting bugs that a hacker would love to exploit. Always play things safe and keep emergency measures limited to those items you can handle as an update.

Performing Simplified Testing

Depending on the nature of the emergency, you may have to release the update with a minimum of testing. As a minimum, you must test the code that the update directly affects and possibly the surrounding code as well. When a hacker is breaking down your door, you might not have time to test every part of the code as normally required. It's important to remember that the update you didn't release might have kept the hacker at bay. The issue comes down to one of balancing risk—the emergency on one side and the potential for creating a considerably worse problem on the other.

Creating a Permanent Update Schedule

Always treat emergency updates as temporary. You have no way of knowing how rushed the fast response team became while trying to get the update out. The team could have made all sorts of errors during the process. Even if the update works, you can't leave the emergency update in place without further scrutiny. Leaving the emergency update in place opens security and reliability holes that you might not know are there and could cause considerable problems for you in the future.

It's a good idea to perform a walkthrough of the emergency after the fact, determine what caused it, and consider how the fast response team responded to it. By performing a walkthrough, you can create a lessons-learned approach to handling emergencies in the future. You can bet that hackers constantly work to improve their skills, so you must improve your skills as well. Taking time to understand the emergency and looking for ways to handle it better in the future are valuable ways to create a better fast response team.

As part of the permanent update process, make sure you perform static testing of the update to verify that the fast response team reacted properly and provided a good fix for the problem. Make sure you schedule the permanent update as quickly as possible to ensure you fix any additional problems before someone takes advantage of them. The new update should rely on all the usual testing procedures and follow whatever plan you have adopted for permanent updates.

Creating an Update Testing Schedule

No matter how you create the update or the timing involved, it never pays to rush an update into deployment without some testing time in place. Rushing an update out the door almost always causes problems in the end. In fact, the problems created by rushing are usually worse than if you had left the update out entirely. Testing provides a sanity check that forces you to slow down and recheck your thought processes in putting the update together. Used correctly, testing ensures that your fellow team members are as certain as you are that the update is solid and won't cause issues that end up being a security nightmare.

Update testing doesn't quite follow the same pattern as upgrade testing because you change less of the application during an update and can focus most of your energy on the features that changed. In addition, you may perform updates during an emergency and need to field the update as quickly as possible to prevent a major security breach. With this in mind, you must perform these levels of testing to ensure the update doesn't do more harm than good:

- Unit
- Integration
- Security

When the update serves to address an emergency, these three levels will usually keep the update from doing more harm than good. However, you must perform these additional levels of testing as soon as possible:

- Usability

- Compatibility
- Accessibility
- Performance

Once the dust has settled and you have additional time for testing, you need to ensure that the update is fully functional. The best way to ensure functionality is to perform these additional levels of testing:

- Regression
- Internationalization and localization
- Conformance

You could perform other sorts of testing, but only as needed. For example, web applications seldom require any sort of installation, so you don't need to perform any sort of installation testing in most cases. The exception is when a web application requires installation of a browser extension, browser add-on, browser service, system agent, or some other required software.

CHAPTER 15

Considering the Need for Reports

Reports help document the status of your application. It would seem as if a note in the code file or a simple discussion in the hallway would be enough to get the ball rolling, but a formal process of accepting input information about applications really is the only way to ensure that everyone understands the application status. Many people associate reports of this sort with negative issues, such as bugs. However, you can use reports for all sorts of needs. For example, a positive report may indicate that users really do like a new feature based on usage statistics. A report like this gives everyone a pat on the back without having to worry about breaking one's own hand to do it.

You generally create internal reports for the application as a whole, but you can use reports to track individual application features as well. For that matter, you might not even focus on the application directly and instead track network bandwidth usage or data access requirements. The point is that internal reports generally focus on your code, users, and resources.

External reports come from third parties. For example, if you hire a third-party tester (see Chapter 12), then you should expect to see a number of reports detailing the status of your application during testing. A third-party report could also list the services that your application actually uses when you obtain access to a library, API, or microservice. By tracking actual usage of these services, you may be able to optimize the application and obtain a reduced fee for the services by ordering fewer of them.

An important form of report involves actively seeking user feedback (or even appointing specific user representatives to ensure each user group has an opportunity to make their wishes known). You won't ever satisfy every user of an application. However, you can reasonably seek to meet the needs of most users. The trick is to ensure that the reports you obtain from users actually do represent a majority view, rather than the angst vented by a minority. Keeping users happy, efficient, and well controlled is always a good goal to meet with application development.

 Reports can benefit your organization in all sorts of unusual ways. For example, you can analyze reports to look for unusual usage or access patterns. Unusual patterns could indicate hacker activity, but could also indicate the need for an application upgrade (see Chapter 13) or update (see Chapter 14). The point is to keep your mind open to the potential for using reports in nonstandard ways when opportunities present themselves.

Using Reports to Make Changes

Before you can do anything with a report, you need a report. Some developers believe there is a standard set of reports that will meet every possible organizational need. Unfortunately, this isn't the case. Reports vary because needs vary. You need to consider precisely how to create the kind of reports you need and avoid useless reports that simply burn up everyone's time. Sometimes you need reports to follow an upgrade or update to ensure that these tasks go as planned. It's possible to generate reports by hand, from easily accessed data, or automatically. Automatic reports could come from any number of sources, such as log files. The important thing is to ensure the reports are consistent so that the people reading them can come to rely on them as a consistent source of information. The following sections describe how to create reports that will actually do something useful for your organization, making it easier to track issues such as security concerns in the process.

Avoiding Useless Reports

Organizations and even individuals generate a plethora of reports in a lifetime, only a few of which are actually useful. A report is a kind of tool, so you must have a need for it to perform useful work. Some people view reports as informational, but this isn't the case. If you can't act on the content of the report, the information is useless and you may as well not take the time to read it. In fact, useless information is a significant contributor to the phenomenon of information overload.

Reports that contain useful information help you perform specific tasks. They provide the basis on which to act. With this in mind, reports that help you enhance the security of your application usually contain topics like these:

- Bugs
- Speed
- Reliability
- Usage

- Data access

The kind of report determines how you act on the information it contains. When you find that you don't perform any actions in response to a report, the report is either faulty and requires change, or you really don't need it. The information in reports generally inspires some sort of action for the following reasons:

Change in pattern

Data consists of patterns. You can see ebb and flow in the way data presents itself. In fact, whole branches of math are now devoted to the study of data patterns. When you see a change in a data pattern, even if that change doesn't appear to present a problem, you need to investigate its source. Some patterns present reliability issues and others security issues. Of course, a change in pattern could simply come from a change in usage or some other factor, but you need to know why the pattern has changed.

Change in status

A change in status can mean many things. However, status indicators tell you that the ongoing flow of information has changed in some way, which means that you need to check for potential interface, reliability, security, or resource problems. Interface issues can result in security problems down the road and resource problems usually end up causing reliability problems.

Anomalous event

Nature constantly presents the potential to provide an anomalous event. For example, the glitch caused by lightning can present itself as an anomalous information event. However, anomalous events also occur when hackers probe a site looking for potential weaknesses. Some hacks can manifest themselves in as few as three anomalous events, so it pays to track down the source of each event.

Unexpected values

When a report contains information outside the expected range, you need to consider why the application generated such information. The unexpected value could come from a bug or it might be the result of hacker probes. Perhaps it's the result of resource limitations on the server or bad data in the database. The fact is that unexpected values occur regularly and people simply dismiss them instead of acting upon them. Always verify the reasons for unexpected values when you can.

Keeping your desk clear of information you can't act upon is an essential part of maintaining a secure application. When you clear away the clutter, you can begin to focus on the information that you truly need in order to locate and verify security issues in your organization. The key is to ask how you plan to act on the information contained in a report before you create a new one. In addition, getting rid of old reports that no longer serve a purpose is essential to eventually gaining control over the information flow in any organization.

Timing Reports to Upgrades and Updates

From a security and reliability perspective, you need good information to act on application changes that simply don't work out. In order to obtain the information you need, it's important to time reports to those times when you make upgrades and updates to the application. Timing may be as simple as changing when the system outputs the report or modifying report frequency so that you get the information a bit more often.

The flow of information should increase in proportion to the significance of the changes you make. However, as mentioned in "Avoiding Useless Reports" on page 298, you also need to avoid information overload. It's when you become overloaded that you tend to miss patterns and critical events presented by the data. It's important to maintain a balance between the information you really can use and the information you really need. When you start finding that reports go for days without initiating any action, then you know you're experiencing information overload and need to reduce the information flow in some manner.

 Many organizations don't place enough emphasis on filtering software. If you can filter the information received by individuals to make it more focused, you can reduce the amount of overload that the individual suffers and improve the chances of locating reliability and security issues in an application upgrade or update much faster. The problem comes in tuning the filtering software so that it does indeed focus attention, rather than leave out critical information. In order to tune the filter, someone must actually compare the raw data with the filtered data to ensure the filter is working properly. Once the filter is tuned, it's possible to start depending on it a bit more to reduce the individual's workload and make them more efficient.

Increases in information flow due to upgrades and updates are temporary. You don't need to continue receiving the additional information beyond a reasonable time-frame. Of course, the problem is determining when to reduce the information flow. Normally, you can start reducing information flow when the frequency of bugs and odd events decreases, and the patterns of application usage return to normal. Using this approach means that you can then divert some of your attention to other matters, such as planning the next update or upgrade.

Using Automatically Generated Reports

Monitoring software and other support tools usually provide you with some number of reports. The vendor creating the software usually develops these reports in response to user requests, so the reports often reflect precisely the data you need to perform general application monitoring. It's important to go through the list of automatically generated reports and select just the reports that meet your needs. Selecting all of the reports and hoping you find the information you need is a bad idea because it leads to information overload and missed opportunities to correct application issues.

 The key here is that automatically generated reports provide general and generic information—the type that all of the vendor's customers can use in monitoring their applications. The vendor has no way of knowing what sorts of applications you run, when users interact with them, what devices the users rely on, or any environmental factors that affect application execution. In short, the automatically generated reports act as a starting point and a potential catalyst for your own ideas on the information needed to safeguard applications and the data they manage properly.

The generated reports will provide generic information, but sometimes you can make it more specific to your needs by selecting report options (when available). In many cases, the vendor will provide the means to customize a report so that it provides just the information you actually need, rather than a lot of information you don't. The important thing is to run the report once or twice with all of the features in place so that you can see what's available and determine how you can act on it. Once you know these two bits of information, you can start customizing the report to make it smaller and more efficient to use.

Using Custom Reports

The generic reports that the vendor provides with the product are a great way to get started monitoring your application for problems, but they usually don't provide enough information about your specific needs. Of course, the vendor doesn't know anything about your specific needs. The only way to obtain information that directly relates to how your specific application works in your environment and with your users is to create a custom report. When the monitoring software you use doesn't provide the custom report creation capability you require, then it's time to write an application that will obtain the information and format it in a manner that works. This section is about the kind of report that you create completely by hand (see "Using Automatically Generated Reports" on page 301 for a discussion of customized reports).

Of course, some organizations go quite crazy with reports and have so many that no one really knows what they're all supposed to do. Exercising restraint when it comes to custom reports is essential. Otherwise, you find yourself buried in information you don't want, need, or understand and also have the extra burden of maintaining the report generation software. The following sections describe methods you can use to make your custom reports better reflect your needs and generate just the information you require to keep your application safe.

Developing reports by hand

In some cases, you develop reports by hand, drawing the data from the logs that the application creates and any other custom data sources you might possess. Data sources vary greatly. For example, you might need to rely partially on user feedback forms to create the desired report. It's essential to plan the report carefully because custom reports are time consuming to create and costly to maintain. They can also be fragile when the reports rely on data coming from a third-party source that might change the data it provides as part of its product.

Obtaining data you need for a report has some serious drawbacks, especially when working with an application. There isn't any such thing as getting data free—it always costs you something. Here are some issues to consider when obtaining custom data from any source:

- Outputting log data adds code to the application or product, which means that you lose speed in exchange for obtaining the information.

- Hackers can use log data to determine better how your application runs, so you might give the very people you want to keep out of the system the keys to infiltrating it further.

- Creating logs and other forms of application or product information uses resources that you might need for working with the application. As a result, the application could experience reliability problems.

- Data creation code could potentially open a security hole that might not otherwise exist—giving hackers a method for accessing your system that they shouldn't possess.

- It's far easier to create misleading or incorrect data than it is to generate precisely what you need, so you need time to test the data output and check it for accuracy.

Custom reports do serve a purpose. However, you must be careful when creating them. Create only the reports you need that output only the information you need to act upon and keep the report active only as long as absolutely necessary. Following this strategy will help keep your network safer and reduce the penalties for creating a custom report.

Developing reports from readily available data sources

Sometimes you can create a custom report from readily available data sources. Some monitoring products provide APIs that let you access the data they create. If the monitoring product will create the data whether you use it or not, it always pays to use the monitor's (or other application's) data, rather than create data of your own. Even so, you still have to create the custom code, ensure it outputs the data you need in the form you want, and then maintain the code afterward. Here are some other issues to consider when creating a custom report based on data generated by a third party:

- The third party could change the output, which would necessitate a change in your report.
- The data may become unavailable.
- It's harder to verify that the data is accurate, so you can't be as certain that the report is completely correct—it could actually provide anomalous data in some cases.
- You might have to jump through licensing or other proprietary data hoops in order to gain access to the data through an API.
- The data might not be in the form you need, so the custom code will need to perform data manipulation to clean and format the data before you can use it.
- Known security issues with the way in which a third party manages the data could provide hackers with access to your system.

Creating Consistent Reports

An issue that is hard to overcome—but important to contemplate—is consistency. When your reports format data in several different ways and present it in different orders, it can cause confusion. Anyone using the report is bound to make mistakes when glancing at the report, and might end up assuming the data means one thing when it says another. The reports you use and create should consider the following consistency issues:

- Data appears in the same format.
- Data ordering is the same whenever possible.
- The report doesn't reference data using multiple, conflicting approaches.
- Any data cleaning and filtering works in a consistent manner to produce the same information for each report (based on the use of the same algorithm).
- Graphically presented data mirrors the textual data.

When you update reports, make sure you poll users for consistency issues. The people who rely on the information to perform real-world tasks will likely notice discrepancies faster than someone who simply manages, maintains, or outputs the report. Some data can be quite nuanced, making it hard to decipher potential problems with its appearance and layout.

Using Reports to Perform Specific Application Tasks

As mentioned quite a few times in this chapter so far, a report is only useful when it provides an actionable output. However, some reports may not have human readers in mind. It's possible to create reports that enhance application automation. Monitoring and management applications can read log files and use the data they contain to determine when to perform application management tasks. You don't want the maintenance actions to happen all the time or on a particular schedule—it's more important to perform the maintenance only when necessary in order to reduce resource usage and improve application availability. Because other software reads and acts upon the information in these reports automatically, you need to create them with an eye toward consistency and accuracy. The application doesn't care whether the report is beautiful or not, but it does care that the data it contains reflects the true state of the application.

 Automation is an exceptionally important part of modern IT because it helps reduce costs and ensures that actions occur reliably. However, hackers also love automation because people tend to forget that it's there and the hacker can often use automation as a means for gaining access to the system. Even if the automation you use is completely accurate and reliable, you still need to monitor it to ensure it remains secure and continues to work as originally intended.

Creating Internal Reports

Internal reports are those that you create and use within your own organization. Even though they tend to focus on the application as a whole, it's possible to focus these reports on any data source you need to track. An internal report can even focus on the uses to which you put third-party libraries, APIs, and microservices. The reports should help you perform some useful task, such as tracking the potential for security breaches. The point of any internal report is to provide data for application changes or to determine when an application is fine as is and doesn't need any change. The following sections help you better understand and use internal reports.

Determining Which Data Sources to Use

Internal reports tend to work with organization-specific data. These reports reflect the precise nature of the applications running on your systems and within the environments that you provide. You can see the usage patterns of your users and anomalous events that are specific to your system. In other words, internal reports tend to focus on the data that a vendor can't provide as part of a generic report.

The problem with internal reports is that everyone seems to assume that everyone else is trustworthy and that the data included in the report will never leave the organization. It's important to realize that many data breaches that occur today happen because a trustworthy employee left their laptop at the airport or someone with fewer scruples sold it to the highest bidder. With this in mind, you need to consider that any data you make available as part of a report will eventually see the light of day in the outside world, whether you want it to appear there or not. The following list provides you with some issues to consider when using internal data sources for a report:

- Ensure the people using the report actually require the data you're including.
- Define protocols, with penalties, for working with sensitive data.
- Create a plan for dealing with data breaches that involve sensitive data (procedures you intend to perform beyond the normal data breach protocols).
- Track the users of sensitive data to make it easier to determine where the source of a data breach occurred.
- Secure the sensitive data and keep it separate from less sensitive data.

 Sensitive data sometimes ends up appearing in public venues due to a series of connected errors. The reason you want to keep sensitive data separated is to make it less likely that it will appear in a public venue, such as a quarterly report or a public presentation. Releasing sensitive data accidentally isn't just embarrassing; it can cause all sorts of publicity issues, not to mention giving hackers fodder for breaking into your system.

Protecting your data is paramount today. Too many organizations are appearing on the front page of the trade press or in the major news media after making a seemingly small mistake that ends up giving hackers access to sensitive information. In many cases, the fault lies with incorrectly using an internal data source that an organization is supposed to jealously guard by making it available to people who really don't need it. The best question you can ask yourself when creating a new report is whether the persons who will view that report actually need to see the data you're providing.

Specifying Report Uses

Internal reports can and do use sensitive data. If you were to lock up every potentially sensitive piece of information, the organization could never function properly. There is a time and place for making the sensitive data that an organization holds known. However, you still want to reduce the security risks associated with sensitive data by ensuring that you define the uses for reports that you generate and spell out how users are to interact with them. An organization requires an enforceable set of rules for dealing with sensitive data contained in reports.

It's important to consider precisely how the report uses the data. Extrapolations and data science techniques can make sensitive data even more damaging when released in the wrong venue. Then again, you can use data cleaning and filtering techniques to make the data less sensitive and possibly acceptable for use in presentations to the organization as a whole. For example, data associated with individuals is more sensitive than disassociated data. Cleaning techniques would allow you to retain the statistical value of the data without associating it with specific individuals.

Reports should also have documentation associated with them. You need to know who created the report and why. The report should have a review date to ensure that it continues to have a pertinent purpose in the organization. As part of the documentation, you need to define some elements of report security:

- Detail who can access and read the report.
- Specify who can generate the report.
- Define how users can view the report and where (some reports may not be suitable for download to a mobile device, for example).
- Create a process for ensuring that all copies of the report are destroyed at some point (except an archival copy maintained in a secure location).
- Provide contact information so that anyone with questions knows who to ask about the report and its content.

The bring your own device (BYOD) phenomenon is creating security issues for many organizations when it comes to reports containing sensitive data. It's unlikely that you can keep users from trying to view sensitive data on their mobile devices without some significant security measures in place. What you need to assume is that some users will take the report out of the building with or without your permission. As a result, you need to prepare for the eventual breach that will occur when the user loses their mobile or other personal device containing your sensitive data. Making things hard for users who don't want to follow the rules will keep some users honest, but not all of them.

Relying on Externally Generated Reports

Third parties you interact with may need to provide you with reports before you can ascertain how the relationship is benefiting your organization, users, data, and application. Without this input, you can only guess as to how the third party views your organization and its use of the services that the third party provides. The point of externally generated reports is to ensure you understand the return you're getting on the investment and that the third party is performing as expected.

Obtaining Completed Reports from Third Parties

Any sort of third-party support product you obtain, such as application or security testing, needs an associated report. The report must detail the service rendered and when. It should tell anyone viewing it why the third party performed the service and the results of performing the service (for example, testing should detail when the tests succeeded or failed and provide the means to look at individual results). Any reports you require need to appear as part of a deliverables list that the third party must complete prior to receiving payment or it's likely that you won't receive all the reports you need.

As with internally created reports, any report you get from a third party should provide an impetus for action. Third parties tend to generate reports that are meant to impress, rather than inform. The glitzy paper and persuasive wording won't help much when you're dealing with a security breach possibly caused by an error on the part of the third party or a lack of attention to detail. In short, you need to view the report in the same way that you do internal reports—always questioning the value the report provides to you and your organization.

Whenever possible, work with the third party to generate reports that specifically address the needs of your organization, rather than accepting generic reports that the third party creates for everyone. The report should reflect your application environment, use of resources, personnel, and other factors that make your organization unique. The custom report will probably cost more, but you obtain more information from it and the savings in employee time often produce a return in excess of the additional cost.

Verification tests should be performed on the reported data as much as is possible. In many cases, you won't have the resources to check every fact contained in the reports, but you can usually make spot checks to ensure the third party hasn't produced a report containing information that the third party thinks you want to hear. In order to create a truly secure environment, you need verifiable facts that help you understand the dynamics of your application better and find ways to keep hackers at bay.

Developing Reports from Raw Data

Some third parties will provide an API you can use to access the raw data associated with your application. Rather than trust the third party reports completely, you can use the raw data to generate your own reports. The service normally costs more and you won't get it with all third-party providers, but it does pay to look for it. When you do create custom reports, use the guidelines in "Using Custom Reports" on page 301 to create them. The important issue is to ensure you get just the information you need, in the form you need it, in order to perform necessary tasks.

Keeping Internal Data Secure

A third party may have access to some internal data for your organization. The data may not be sensitive, but you still want to protect it because you know that a third party has access to it. When working with a third party, you want to treat all data the third party can access as sensitive data, following the rules found in "Creating Internal Reports" on page 304. In addition to following these rules, you want to know as much as you can about the third party. Trusting the third party comes only after you perform the proper steps to verify you truly can trust them. Here are some suggestions for ensuring that your application, its data, and your organization's data remain secure when working with a third party:

- Verify the identity of any third party who will work with the data.
- Perform a background check to ensure the third party is trustworthy.
- Track any access the third party makes to shared data and ensure you follow up immediately on any anomalies you experience.
- Ensure the third party signs a nondisclosure agreement (NDA).
- Monitor the third party to ensure there aren't any attempts to access sensitive data.
- Create a procedure for handling third-party data breaches or managing an issue regarding compliance with security protocols.

Providing for User Feedback

User feedback is an essential element of any reporting scenario because applications are useless without users. If you can't be sure that the users of an application are happy with it, then you can't truly be sure that the application itself is useful. Unfortunately, the smallest group of users with the loudest mouths usually provides user feedback—the silent majority goes unheard. For this reason, you must rely on various techniques to solicit user input and ensure that it's actually useful. Once you make this determination, you can begin using the feedback to make changes to the application that will improve security in various ways. For example, user interface changes that make the application easier to use and more understandable will reduce the potential for security issues that occur due to user error.

Obtaining User Feedback

User feedback is a kind of report and it's an essential part of maintaining a secure environment for your application. At one level, users who are dissatisfied with the performance of an application and believe that their requests for service will go unanswered tend to find solutions to the problems on their own—usually with the resulting security breaches and reliability issues. At another level, user feedback tells you how your application is actually serving user needs. In many cases, users require help and service that they can't verbalize, partly because they don't know the application isn't working as you had intended for it to function.

It's possible to obtain user feedback in all sorts of ways. Some methods work better than others do at obtaining specific kinds of feedback. For example, a comment form will tell you how a user feels about the application, but it won't tell you how a user is actually interacting with the application because the user input is biased (more on this issue in "Determining the Usability of User Feedback" on page 310). When working with a group of users, you often have to derive a middle position based on the varying inputs you receive. Each user may feel that his or her own input is unbiased, but everyone presents bias when expressing an opinion. The bias affects the input you receive, which affects its usability. The following list provides you with some ideas for obtaining user feedback, but it's important to remember that some of these methods are invasive and others tend to produce biased results:

- Create feedback forms that the user can send to you to request new features or simply comment on existing features.
- Sponsor group discussions where a number of users can talk about the relative merits of the application and define what they would like to see changed.
- Log the user's interactions with the application by adding checks to the software.
- Monitor user interactions with the application platform so that you can better understand how the user works within the application environment.
- Track user access outside the application environment, such as through access to a database, API, or microservice.
- Request user input whenever a special event (such as a crash due to a bug) occurs.

Most users will frown on monitoring techniques that involve technologies such as key logging. The feeling is one of being spied upon. When using a secretive approach to obtaining user data, you must consider the cost in negative user feelings against the benefits of obtaining the data. It's important to consider the trade-off not just for the current application, but for all of the applications that an organization employs, because the user will assume that you're monitoring them at all times (even if you aren't). The loss of privacy and trust that using products such as key loggers engender is one of those issues you need to consider carefully before employing one. It's also important to consider the fact that hackers often use the very monitoring software you rely upon to break into your network.

Determining the Usability of User Feedback

Obtaining user feedback is helpful, but only when you consider the circumstances under which you obtained the data. Talking directly with the user will always produce a biased result. Monitoring the user may produce an unbiased result, but if the user knows that the monitoring is taking place, his or her actions won't reflect actual usage conditions and the data you receive will be suspect. Logging user interactions through software checks doesn't provide the depth of information that monitoring provides. The point is that you must consider how you received the information before you can make any decisions about its usefulness in accomplishing a specific task.

To put this into perspective, a user might request a particular feature because it seems like an interesting thing to do. However, testing shows that the feature will likely increase the risk of a data breach because of the way in which it accesses data. In addition, monitoring shows that the user doesn't receive much benefit from the feature—it's rarely put to use in a real-world setting. Consequently, you have three bits of information you need to correlate in order to determine whether to keep the feature. Removing the feature will almost certainly elicit comments from the user, so you need a good reason to remove it. In situations such as this one, you need to consider what other sorts of usable user feedback might help. For example, you might bring up the issues with the feature in a group session and rely on the group's input to help you understand the need for the feature.

Application security often hinges on the user's participation. Social engineering attacks are devastating enough, but trying to thwart the efforts of a disgruntled employee can be even harder. Part of the purpose of user feedback is to ensure the user remains committed to working with the organization as a whole to keep the application and its data safe. In some cases, you need to weigh the effects of accepting user feedback that may not seem very helpful at the outset in order to maintain the user's good feelings toward the application.

Some developers view group sessions as a painful process best avoided by any sane individual. However, group sessions and the conclusions they provide help bring social pressure to bear on the issue of security. In some cases, the social pressure is enough to keep users from making some of the errors that they'd make without the introduction of social pressure. When working through a difficult decision, a group session can also keep you from looking like the bad guy when it comes time to cut a feature that could potentially present a security risk with little value to the user. Used properly, group sessions can provide an invaluable form of user feedback that will also help create a more secure environment for your application.

During the process of evaluating user feedback, you must also consider the politics of the organization. User feedback is always biased, but how biased often depends on the perceived value of the application to the user and the politics behind the decision-making process. Some situations require that you partially disregard the direct user feedback and try to obtain feedback through indirect means (such as monitoring) in order to determine where politics end and the true bias begins.

Make sure you consider all user feedback with the assistance of your development team and keep management informed about your progress. However, it's important to remember that your development team and management are both made up of people with their own biases and political agendas. It's human nature to disregard the user input you really didn't want to hear in favor of the opinions of the development team that correspond closely with your own. However, sometimes the user really is correct and you need to consider that view before making decisions.

As part of the decision-making process, also consider the other information sources at your disposal. The reports you generate not only tell you about the application, platform, third-party services, and so on—they also tell you about the state of your organization and help you make better decisions about user feedback you receive. Don't forget to consider the input from outside sources, such as trade press articles. A report that a certain type of hack is taking place might weigh heavily against including specific application features that would make it easier for a hacker to gain access to your application. In short, use all of your resources to get the big picture, rather than taking a myopic view of just the user input you receive.

PART V

Locating Security Resources

This book has provided you with a wealth of information about security threats, sources, fixes, and monitoring techniques. You've discovered all sorts of ways in which hackers often gain access to your organization and make life difficult for everyone. The data breaches hackers create come in a wide range of forms and have significantly different effects. However, you really need more information about these issues and that's what this part of the book is all about.

Chapter 16 discusses the methods you can use to track security threats. These threats are continuously changing and you need to keep on top of them. However, you also don't want to succumb to information overload, so getting the right information as quickly as possible is essential. This chapter helps you locate the information you need without expending a lot of time or energy to do it.

Chapter 17 talks about training. Everyone requires training. In fact, if you look at a lot of the detailed reports on security breaches, you soon discover that more training might have prevented them in the first place. Of course, you need to know what sorts of security training to get and who should get it. This chapter fills in all the details for you.

CHAPTER 16

Tracking Current Security Threats

Knowledge is an exceptionally powerful tool in the right hands. In order to stay on top of the security issues that could affect your application, you need to track the current security threats. However, if you pay any attention at all to the news media, you know that trying to track every potential security threat could become a full-time job. If you add in the stories from the trade press as well, then you really do have a full-time job and possibly a task that would require a team to manage the information flow. Clearly, you need some method of discerning which threats really do require your attention, or you could end up spending too much time tracking information and not enough time actually avoiding the threats.

Once you decide that the security threat is real, you need to decide what sort of action to take. Remember from Chapter 15 that the only report you really need is the one that provides for some type of action. You can say the same thing about security threat reports. The security threat discussion you need to investigate fully is the one that requires some sort of action on your part. Everything else is excess information that wastes your time. Of course, you need to decide between an update or an upgrade of your application when the situation requires. The point is that you need to be thinking about how to react to security threats and then take the required actions when necessary (or simply put the report in the circular file where it belongs).

This chapter isn't solely about researching security threats—it's about acting on information about security threats. In order to keep your application and its associated data safe, you need to know about the security threats and then act upon the information you receive. The worst thing you can do is arrive at a crisis situation unprepared, without a plan, and lacking the information you need to deal with the threat.

Avoiding Hype, Hysteria, and Helplessness

A problem exists in the security industry. Actually, a number of problems exist, but they all come from the same sources: hype, hysteria, and helplessness. The security industry thrives on these three words and many security professionals buy into them too. Often the media plays into it as well because sensational headlines sell content. The point is that the people who are supposed to make you calm, cool, and collected do anything but. It's easy to become a basket case in the security industry—everyone wants to make you paranoid of everything, all the time.

Hype continues unabated because it's the basis for selling you false promises—some product-related and some not. For example, you've probably heard that a particular virus or hack was going to end the Internet as we know it a number of times, but the Internet is still here. The fact of the matter is that a security breach will cause damage and it may ruin your day (or even your career), but the earth-shattering sorts of prognostications rarely, if ever, come true. When you hear a statement that seems outlandish, it probably is.

Even when a statement is true, those in the lead positions of the security industry often promote a hysterical perspective of it. The sensational headline you read might create a desire for content, but it doesn't really serve your needs. Hysteria never won a war and it doesn't work particularly well in the security industry either. What you really need to do is consider what effect a threat has on your organization, do what you can to mitigate it, and then monitor your systems to determine when (or if) someone managed to get in. The calm head usually wins the day.

It all comes down to an issue of making you feel helpless. After all, unless you feel truly helpless, the various security vendors can't charge in to your rescue. If this book has taught you nothing else, you should know by now that knowledge empowers you to take charge of security in any number of ways and that tools, while useful, are only a small part of a much larger solution. You really aren't helpless because you have all sorts of resources at your disposal.

Developing Sources for Security Threat Information

Because there is so much security information so widely available, you need to cultivate sources of security threat information that provide the material in a form you need and proves succinct enough to discover threats without wasting a lot of time. You want input from security professionals because the professionals have the time and resources to research the information fully. However, you need information from sources managed by professionals with a perspective similar to your own and not subject to the usual amount of hype, hysteria, and helplessness. The following sections review the most commonly used sources of security threat information and help you understand the role that each source has to play in helping make your application secure.

Reading Security-Related Articles by Experts

You don't have enough time to research every potential source of security threats. Of course, you could hire your own team to help out, but you need to consider the availability of security experts that write for the trade press magazines as a good second choice. These experts tend to spend most of their time enmeshed in security issues, so they know all the ins and outs of the various threats. For example, Jeremy Kirk recently revealed that, "Even Encrypted Medical Record Databases Leak Information" (*http://www.computerworld.com/article/2980593/data-privacy/even-encrypted-medical-record-databases-leak-information.html*). It's the sort of article that you need to pay attention to because most businesses rely on databases to store information and the databases that store sensitive information normally rely on encryption of some sort. The kind of article to look for has these characteristics in common:

- A clear title that lacks sensational language (as much as this is possible, anyway)
- A short overview of the problem so that you can decide whether the threat requires further research
- Short descriptions of the methods hackers employ to use the hack
- Links to additional information so you don't spend hours just looking for the details
- Statistics on the effect of the threat (making it possible for you to assess the risk to your organization more intelligently)
- Case study examples that demonstrate the viability of the attack against a real-world target

Scanning the article takes a few seconds, but by looking for these characteristics, you can usually save yourself from reading an article that really doesn't tell you anything. The important thing is to get the information you need without wasting a lot of time doing it. After a while, you begin to know which trade press authors best suit the needs of your business and you start paying more attention to the articles they write —saving you additional time. (Likewise, you figure out which authors write articles that are a total waste of your time and disregard them more often than not.)

When dealing with articles from the press, remember that the author's main job is to attract viewers to sell products from ads. That's how the online magazine pays for the author's services. As a result, you need to exercise care when you see headlines such as, "Is Your Connected Car Spying on You?" (*http://www.bbc.com/news/business-29566764*). The material in the article is probably technically accurate, but the author has used language to make the threat seem more significant than it really is; another such story relates to baby monitors—"9 Baby Monitors Wide Open to Hacks That Expose Users' Most Private Moments" (*http://arstechnica.com/security/2015/09/9-baby-monitors-wide-open-to-hacks-that-expose-users-most-private-moments/*). The purpose is to gain views, but the effect is to breed hysteria. Of course, you might wonder just what cars or baby monitors have to do with web applications. The fact of the matter is that many web applications now run in cars and baby monitors to perform all sorts of tasks—everything from providing entertainment to monitoring the environment. Even if your organization isn't involved in creating this sort of web application, the same principles apply.

The best reason to use trade press articles to locate information about security threats is that you can get information on a lot of threats in an incredibly short time. Just scanning for the kinds of clear headlines by authors you know makes it possible to locate the most important threats in just a few minutes.

The main disadvantage of using trade press articles is a lack of depth and the need to watch for writing that is less informative than it could be. You want to be sure that you rely heaviest on authors who provide you with links to the details you need to know everything you can about a threat without having to spend hours looking for it. If you start to find that the trade press article is getting into too much depth, you have a good reason to suspect that it might be more about selling products to you than informing you. Always look for the short, informative article with lots of links.

Checking Security Sites

Security sites tend to provide you with detailed information for a wide range of security threats. The security site may not discuss every current threat, but you can be sure of finding most of the threats that are currently active (and probably a history of all of the threats that security professionals have destroyed in the past). In fact, the sheer weight of all that information makes security sites a bad choice for your first visit. What you really want to do is create a list of threats to research and then visit the security sites to look for those particular threats.

Not all security sites are created equal—a fact that is lost on many people who cruise the Internet looking for security information. In fact, security sites come in four different forms (summarized in Figure 16-1), each of which has its own advantages and disadvantages:

Organization-based sites

Organization-based sites often provide the most concentrated information in a particular area, but lack the breadth of information that other kinds of sites support. For example, the SANS Institute (*http://www.sans.org/*) provides you with phenomenal research sources. It also sponsors various kinds of training events. This particular organization (like many others) is vendor supported, but at least you don't get a single vendor's perspective of how you should work through security issues.

Government-supported sites

These sites are obviously biased toward the needs of the government that sponsors them, but they're mostly unbiased in the kinds of information they provide. These sites are good places to locate information about current threats of an international nature. Sites such as the United States Computer Emergency Readiness Team (US-CERT) (*https://www.us-cert.gov/*) and National Vulnerability Database (*https://nvd.nist.gov/*) provide you with an abundance of useful tips and publications that you can obtain without cost.

Community-supported sites

Of the security sites you can visit, community-supported sites can prove the most interesting. They often offer insights you won't find anywhere else. Like every other site you visit, they do have an agenda of some sort and this agenda biases the information you receive, but the bias usually isn't strong enough to affect the quality of the information you receive. Sites such as Vmyths (*http://vmyths.com/*) can help you avoid the hysteria that normally comes with security incident disclosures.

Vendor-based sites

When you visit a vendor-based site, you often obtain a depth of information unparalleled by any other source, partially because the vendor wants to impress you. However, because the vendor is also actively engaged in trying to thwart various security threats, you can also gain better insights into what you need to do to prepare for a particular threat. Sites such as Symantec Security Response (*http://www.symantec.com/security_response/*) make it possible to ascertain things like the current threat level on the Internet quickly and determine which threats present the greatest potential for problems for most people.

Vendor-based security sites are there to sell you security products from that vendor. You need to realize this fact when you go on the site because the articles will contain biases that lean toward getting a product that will solve the security threat. Sometimes you really do need a third-party product to solve a problem, but careful research, attention to detail, proper system configuration, and an update or two often do more to solve the threat than buying a product ever will. Make sure you review and validate the facts you get from a vendor-based security site before you act on them. Think about the methods you already have at your disposal to solve a problem before you buy yet another product.

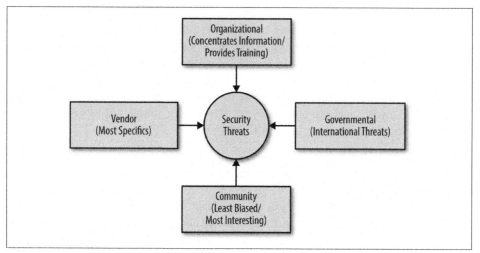

Figure 16-1. Choosing the correct security threat source is important

Some sites specialize in consolidating information from other sources. For example, Security Focus (*http://www.securityfocus.com/*), Open Source Vulnerability Database (OSVDB) (*http://www.osvdb.org/*), and Common Vulnerabilities and Exposures (CVE) (*https://cve.mitre.org/*) provide indexes of information also found on other sites. Using a consolidated site can save you time, but also makes it possible that you'll miss an important security notice because the site owner has a bias that is different from the needs of your organization.

An important thing to consider is that you really only need to visit a security site when you feel there is a security threat you need to research. Otherwise, your time is better spent looking for overviews of security threats you might need to deal with. Make sure you visit the kind of site that will best serve your needs for a particular threat. For example, an international threat perpetrated by one country against another will likely receive the best coverage on a government-supported site. Hackers who are trying to extort funds from you after encrypting your hard drive data are often detailed better at vendor-based sites. If you feel that a threat is likely pure hoax, make sure you visit a community-supported site first to verify it.

Getting Input from Consultants

All of the sources discussed so far in the chapter have one thing in common—they provide general information supported by an outside source. However, your business isn't a general entity and has specific security needs based on the kinds of applications you run, the environment in which you run them, and the level of training your users have. In some cases, the general sources don't provide enough information because they simply can't provide it—the authors of those bits of information know nothing about your organization. In this case, you usually need to employ the services of a consultant to consider the security threats.

 It's important to remember that consultants are a paid resource, which means that they could (and probably will) provide a stronger level of bias than other sources you use. After all, the consultant is in business to make money. Some consultants are quite ethical and would never overcharge you on purpose; however, the fact that money is exchanging hands and the consultant has a more personal relationship with you than other sources do, will likely make the consultant a cautious source of information. You need to balance the deeper understanding that a consultant has about your particular setup with the fact that the level of bias is stronger as well.

A consultant can provide specific information about the specific threats faced by your organization in particular. The advice will make it possible to deal with the threats a lot faster than if you had to create a strategy of your own. Of course, the quality of the information comes with a price. Using a consultant is also the most expensive way to deal with security threats. For the most part, the majority of the sources provided in this chapter offer some level of free support. It's best to use consultants when:

- You already know that the threats are serious
- You can't create a strategy to handle them quickly
- The methods required for handling the threats are outside the realm of skills your organization has to offer
- Handling the threats requires coordination between several groups or contact with other companies
- There is some other mitigating circumstance that makes handling the security threat yourself untenable

Avoiding Information Overload

So many hackers are doing so many things to make your life interesting that it would be exceptionally easy to go into overload on the issues that affect security today. Most people are facing a terrible case of information overload anyway. It's possible to have an entire inbox filled with links to articles you really should read, but never get to due to scheduling concerns (such as those endless meetings that most organizations have). Even so, you need to spend some time trying to figure out which threats are terrifying enough to require action on your part, which is why you need to keep from getting overloaded in the first place. The following steps summarize techniques you can use to avoid information overload and potentially avoid the security threats you read about completely:

1. Choose security sources carefully. Make sure the security information sources you choose relate to your organization's needs, present the information you need in a succinct manner, and provide just the details you need without becoming overwhelming.

2. Locate potential security fixes that don't depend on changing your application. In some cases, the best security sources can provide you with a quick fix to your problem, such as installing a browser or other update.

3. Create a task-based approach to handling threats. If you can't summarize a security threat in a single sentence, you don't really understand it well enough to know whether you need to do anything. Developing the habit of summarizing the threat quickly as a single sentence description will save your time and effort in the long run.

4. Discard information sources that tend toward sensationalizing security threats. What you need is just the facts and nothing but the facts. When a source starts to peddle hype, you can't depend on it to tell you about the real security threats that you really do need to fix.

5. Develop critical-thinking skills. Some of the smartest people around base their actions on the worst that could happen if they didn't act. Thinking about threats in the form of a worst-case scenario helps you figure out which threats present the greatest risk so you can devote your time thwarting them.

6. Avoid the flash in the pan threat. Some threats only appear in a headline once and then you never read about them again. Even when the predictions about such threats are dire, you have to wonder just how dire they are when they don't stick around long enough to make a second headline.

As part of your strategy for avoiding becoming overwhelmed, make sure you spend the time required to understand how threats really work. For example, you might have heard about some threats like rowhammer (*http://www.rowhammer.com/*) that can wreak havoc with a system. However, when you start reading further, you begin to understand that it's an interesting hack, but requires the sort of system access that hackers normally lack when dealing with web applications. Consequently, you can probably ignore rowhammer for now. Of course, a great security resource would have told you that fact from the outset, but sometimes you need to perform the research on your own in order to avoid being inundated with information you really can't use.

 Be sure to employ data filtering when you can. Performing quick searches on your accumulated information sources for particular keywords can help you determine whether a threat really is something you should consider overcoming. Many of the tools available on the market today make it possible to filter and reorganize information in various ways. Knowing how to use these tools effectively will save you time in the long run for a little extra effort learning the tool today.

Creating a Plan for Upgrades Based on Threats

When you receive information about a potential threat soon enough and the amount of code required to fix the problem is large enough, you may need to perform an upgrade of your application. Of course, you must first figure out whether you need to do anything at all. Some threats do merit attention, but are of a sort that won't affect your application because they require some sort of special access or affect the use of software you don't even have. The following sections help you determine whether an upgrade is needed based on security threat information and how to approach the upgrade once you know one is needed.

Anticipating Situations that Require No Action at All

Whenever you read about a security threat and research its implications, you need to keep in mind that the documentation you read will make the threat sound dire. And the threat is, in fact, dire for someone. However, the threat may not matter at all to you. Organizations often spend time and money reacting to threats that don't pose any sort of problem for them. In short, they buy into the hysteria that surrounds security threats when there isn't any need to do so. One of the things you need to consider as you review current security threats is whether they actually do apply to you. In many cases, they don't apply and you don't need to do anything about them. You can blithely slough them off without another thought.

Of course, the problem is in getting to the point where you know the threat doesn't affect you. A missed threat represents a serious problem because it can open you to attack and the things that follow (such as a downed site or breached data). Assessing the potential risk of a particular security threat involves:

- Determining whether you use the technology described as the entry point for the security threat
- Considering whether the kind of access required to invoke the threat actually applies to your organization
- Defining the circumstances under which your organization could be attacked and when the attack might occur
- Reviewing the safeguards you currently have in place to determine whether they're sufficient to thwart the attack
- Ensuring that you have a strategy in place should the attack occur and you're wrong about the hacker's ability to invoke it on your organization

Deciding Between an Upgrade or an Update

Chapter 13 and Chapter 14 discuss naturally occurring upgrades and updates. However, in this case, you're thinking about an upgrade or an update due to a security threat. Many of the same rules apply. An upgrade always indicates some type of significant code change, while an update may not require a code change at all, but may instead reflect a change in user interface or some other element that you can change quickly without modifying the underlying code. Consequently, the first demarcation between upgrades and updates are those that you normally apply when making any other change.

A security threat can change the intention and urgency of an upgrade or an update. In some cases, you need to tackle the problem in several parts:

1. Address the specific issue that the security threat focuses upon as an update.
2. Upgrade or update any supporting software (such as firewalls or the operating system) to ensure the security threat can't attack the application from another direction.
3. Train users to avoid performing tasks in such a manner that they provide hackers with valuable information or access that the hacker can use to initiate the attack.
4. Modify any code surrounding the target code to ensure the application continues to work precisely as designed as an upgrade after you've deployed the update.
5. Perform an upgrade of any dependencies to ensure the entire application is stable.

6. Verify that the upgraded application continues to thwart the security threat by performing extensive testing targeted in the same manner that a hacker would use.

Not every security threat requires this extensive list of steps to overcome, but it's important to consider each step when deciding how to proceed. You may find that just an update will suffice to thwart the attack or that an operating system upgrade is really all you need. The point is to consider every possible aspect of the security threat in relation to your application and its supporting data.

 When faced with a zero-day attack, it's always best to start with an update that you create and test using the shortest timeline possible. The hackers won't wait for you to deploy the update before attacking your system. In fact, hackers are hoping that you'll become embroiled in procedure and organizational politics—giving them more time to attack your application. Speed is an essential element of keeping hackers at bay, but make sure you always test any software before you deploy it to ensure you aren't actually making things worse. Mitigating the security threat requires an accurate strategy delivered as quickly as possible.

Sometimes you really do need to make quick decisions regarding the use of an upgrade or an update to fix a security threat. The steps in this section are certainly helpful, but the flowchart in Figure 16-2 provides an even faster method of making the determination.

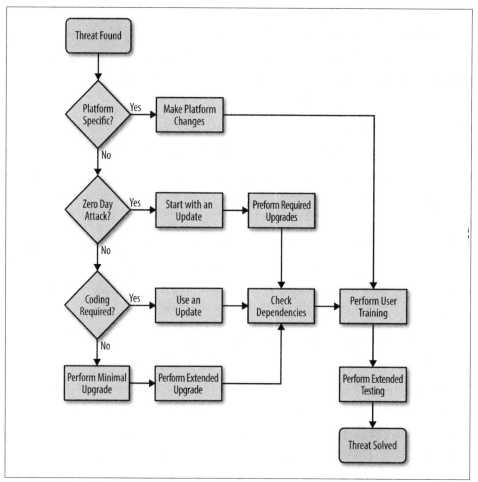

Figure 16-2. Making the decision between upgrade and update quickly is sometimes necessary

Defining an Upgrade Plan

Chapter 13 describes the process for a standard upgrade for your application. It details a process that could require months to complete. Of course, you have time when you're performing an upgrade of your application to perform every task carefully and completely. Security threats seldom wait long enough to provide you with months of waiting time to create an upgrade and deploy it. The only way that you obtain the level of advance warning to perform a long-term upgrade is to have someone in the right place to obtain information when it first becomes available (many ethical hackers give vendors three months to a year to fix problems before making them public knowledge).

Constant testing of your application by an organization that specializes in security testing can provide you with longer lead times for upgrades. A security testing firm can make you aware of potential deficiencies in your application long before they become public knowledge. Of course, in order to get this level of advance knowledge, you must be willing to pay for the service, which can become quite expensive.

When working through an upgrade in response to a security threat, you need to consider methodologies that allow you to create the upgrade and test it incrementally as you work in order to deliver the upgrade in a shorter timeframe. Agile programming techniques (*http://agilemethodology.org/*) can help you accomplish this task. Of course, if your organization doesn't normally use agile programming techniques, the time lost in learning them won't help much. Even so, part of your upgrade plan should include some methodology for creating the code and testing it on a much shorter schedule than is normal. After the threat has passed, you need to go back through the code and ensure you didn't introduce yet more security holes in fixing the hole presented by the security threat.

In Chapter 14, "Performing Emergency Updates" on page 293 discusses the need for a fast response team. In many cases, using this team to put the upgrade together will save time and possibly expense. The team is already used to working together to create updates quickly. Using it to create an upgrade in response to a security threat makes sense. However, you need to ensure that the team has the proper staffing to handle an upgrade. It may become necessary to add team members to provide services beyond those normally required for an update.

A deadly problem faced in many organizations is managers who have become hysterical and require constant updates. The "are we there yet?" problem slows progress on the upgrade considerably. The development team responsible for the upgrade should make regular reports to management, but management should also realize the need to let the development team work in peace. Otherwise, while an important team member is delivering yet another unnecessary report, hackers will invade your system and make your worst nightmares come true.

Creating a Plan for Updates Based on Threats

In some cases, you receive security threat information with such short lead time that you need to perform an update now and an upgrade later. Updates make fewer changes to application code and sometimes don't affect the code at all. As part of planning for an update based on threat information, you need to consider whether the update is an emergency or not. In addition, you need to create a plan that considers the effect on any third-party software you may rely on to make your application work.

Verifying Updates Address Threats

The focus of this chapter is on speed of execution. When you identify a security threat, you need to act upon the information as quickly as possible. Consequently, an update is the preferred method of attacking the problem because updates require less time, fewer resources, and potentially cause fewer issues during testing. In this case, updates mean more than simply your application. Updates can include:

- Adjustments to the security software already in place
- Alterations of the host platform
- Modifications of the host browser
- Changes in procedure based on user training or other means
- Updates to the underlying application through noncoded or lightly coded means
- Modification of dependent software such as libraries, APIs, and microservices

Unfortunately, updates don't always fix the problem. If the goal is to thwart a security threat, then finding the correct course of action first is the best way to proceed because time you waste trying other measures will simply delay the approach that works. The hackers aren't waiting. Sometimes speed of execution comes down to performing more detailed fixes and simply admitting that you need more time than is probably convenient to effect a repair.

The crux of the matter is to look at the kind of attack that the hacker uses. For example, a man-in-the-middle attack may simply require that you encrypt incoming and outgoing data correctly and with greater care. In addition, it would require additional authentication and authorization measures. A hack of this sort isn't easily fixed using an update because you're looking at the way in which data is prepared, sent, and processed, which are three tasks that the underlying code must perform.

On the other hand, a distributed denial-of-service (DDoS) attack does lend itself to the update model because you can change the security software settings, provide additional system resources, and reconfigure the platform to make such an attack harder. You can also fix social engineering hacks through user training, modification of the user interface, and changes to the application's security settings. The kind of attack determines whether an update is a good choice. In many cases, you find that you can at least reduce the likelihood of an attack through an update, but may not be able to fix it completely.

Dealing with Application Downtime

Most people don't want to talk about application downtime, especially in relation to security issues. The moment an application goes down, people start asking questions, and questions naturally lead to suspicions (true or not). At some point, the question becomes one of whether you can continue to keep an application active in an attack situation or whether you must take it offline to prevent the sorts of damage that come back to haunt you later. In some cases, the hacker won't give you a choice; the hack itself causes the application to crash in a specific manner. The point is that hackers do cause application downtime, and it's never pleasant for the IT staff that allows the downtime to occur.

Downtime does occur, despite the ads you see for 99.999% uptime from some companies. Of course, the downtime always appears in a major trade press article when you're a larger organization, making it even more embarrassing. It's interesting to note that the articles usually contain a nebulous (and probably incorrect) reason for the downtime (see *http://www.zdnet.com/article/microsoft-explains-roots-of-this-weeks-office-365-downtime/*). However, sometimes the downtime and subsequent data loss come from other sources, such as Mother Nature (see *http://www.computer world.com/article/2974260/data-center/mother-nature-teaches-google-a-lesson.html*). The point is this: downtime occurs for everyone and for various reasons.

When an attack becomes such that you begin to worry about data loss, loss of system integrity, or grievous damage, it's time to take the application and perhaps the entire system offline. Doing so will give you time to perform any required updates and attempt to bring the system back online—hopefully with better results. Although downtime is viewed by management as a negative solution for any problem, it's sometimes the best solution to prevent serious damage that will take you weeks or months to repair (usually with yet more downtime involved).

Determining Whether the Threat Is an Emergency

When talking about security threats, it's important to make a determination of whether the threat presents an emergency. Chapter 14 discussed the criteria for an emergency from a general update perspective. Here are some things to consider in addition to the general considerations when working through security threat issues:

- Any zero-day security threat that actively targets your system or application
- Any in-progress attack
- Significant, verifiable threats delivered directly to the organization or one of its staff

- Attacks against libraries, APIs, or microservices that your application depends upon

Defining an Update Plan

Chapter 14 defines the requirements for an update plan. When working through an update that addresses a security threat, you want to use the fast response team to ensure the update is completed and tested in a timely manner (see "Creating a Fast Response Team" on page 294 in Chapter 14). It's also important to ensure that you consider the same sorts of issues discussed in "Defining an Upgrade Plan" on page 326. For example, using agile programming techniques will only make things go faster and reduce the time required to obtain a good update.

Asking for Updates from Third Parties

Something that many development teams forget in the rush to get a security update out the door is the need to address dependencies. If the dependent code is rock solid and you're using the latest release, you might not have to check into an update immediately, but you do need to make the third party aware of potential security issues with their product and ask that these problems be addressed. Otherwise, any fixes you create might not continue to work—the hacker will simply choose another avenue of attack.

CHAPTER 17

Getting Required Training

Secure applications that follow best practices and employ all the latest anti-hacking strategies are easy prey to users who are unaware of the need to keep things secure. Social engineering attacks are still the most effective way to break into an organization. Users aren't inept and it isn't that they lack the ability to make good decisions—it's the fact that they often don't have appropriate training and lack a requirement to retain the knowledge gained. Simply training someone to perform the task well won't achieve anything unless that knowledge is tested from time to time with repercussions for failure (or perhaps rewards for success).

However, developers, administrators, managers, and all other personnel in your organization also have training requirements. Without proper training, you can't expect your organization to have even a small chance of keeping hackers at bay. Developers need to keep an eye out for new threats and fix security holes, administrators need to remain vigilant to potential breaches, and management needs to know about the need to provide resources to keep applications safe. In short, everyone has a task to do that requires some level of training to achieve.

This chapter discusses some of the ways in which you can help keep the human element of an application trained so that the application performs better and hackers are less inclined to attack. No, training won't solve all your problems, but training mixed with secure applications, appropriate support software, and well-designed libraries, APIs, and microservices will give hackers a reason to have second thoughts. A determined hacker will always break your security, but if you can give a hacker a good reason to look for a target with less effective defenses, it certainly pays to do so.

Making Training Specific

This chapter uses the term *training* in a generic sense because most issues discussed affect all forms of training equally. You must still set space aside for training no matter what form of training you perform.

Some forms of training really are generic. For example, every group in your organization requires training in organizational security procedures. It doesn't matter whether the group contains users, developers, administrators, or management—everyone needs to know the organizational policies in order to ensure the security process occurs as expected.

However, some types of training are quite specific. Users may require specific training for data entry. In this case, you would size the training area to accommodate a smaller group consisting of just users. Developers, an even smaller group in most cases, may require special training in library, API, or microservice access. Perhaps some of this information is sensitive, so you need a smaller training area that provides the level of privacy required.

Making the training specific to the needs of the group or groups receiving it is important. Ensuring you meet the privacy, size, and technical needs of these groups is important. Consider how the group will learn as part of your search for a particular space. For example, if the group requires the use of a projection system, then you need a room with the appropriate equipment and enough electrical circuits to accommodate such needs. This book isn't about giving presentations, but trying to discuss security without first meeting the needs of the individuals in the group will doom your presentation to failure.

Creating an In-House Security Training Plan

Depending on the size of your organization, an in-house training plan can be less expensive and better than using a third-party trainer or school. The advantage of this approach is that you can teach security as it applies to your organization, which means that your staff gets more in the way of pertinent information in significantly less time. The disadvantage is that it's unlikely that the in-house trainer will have the skills, education, or experience that a professional trainer will provide. The following sections discuss the requirements for an in-house security training plan.

As with many areas of security, you must consider risk as part of the equation when choosing in-house security training. Yes, your trainer will know all of the security requirements for your organization, but the documentation your organization provides may be incomplete or simply wrong. The risk is one of providing the wrong information to your staff, even when this information more closely aligns with what your organization believes is correct. Using an outside training option often gets staff talking about the latest trends in security and may prompt your staff to make changes to the security plan to better promote good security processes within the organization.

Defining Needed Training

Before you can embark on a training crusade for your organization, you need to have some idea of what sort of training your staff requires. Everyone in the organization requires some level of training, even those who already have some professional training. Creating a list of the kinds of training needed will make it possible to tune the training sessions and obtain better value for your investment. In addition, because the training resources of an organization are usually quite limited, you need to get the maximum value from them. With this in mind, consider the following issues as part of any training plan:

- The current skill level of your staff
- General training requirements (those used throughout the industry)
- Organization-specific training requirements (such as the use of forms or processes)
- Staff availability
- Trainer availability
- Trainer familiarity with specific staff needs
- Potential training locations

Unless you create a usable plan for meeting training goals, the outcome is that the staff will learn little, trainers will become frustrated, and the value you receive for the time invested will amount to nearly nothing. It's important to understand that in-house training only provides a benefit when you tailor the setting and goals to take advantage of the in-house environment. For example, a quiet room where the trainer can meet with staff members who require special help one on one usually nets better results than attempting to accomplish the task in a noisy classroom.

Setting Reasonable Goals

A major problem with in-house training is that management tends to set unrealistic goals and the trainer lacks the experience to steer management in the right direction. Because staff members can be unwilling participants, they sometimes feel the trainer should give them a break—a free ride—simply for attending the training sessions. The lack of clearly defined goals makes it impossible for anyone to get what they want or even to know what they have achieved. A lack of reasonable, clearly defined goals often causes even a well-organized training session to fail. In short, goal setting is an essential part of making training work. Here are some things to consider as part of setting training goals for the organization:

- Develop a plan based on what the organization actually needs for training, rather than what would be nice to have.

- Specify goals that everyone can understand, using a language that everyone understands, rather than relying on jargon.

- Ensure the goals fall in line with what the staff is able to learn, rather than what you think the staff should learn.

- Create goals that use the time you have available efficiently and allow extra time for harder topics because staff members will definitely have questions or simply not understand the material.

- Provide time for staff members who require individual training or who aren't able to meet at a specific training time.

- Use input from all stakeholders in the training arena: management, trainer, and staff should all have a say in what the training sessions provide.

Only when a training plan includes reasonable goals can you hope to achieve anything. It's important to understand that you might not meet all your goals, so having levels in the list of goals (where meeting a specific level is still considered a win for everyone) is important. You can always create another training session to handle harder goals later—the important thing is to achieve demonstrable results during each training session so you can point to the goals when management asks what the training accomplished.

It might seem as if the trainer should set the goals for training, but this isn't the best route in many cases. The trainer will spend time getting ready to train staff members in new techniques, so coordinating the training sessions will place an unnecessary burden on the trainer. In many cases, you can accomplish more by assigning another individual to coordinate everyone's efforts. That way, the stakeholders can concentrate on their specific area of concern.

Using In-House Trainers

Many organizations will require a staff member to perform required training. In many cases, using an in-house trainer does work acceptably, but some situations call for use of a consultant or professional trainer to obtain good results. There are advantages and disadvantages in using an in-house trainer. The advantages are:

Cost
> It's a lot less expensive to use in-house staff than it is to hire a professional trainer in most cases.

Familiarity
> An in-house trainer will already be familiar with company policies and the staff that implement them, so it's easier for an in-house trainer to provide personalized attention.

Availability
> Using an in-house trainer means that it's possible to schedule training around organizational needs, rather than the needs of the trainer. In addition, staff with questions can access the trainer as needed.

Convenience
> In most cases, using an in-house trainer is more convenient than having to find someone with the requisite knowledge on the outside. Hiring an outsider effectively means having to hold interviews for someone you don't plan to retain as an employee.

Known quantity
> An organization already knows the knowledge level, credentials, and abilities of the in-house trainer. Some outsiders represent themselves in one light during the interview and deliver something different—something less than expected.

In order to gain these advantages, management must work with the trainer and staff must be willing participants in the training process. Even under ideal conditions, using an in-house trainer comes with at least some of these disadvantages:

Lack of respect
> The staff members are already familiar with the trainer as a peer. The classroom environment demands someone who commands respect and the other staff members may refuse to provide it.

Loss of time
> An in-house trainer will focus attention on the training task, rather than attending to normal business matters. You can't expect them to do both. What this means is that you effectively lose an employee before and after the training sessions.

Lack of skill

In general, any in-house trainer is not going to possess the same skills as someone who trains full time. The exception is someone who happened to go to school to become a trainer.

Lack of experience

Even if someone has the required skills and training, the fact that they don't perform training tasks full time means that they lack the experiential knowledge a full-time trainer will have.

Monitoring the Results

Training is a process of monitoring and adjustment. You can't simply pour information into people's heads and expect it to stick (at least, not yet). The reason that schools are supposed to give exams is to help the teacher understand deficiencies in the current curriculum and to aid in making adjustments to it. The same is true of corporate training. In order to achieve the best results, you must monitor the training effort and make adjustments to it to allow for the differences in people and their understanding of the topic. Of course, work-related exams can take many forms. Here are some ideas for monitoring the effectiveness of training:

Written exams

Using an exam to measure the effectiveness of training works in the classroom to some degree and it also works in the corporate environment. Of course, some people know how to bend a test to their will (without actually becoming competent) and some people simply don't take tests well (despite being quite competent), so this shouldn't be your only measure of success.

Hands-on testing

Creating a test scenario and having the staff member demonstrate the training they received is another way to check for the desired results. Often the people who fail written exams do much better with hands-on testing. However, hands-on testing still has the same problems that written exams do—some people simply do better at them without really knowing the material.

Practical factors

Training should produce a demonstrable effect in overall workplace efficiency and productivity. Simply watching how the training affects the business can prove that the training is working. For example, a significant drop in security-related errors can show that the security training is achieving the desired goal.

Monitored results

Watching the business as a whole may not tell you everything you need to know about the effectiveness of the training. Sometimes you need to monitor specific business areas, such as a reduced incidence of successful email attacks, to know whether the training is working as desired.

Cross-training

Teaching someone else to perform a task correctly is one method that many businesses fail to think about for assessing the success of a training situation. In order to train someone else, the staff member must absorb the knowledge well enough to use it effectively. A cross-training scenario demonstrates that a staff member actually understands the material and can put it into words that someone else understands.

 A serious problem that occurs during the monitoring process is that people feel threatened and can become unproductive. For one thing, it seems that everyone has this need to blame someone or something for a failure to achieve a specific training goal. However, failure simply points out the need for additional training, not the need for blame (see the article "Defining the Benefits of Failure" (*http://blog.johnmuellerbooks.com/2013/04/26/defining-the-benefits-of-failure/*)). A failure can occur for reasons other than an error on anyone's part. Wasting time playing the blame game is unproductive. It's far better to look at the fact that a failure occurred and to provide remedial training to address it.

As you monitor the results of training, you can check off items where the staff has demonstrated adequate knowledge. Where the staff fails to meet training goals, you can re-create the goal and try some other approach in presenting the material. Repeating the same approach to training will generally create the same result—the ability to create multiple methods for learning the same material is essential to ensuring that the staff members actually absorb it.

When training is ongoing, you can use the opportunity of checking off learned goals to generate new goals that build on the knowledge the staff accumulates. It's important not to overwhelm anyone by creating huge lists that make the task of learning the new material seem insurmountable. What you want to do is create smaller steps with frequent successes so that the staff can maintain a positive attitude toward the training.

The overall goal of any training scenario is to ensure your application and its associated data remains safe. As mentioned earlier in the book, the only way to achieve a secure environment in any organization is to procure staff support for it. Training is part of the process for gaining the staff member's trust in the application and ensuring that everyone understands the role security plays in making the work environment better. The only way you gain this sort of result is to maintain a positive environment.

Obtaining Third-Party Training for Developers

Third-party training usually promises generic security information that works well for most organizational needs. Of course, you pay more for this generic training than you would using in-house staff, so you're getting information that is less pertinent to your organization and it's costing more to obtain it. However, the training the staff receives is more professional and current than an in-house instructor can provide in most cases. What you gain is the quality of training.

Not all third-party training is alike. You can obtain third-party training in several different ways—each of which has advantages and disadvantages. The following list summarizes the most common third-party training options:

In-house security training

A security consultant with training experience comes to your organization and sets up shop in an area you provide. You can provide input to the trainer on the sorts of information that your staff needs. As a result, you can customize the training to some degree and obtain a better balance between generic and organization-specific information. In addition, your staff learns in the environment they work in and use the equipment they normally use. One downside of this option is that you must provide an area for the trainer to work that is sufficiently large to house the staff that you want to train. In addition, this tends to be the most expensive option.

Online schools

When working with an online school, staff members can usually proceed at their own pace, which could mean a better level of training. However, staff members must be self-motivated for this option to work well. The advantage of this training option is that it costs significantly less than most other options and provides high-quality training in most cases. The disadvantage is that staff members aren't learning in a classroom environment and may find it difficult to get questions answered in some cases. You may also find that the course material is a little more limited than other options.

Training centers

A training center offers a specialized classroom environment with trainers who do nothing all day but teach security. Consequently, this option offers the best generic training and staff members obtain the best level of interaction with the instructor. Training centers normally keep class sizes quite small so that the instructor can spend personal time with each student and motivate the students to do their best. This tends to be a moderately expensive training option and you may find that you're out additional expenses for the staff members who attend the classes when the training center is located some distance away.

Colleges and universities

In most cases, students gets the same level of training as they obtained when going to school for their degree. The classes may be crowded, the instructor overwhelmed, and the material outdated. In some cases, this option is free or of minimal cost, with the exception of required classroom materials. A downside of this approach is that the school holds classes when it's most convenient for the school, not for your organization, so you may end up losing staff members when they go for training.

You may not find a perfect third-party option, but you can usually find one that fits well enough. The goals in this case are to find the level of training needed (or get as close as possible to it) for the price you can afford. The following sections provide additional information about how third-party trainers can help your staff members get the kind of training they require.

 Some levels of training offer a certificate that an in-house trainer can't provide. The certificate may be meaningless for your business or it might be something you can show to potential customers to demonstrate that your staff has received the required security training. Having the certificate makes you more attractive to some customers and can improve business—making it possible to earn back some of the additional money spent on training needs.

Specifying the Training Requirements

When working with a third party, you still need to perform the tasks described in "Defining Needed Training" on page 333 and "Setting Reasonable Goals" on page 334. However, you must now perform these tasks for someone who doesn't know anything about your company's culture or needs. In order to obtain the training requirements you need, you must provide a blueprint for the person or organization providing the training service. Any staff members involved with looking for, querying, and interacting with a third-party trainer must understand the training requirements fully and communicate them clearly to the provider. Otherwise, the training your staff receives won't do the job and you'll continue to have security issues that you could avoid with the proper training in place. The following list describes some of the things you should consider during any conversation with a third-party trainer:

- Discuss training times to ensure they work for your organization
- Specify the venue for the training
- Ensure the trainer actually offers the services needed
- Verify that the trainer has the proper credentials
- Create a list of needs the trainer has in order to obtain a desirable result

- Obtain a list of any required special equipment

 The value provided by third-party trainers and training organizations varies greatly. Make sure you get any promised services in writing and that the training service you obtain has a proven record of accomplishment. If possible, take time to talk with previous clients to discover any potential problems. Of course, the people that the trainer will recommend will have mostly positive things to say because they likely had a positive experience. Even so, you can usually obtain enough information to make a good decision by being careful in how to talk with past clients. As with any other business dealing, it's important to remain cautious when hiring a third party to perform training tasks in your organization.

Hiring a Third-Party Trainer for Your Organization

When hiring a third-party trainer to teach on site, you need to set up several meetings to ensure the trainer understands what you want and to verify you have everything the trainer needs to do a good job. The first day a trainer arrives on site to teach shouldn't be a tragic waste of time for everyone. Doing your homework will reduce first day issues so that everyone begins on the right foot. Here are some things to consider discussing with the third-party trainer:

- Discuss specific security issues that your organization has and provide demonstrations of how these issues take place within the organization. It's essential that the trainer know precisely which security areas to address and emphasize during the training sessions.

- Ensure the trainer understands the history behind any security-related issues and knows what you've done in the past to alleviate them. This step ensures the trainer doesn't waste time trying things that you've already tried and ruled out.

- Address any potential restrictions on training with the trainer to ensure the staff members don't feel uncomfortable receiving instructions that are contrary to company policy.

- Verify that the physical location you select for training will meet the trainer's needs. In addition, check on issues such as the kind of equipment the trainer needs and what equipment the trainer will provide.

As with any other visitor to your organization, you need to ensure the trainer feels welcome, but doesn't have free access to sensitive areas or sensitive information. A trainer isn't somehow above the security requirements for your organization. In fact, the trainer could be in the business specifically to carry out social engineering attacks.

Always treat your third-party trainer with respect, but also ensure the trainer receives the proper level of monitoring so that you keep your organization safe.

Using Online Schools

Online schools offer little in the way of customization and the curriculum you see is the curriculum you get. Ensure that the online school provides good access to the instructor through some asynchronous means (such as email). You want to be certain that your staff members can contact the instructor when it's convenient for them. It's also important to realize that communication in an online school setup has limits, so you may need a knowledgeable staff member standing by to help.

As previously mentioned, the advantage of using an online school is that everyone can proceed with training at a comfortable pace. However, human nature being what it is, many people will procrastinate and then try to cram for exams at the last minute. This form of training requires additional support by management and monitoring by a knowledgeable staff member. You should see a definite progression of knowledge by staff members as the training proceeds. Otherwise, you need to ask whether the staff member is fully participating with the program.

It's important to realize that not everyone can learn online. People have all sorts of ways to learn. In fact, some people don't learn well in the classroom environment at all—they need some sort of hands-on training or they may need to see someone else perform a task. You may find that some staff members simply can't use this option and will need to rely on an in-house trainer or some other method of obtaining the required training. The problem isn't one of the staff member not trying, but simply a matter of ability to learn using a specific approach.

Relying on Training Centers

Training centers can offer the best of breed training as long as you have willing staff members. The main thing to remember in this case is that the training the staff members receive is not only expensive, but it's also generic. Training centers make their money by providing intensive training using scripted techniques. The training really is good, but the staff members have to be willing to participate in the process fully and then study during their off time (after class).

In order to make this option work, you essentially need to give up on getting anything from the staff member during the training time. Disruptions will only distract the staff member and reduce the effectiveness of the training (and at the prices these places charge, disruptions really are quite expensive). Because the training time and venue aren't negotiable, you may need to compensate the staff member in various ways to ensure training goes as anticipated.

When the staff member returns from training, make sure you test the new knowledge gained fully. In addition, it's often helpful for the staff member to provide a presentation on new skills learned. Using this approach helps to reinforce the knowledge that the staff member has gained and to inform other staff members about new techniques. The presentation falls into the cross-training category described in "Monitoring the Results" on page 336. You can use other techniques from that section to ensure that you got your money's worth from the training center.

Using Local Colleges and Universities

Not every organization has the time, resources, or funds to use any of the other training techniques described in this section. Your staff members still require training. Even if you don't have someone capable of performing in-house training and can't afford any of the other options listed in this chapter, there is still a good chance that you can afford the services of a local college or university. Depending on how your locality handles schooling in this venue, you may need to pay some amount of tuition for the staff member, but you'll likely find it a lot less expensive than other options.

Colleges and universities don't teach anything quickly. The staff member will proceed at the same pace as everyone does, so this option won't provide the sort of training needed in the short term. A staff member using this option may end up going for the entire semester or the school year to obtain the required information. Consequently, you need to perform advance planning to use this option.

The training is usually a bit more flexible than going to a training center. For example, the staff member may find that classes occur several times during the day and at night as well. Even so, you'll often find that the schedule isn't nearly as flexible as other training options mentioned in this chapter—the school will definitely meet its own needs before it meets yours.

As when using a training center, make sure the staff member demonstrates knowledge gained and provides presentations to cross-train other staff members. However, because the timeframe for training is so long, you can usually perform these tasks in segments. In addition, the longer training time means that the staff member won't be quite so rushed in gaining the new skills and there is a good chance that the staff member will retain more because there is more time to absorb material between training sessions.

Ensuring Users Are Security Aware

Everyone requires some level of training to ensure you have good security at your organization. However, users often require specialized training because they don't possess the knowledge that your development staff obtained during certification or while in school earning a degree. In addition, users lack the experience that the development team and other staff members have obtained through years of working through security issues. Therefore, you need to make some additional plans when it comes to user training in order to create a secure environment. The following sections provide some ideas on how you can make your users more security aware.

Making Security Training Specific

A problem with much of the security training in use today is that it isn't specific. You must make security training specific to the organization—reflecting organizational policies. Otherwise, you can't expect staff members to follow these policies when performing daily tasks and the result is often a security breach that the organization could avoid by following the policies.

Training also needs to consider any legal or other requirements. Not every business has the same security requirements placed on it. In order for staff members to know how to perform tasks securely in your specific organization, you need to make them aware of all the legal and other requirements that affect your organization. It's important that staff members not only understand the legal or other requirement, but also understand how your organization meets that requirement.

It's also important to focus on particular problem areas for your organization. Use actual examples of security issues (names, dates, and other particulars removed to protect the innocent). By focusing on your organization's specific needs, you make the training more pertinent and help ensure that staff members see the practical benefit of following any requirements defined by the training. More importantly, help the staff members understand the cost of the security breach to them personally as part of the training. It's essential that staff members understand the stake they have in following organizational guidelines when it comes to security.

Combining Training with Written Guides

No one will remember every word said during a training session. Testing of various sorts does help extend memory, but they also have limits. In addition to training, your staff members need written guides that reinforce the training. In fact, you should use these written guides as part of any in-house training that you perform. Make sure that your written guides always reflect the actual training that people receive. As you update the training, update the guide as well.

Whenever you perform an update, make sure that everyone receives a copy of the updated guide. In addition, don't let long-term staff members fall through the cracks. Any update in training should include updated training for existing staff members as well. Someone who is with an organization for a long time can get out of step with current security protocols and inadvertently cause a security breach through a lack of information.

Don't focus on making your written guide ostentatious or flowery. What you want is a practical, simple guide to company policies. The staff members don't have time or patience to deal with a guide filled with legalese or jargon. A guide that spells things out simply and concisely works far better. Remember that most people nowadays have an attention span of well under a minute, so if staff members can't find any given answer in the guide you create in less than a minute, they won't use it.

Make the written guide as short as possible. The less you bloat the language used to convey important security issues, the more people will pay attention to it. Keep things short and easy to remember. In addition, make sure you produce the guide in both printed and electronic form. Doing so allows a staff member to place the guide on an alternative device, such as a smartphone, to keep it available at all times.

Creating and Using Alternative Security Reminders

Users get fixated on using an application and won't think about security at times unless you provide an appropriate reminder. For example, an organization could create posters with security reminders and place them in public locations. The technique seems like something out of yesterday's bad movie, but it actually does work. Keeping the need for security in front of the user, even during breaks, is one way to maintain the perception that security is important.

The application should also include security reminders. You don't want to make them annoying. The reminder that says "Are you sure you want to do this?" and then displays another "Really?" reminder is just plain annoying and users will ignore it. One effective way to spell out security reminders is to provide a tip of the day as part of starting the application. Not every tip has to have a security focus. Sometimes you can add a fun tip into the mix. The point is to keep users guessing as to the content of the tip so that they'll continue to look at it.

One organization had a creative security administrator who sometimes ran contests, such as, "The first person who can locate the correct security principle to apply to giving people your password receives a free pizza at lunch." The contests didn't occur often and cost management almost nothing, yet they kept the staff alert to the security tips and greatly improved organizational security. Creativity in getting people to continue learning more about security is an essential part of gaining their cooperation to keep the application and its data safe.

IT staff should also receive human relations training. One of the biggest problems in gaining the attention and cooperation of staff members is that IT tends to make everyone feel like an idiot. If you tell someone often enough that they're an idiot, they may tend to believe you and start acting the part. Positive reinforcement and a good attitude toward helping other staff members really will garner better results than constantly telling them that they can't possibly understand security issues.

Holding Training Effectiveness Checks

You may find that the various techniques you try to get the staff members enthusiastic about security just aren't working as well as you planned. Of course, the problem is figuring out how to change things so that security does improve. The first thing you need to think about is that security will never be bulletproof—all you can do is to continue to improve it as much as possible and deal with each new threat as it arrives. However, you can get close to perfect. Part of achieving that close to perfect mark is to check on the effectiveness of the various methods you use. Obtain statistics on what is and isn't working using the various techniques described throughout the book (especially those found in "Providing for User Feedback" on page 308 in Chapter 15). What you want to ascertain is the sources of potential security failures.

These potential security failure points tell you more about how well your training is working. You can also test staff members randomly using the techniques found earlier in the chapter. The point isn't to locate staff members who are falling down on the job, but to locate places where current training strategies aren't getting the results you had intended. As you find these problem areas, you need to consider how best to convey the required information, provide motivation for following the rule, and ensure penalties for purposely failing to follow procedure are implemented. However, the focus is always on getting better training to ensure people truly understand what is required.

Index

Symbols
/ (forward slash), 4
; (semicolon), 134
\ (backslash), 4

A
Accellion (cloud services), 22
accessibility issues, 76, 79-82
AES (Advanced Encryption Standard), 4, 248
AirGap sandbox solution, 219
AJAX (Asynchronous JavaScript and XML), 90
alert() function, 125
alt attribute, 79
Amazon APIs, 24
analyzing applications
    about, 11
    constraint aspect, 13
    data aspect, 12
    interface aspect, 13
    logic aspect, 11
AngularJS framework, 140
API aggregation, 223
API mashups, 223
API safety zones
    about, 205-207
    defining need for, 207-217
    developing with sandboxes, 217-222
    virtual environments and, 223-226
API virtualization, 214-216
APIs (application programming interfaces)
    accessing safely from JavaScript, 157-159
    creating testing scripts for, 241
    differentiating libraries and, 144-147
    differentiating microservices and, 117, 164

examples of, 66
    extending JavaScript with, 147-152
    load testing, 216
    locating, 147
    packaged solutions issues, 112-114
    sandboxing and, 159
    security threats posed by, 153-157
    testing external, 239, 286
    testing internal, 238, 286
    updating, 285-287
    usage considerations, 24, 65, 143
    verifying security, 157
Applause tester, 198
application downtime, 329
application environment
    allowing access by others, 28
    cloud storage and, 20-22
    CRUD acronym, 1
    endpoint defense essentials, 17-20
    external code and resources, 22-28
    language-specific issues, 14-17
    Software Security Assistance, 7-14
    user needs and expectations, 49-51
    web application threats and, 2-6
application virtualization, 225
AppScan tool, 237
arrays (JSON), 168
Ashley Madison hack, 32
assert() function, 240, 247
ASTQB (American Software Testing Qualifications Board), 254
authentication
    hardcoded, 3
    missing or incorrect, 4

About the Author

John Mueller is a freelance author and technical editor. He has writing in his blood, having produced 99 books and more than 600 articles to date. The topics range from networking to artificial intelligence and from database management to heads-down programming. Some of his current books include a book on Python for beginners, Python for data scientists, and a book about MATLAB. He has also written a Java e-learning kit, a book on HTML5 development with JavaScript, and another on CSS3. His technical editing skills have helped more than 60 authors refine the content of their manuscripts. John has provided technical editing services to both *Data Based Advisor* and *Coast Compute* magazines. Be sure to read John's blog at *http://blog.john muellerbooks.com/*.

When John isn't working at the computer, you can find him outside in the garden, cutting wood, or generally enjoying nature. John also likes making wine, baking cookies, and knitting. When not occupied with anything else, he makes glycerin soap and candles, which come in handy for gift baskets. You can reach John on the Internet at *john@johnmuellerbooks.com*. John is also setting up a website at *http://www.johnmuellerbooks.com/*. Feel free to take a look and make suggestions on how he can improve it.

Colophon

The animal on the cover of *Security for Web Developers* is a bearded vulture (*Gypaetus barbatus*), which is also known as a lammergeier or ossifrage. The bearded vulture is a bird of prey, eats mostly carrion, and lives in the mountainous areas of southern Europe, the Caucasus, Africa, the Indian subcontinent, and Tibet.

Being a scavenger means that the bearded vulture subsists on a diet of the remains of dead animals. Instead of eating the meat, however, this bird prefers the bone marrow, which makes up 85%–90% of its diet. Occasionally, bearded vultures have been known to attack live animals, and they seem to have a preference for tortoises. They have been observed catching tortoises, bringing them to great heights, and dropping them to split the shells and access the soft body underneath.

Bearded vultures can be anywhere from 37 to 49 inches long and weigh up to 18 pounds. Females are slightly larger than males, and both members of a bonded pair contribute to building the enormous (up to 3.3 feet across) nest. Their long narrow wings make them easy distinguishable from other vulture species. Bearded vultures also do not have a bald head like many other types of vultures, and the species gets its name from the long black feathers under the chin.

Its large size and majestic presence have earned the bearded vulture a place in the mythologies of many societies. To Iranians, this bird is a symbol of luck and happiness, and it was believed that being under its shadow would predict a person's rise to kingship. It is said that the Greek playwright Aeschylus was killed when an "eagle" dropped a tortoise on his head, mistaking his bald scalp for a stone. Given the region, time period, and behavior, the bearded vulture is a likely candidate for the "eagle" in the story. Also in Greece, the bearded vulture was one of the few species of birds that could be used to predict the future, the practice of which is called augury. Finally, in both the Bible and Torah, the bearded vulture is among the birds that people were forbidden to eat.

Many of the animals on O'Reilly covers are endangered; all of them are important to the world. To learn more about how you can help, go to *animals.oreilly.com*.

The cover fonts are URW Typewriter and Guardian Sans. The text font is Adobe Minion Pro; the heading font is Adobe Myriad Condensed; and the code font is Dalton Maag's Ubuntu Mono.

Get even more for your money.

Join the O'Reilly Community, and register the O'Reilly books you own. It's free, and you'll get:

- $4.99 ebook upgrade offer
- 40% upgrade offer on O'Reilly print books
- Membership discounts on books and events
- Free lifetime updates to ebooks and videos
- Multiple ebook formats, DRM FREE
- Participation in the O'Reilly community
- Newsletters
- Account management
- 100% Satisfaction Guarantee

Signing up is easy:

1. Go to: oreilly.com/go/register
2. Create an O'Reilly login.
3. Provide your address.
4. Register your books.

Note: English-language books only

To order books online:
oreilly.com/store

For questions about products or an order:
orders@oreilly.com

To sign up to get topic-specific email announcements and/or news about upcoming books, conferences, special offers, and new technologies:
elists@oreilly.com

For technical questions about book content:
booktech@oreilly.com

To submit new book proposals to our editors:
proposals@oreilly.com

O'Reilly books are available in multiple DRM-free ebook formats. For more information:
oreilly.com/ebooks

CPSIA information can be obtained at www.ICGtesting.com
Printed in the USA
BVOW09s2310151115

427037BV00010B/6/P